C0-AKA-575

TURN-TAKING IN JAPANESE CONVERSATION

Pragmatics & Beyond New Series

56

Hiroko Tanaka

Turn-Taking in Japanese Conversation
A Study in Grammar and Interaction

TURN-TAKING IN JAPANESE CONVERSATION

A STUDY IN GRAMMAR AND INTERACTION

HIROKO TANAKA
University of Essex

JOHN BENJAMINS PUBLISHING COMPANY
AMSTERDAM/PHILADELPHIA

The paper used in this publication meets the minimum requirements of American National Standard for Information Sciences — Permanence of Paper for Printed Library Materials, ANSI Z39.48-1984.

Library of Congress Cataloging-in-Publication Data

Tanaka, Hiroko.

Turn-taking in Japanese conversation : a study in grammar and interaction / Hiroko Tanaka.

p. cm. -- (Pragmatics & beyond, ISSN 0922-842X ; new ser. 56)

Includes bibliographical references and index.

1. Japanese language--Discourse analysis. 2. Conversation analysis--Japan. 3. Dialogue analysis--Japan. I. Title. II. Series.

PL640.5.T36 1999

495.6'0141 99-049419

ISBN 90 272 5070 7 (Eur.) / 1 55619 819 1 (US) (alk. paper) CIP

John Benjamins Publishing Co. • P.O.Box 75577 • 1070 AN Amsterdam • The Netherlands
John Benjamins North America • P.O.Box 27519 • Philadelphia PA 19118-0519 • USA

for Noë

Contents

Acknowledgements

I would like to extend my profound appreciations to friends, colleagues and teachers who kindly read earlier chapters of this manuscript and made many helpful suggestions, including David Greatbatch, Max Atkinson, Robert Dingwall, Paul Luff, Robert Sanders, John Scott, Drew Gerstle, Kanji Kitamura, and Junko Mori. Also, a special word of thanks to Ken Plummer, Tony Woodiwiss, Paul Thompson, Roger Goodman, Christian Heath, and Laurien Berkeley for their support and encouragement.

This book owes a great deal to the participation of the many people who happily agreed to be audio- or video-taped. I would like to record my sincere thanks to all those who have been so helpful and accommodating.

I am extremely grateful to John Heritage, who through the generosity of his heart, gave me much inspiration and advice. He kept me informed of the latest developments in the field of grammar and interaction and made comments and criticisms of my work, which contributed immensely to setting the direction for this study. I am most thankful to Paul Drew for his invaluable guidance and support, without which I would not have been able to complete this book, and for always having a sympathetic ear to listen to any questions or problems I may have.

My heartfelt thanks goes to my friend and co-worker Makoto Hayashi, who took much of his time and effort to make countless constructive comments and criticisms on earlier versions of this manuscript. If it had not been for his insightful input, this book would have been very impoverished. However, I am responsible for the inadequacies which remain.

I would like to express my sincere gratitude to Andreas Jucker and Bertie Kaal of Benjamins for providing this opportunity to publish my research and for their helpful advice in the preparation of the manuscript. I am also very grateful to successive editors of *Research on Language and Social Interaction* for permission to reprint Chapter 4, which is a slightly revised and expanded version of the paper entitled "Turn-projection in Japanese talk-in-interaction", to appear in the journal.

Finally, I wish to thank my family, and especially Noë and Satoshi for their infinite patience, love and encouragement throughout the writing of this book.

Transcription conventions

The transcripts follow the conventions developed by Gail Jefferson, with a few modifications: (1) the original Japanese talk is presented in italics in the first line; (2) a word-by-word translation or grammatical description is provided in the second line, and a vernacular gloss in English appears in quotation marks in the third line; (3) only one line of translation is provided in cases where the word-by-word translation coincides with the vernacular gloss, as in certain lexical turns; (4) unexpressed elements in the Japanese original are supplied in double parentheses in the English gloss; and (5) bold typeface is employed to draw the reader's attention to particular portions of the transcript, and does not indicate aspects of the delivery. Since the word order and location of overlaps in the Japanese original often cannot be represented accurately in the English gloss, the reader is asked to examine the Japanese transcription (or the word-by-word translations) in addition to the third line. The transcription notations based on Gail Jefferson's system are summarised below.

A:	code for name of speaker
·hh	inbreath or inhalation.
h	(or (*h*)) aspiration, breathiness, or laughter tokens
↑	rising intonation
↓	falling intonation
<	a hurried start in speaking
> <	talk delivered at a quicker pace in relation to surrounding talk is enclosed in these two symbols
[ ]	overlapped speech in contiguous lines
	[is used to mark where two or more speakers begin simultaneously or where a speaker overlays the talk of another speaker
	] denotes where overlapped speech ends
	[. . .] denotes where overlapped speech begins and ends
	[ ] mark the point where one speaker stops and another starts up contiguously.
=	"latching" or contiguous talk: i.e. there is no pause after the completion of one utterance and the beginning of another
(.7)	the number indicates the length of a pause or silence measured in seconds

(.)	unmeasured micropause
( )	transcriptionist doubt of what was said
(( ))	commentary by transcriptionist
:::	sound stretch, e.g. *Ah*:::
CAPITALS	mark passages delivered in a louder voice than surrounding talk
Underlining	highlights parts produced in a louder or more emphatic tone than surrounding talk.
° °	portions which are delivered in a quieter voice than surrounding talk is enclosed between degree signs
-	cut-off
,	continuing intonation
.	(full stop) falling intonation
?	rising intonation
ṭ	(underdot) a hardened or dentalised quality of sound
→	points out a phenomenon under scrutiny

Abbreviations in transcripts

ACC	accusative particle	LOC	locative particle
ADVP	adverbial particle	N	nominaliser
AP	appositional	NEG	negative
CAUS	causative	NOM	nominative particle
CONJ	conjunctive particle	NP	noun phrase
CONT	continuation	P	particle
COP	copula	PASS	passive
DAT	dative particle	POTEN	potential
DESI	desiderative	PRES	present tense
DF	disfluency	QP	question particle
EXC	exclamation	QUOT	quotative particle
FP	final particle	SFX	final suffix
GEN	genitive particle	TOP	topic particle
INT	intensifier	VN	verb nominaliser

A note on names

Japanese names which appear in the body of the text in Chapter 1 are written surname first, given name last, without a comma. However, they are listed according to English conventions in the bibliography.

Chapter 1

Introduction

1.1. Preliminaries

This book explores the interpenetration of grammar and turn-taking in Japanese talk-in-interaction from the perspective of conversation analysis (CA). Turn-taking has been described as a generic organisation of conversation with the aim of achieving "one at a time while speaker change recurs" (Sacks, Schegloff, and Jefferson 1974: 726). Specifically it regulates the construction of turns, transition from one speaker to the next, turn allocation, the resolution of gaps or overlapping speech, and the like. Turn-taking is also a basic mechanism for managing diverse activities in social interaction: "the process of turn-taking can be exploited as a resource for pursuing individual ends, making social identities visible and effective in concrete form, and assembling social occasions and pursuing socially organized sequences of activity within them" (Wilson and Zimmerman 1986: 375). For the purposes of this book, turn-taking will be regarded as a set of structured solutions to the fundamental interactional problem of constructing and allocating turns at speaking together with the range of conversational resources to implement them.

Recently attention has increasingly been focused on the question whether turn-taking is a universal interactive mechanism or if its basic structure is affected by variations across cultures and languages. The very fact that conversation is possible in any language implies that some system of turn-taking is operating to co-ordinate turns at talk in that language. If we grant that turn-taking is an activity that needs to be dealt with in any language, it becomes pertinent to ask to what extent members' concrete turn-taking practices are shared or differ from one language to another.

This wider question is addressed in this book through an investigation of selected aspects of turn-taking in Japanese conversation and "informal" meetings. A circumscribed comparison is also made with what is known about Anglo-American English. The main aim is to discover potentially generalisable features as well as ways in which socio-linguistic particularities may have implications for the performance of turn-taking operations in the respective languages. A related objective is to show that language and interaction are deeply interconnected, and combine with other features of talk to provide resources as well as constraints for the construction, recognition, and allocation of turns at speaking. Of the various facets of language, special attention is paid to the role of grammar and prosody in Japanese for the performance of turn-taking operations. Features of both grammar and prosody are utilised by participants to project and anticipate how a turn is developing or where it may come to an end, and therefore are vital tools for the production and understanding of what is happening in interaction.

The choice of turn-taking as the topic of this book was motivated by a belief in the primacy of turn-taking as a feature of human communication. It is perhaps one of the most primordial and generic of the structures which we depend on in the performance and understanding of social interaction. Arguably talk would simply break down without it. Turn-taking operations not only accommodate features of conversation, but also coexist and are co-ordinated with infinite variations in the structures of language, cultural orientations, and the particular occasions for which they are enlisted (see Sacks, Schegloff, and Jefferson 1974). Therefore a deep interpenetration of turn-taking with linguistic, cultural, and pragmatic features can be expected. The arena of turn-taking promises to be a rich locus of a complex interplay of the most fundamental to the most culturally singular features of social interaction. For these reasons, the scope of issues relevant to turn-taking is potentially colossal. There is space here only to investigate a few of the myriad aspects of the turn-taking system in Japanese. It is hoped however, that this book will begin to illuminate its complex but orderly properties, and pave the way for more detailed and comprehensive future research.

CA research on Anglo-American interaction has proven to be an innovative and fruitful field of investigation into the detailed organisation of a wide variety of naturally occurring interactional phenomena. Some researchers have also been conducting intensive work with respect to Japanese as well as comparisons of Japanese and Anglo-American English using CA and related approaches, though the volume of research produced by no means matches that for Anglo-American English (e.g. Saft 1996; Nishizaka 1995; Yamada, Yoshii, and Yamazaki 1987; Yoshii 1992; Szatrowski 1993; Maynard 1989). This book attempts to make a contribution to the area through an examination of Japanese interactional organisation—and turn-taking in particular—while making a restricted comparison with Anglo-American English. However since basic research on Japanese interactional organisation is still relatively sparse, this book will be centred on Japanese, while relying extensively on existing work on turn-taking in English conducted by others (e.g. Sacks, Schegloff, and Jefferson 1974; Schegloff 1987b; Wilson, Wiemann, and Zimmerman 1984; Ford and Thompson 1996) for comparative purposes.

In recent years, there has also been a growing interdisciplinary interest among conversation analysts and linguists in the interpenetration of social interaction and grammar. Studies driven by such concerns are beginning to highlight the significance of grammar as a resource in the production and recognition of "coherent" conversation (i.e. conversation coherent to participants) and for the accomplishment of diverse interactional activities (Ochs, Schegloff, and Thompson 1996; see also Ford 1993; Ford and Mori 1994; Lerner 1991; Lerner and Takagi, to appear; Mori 1994, 1996a, b; Hayashi 1997; Hayashi and Mori 1998), inter alia how grammar may be consequential for the organisation of turn-taking (Ford, Fox, and Thompson 1996; Hayashi, Mori and Takagi, to appear; Schegloff 1996a). This book draws its inspiration from this newly emerging field, and builds on the above studies. In particular there are vast insights into both grammar and social interaction which can be gained by studying turn-taking in relation to grammatical organisation. According to Schegloff,

> grammar stands in a reflexive relationship to the organization of a spate of talk as a turn. On the one hand, the organizational contingencies of talking in a turn . . . shape grammar—both grammar as an abstract, formal organization and the grammar of a particular utterance. On the other hand, the progressive grammatical realization of a spate of talk on a particular occasion can shape the exigencies of the turn as a unit of interactional participation on that occasion, and the grammatical properties of a language may contribute to the organization of turns-at-talk in that language and of the turn-taking device by which they are deployed. (Schegloff 1996a: 56)

These observations are played out over and over again throughout the discussions in this book. While the generic organisation of turn-taking shared between Anglo-American English and Japanese can be described more or less independently of grammar (see Chapter 2), differences in the specific practices involved in turn-taking are found to be deeply interrelated with the divergent grammatical organisations of the respective languages (see Chapters 3–6).

There are two major aspects of talk-in-interaction with relevance to turn-taking which are not covered in any depth in this book. First, analysis of non-verbal conduct has been largely left unexplored, though this would be the next logical direction in which a comparative study of turn-taking might be pursued, as already undertaken by researchers in specific languages (e.g. Goodwin 1979b, 1981, 1986; Schegloff 1984; Ford, Fox, and Thompson 1996; Hayashi, Mori, and Takagi, to appear). These works provide insight into the co-ordination and integration of non-verbal and verbal features of interaction in the performance of social actions. Another major area not dealt with here is the salience of cultural orientations for turn-taking. For instance, preliminary work on "next-speaker selection" (this term is due to Sacks, Schegloff, and Jefferson 1974) suggests that the situated avoidance of second-person pronouns and the use of honorification in Japanese are deeply implicated in turn-allocation techniques (see Tanaka 1996). Again a fuller investigation of these themes must await future research.

One caveat is in order with respect to what is referred to here as "Anglo-American" interaction. The CA literature has in the past, neither specified nor addressed substantially the possible differences that may exist between British and American patterns of interaction (nor with respect to other versions of English). Accordingly the term "Anglo-American English" will be used interchangeably with "English", except where specifically noted as "American" or "British". However the collapse of the two types of English has been made for practical purposes, and does not imply a view that there are no significant differences between the two domains of interaction.

This chapter deals with various preliminaries before entering into a detailed analysis of turn-taking in Japanese. Section 2 reviews a number of representative works of the *Nihonjinron* genre which emphasise the "uniqueness" of Japanese society, culture, or language. It is important to be aware of these popular theories and the closely related ideologies of language-use which, despite their limited explanatory power, sometimes enter surreptitiously into contemporary linguistic and sociological research relating to Japan. Section 3 highlights some distinguishing features of the methodological strategies of CA in contrast to the holistic approach of the *Nihonjinron* theories, and Section 4 touches on issues pertinent to the utilisation of the techniques of CA for cross-cultural research. The data employed in this book are noted in Section 5, and Section 6 describes basic aspects of Japanese conversational grammar relevant to the ensuing discussions. Finally, Section 7 outlines the organisation of the chapters of this book.

1.2. *Nihonjinron* and ideologies of language-use

The existing literature on cross-cultural communication frequently contains implicit or explicit characterisations of the Japanese people and behaviour in blanket terms as unique, homogeneous, and group-oriented. As is well known, Japan's miraculous economic success since the 1960s has coincided with the efflorescence of the so-called *Nihonjinron* (variously known as "Japanology", "treatises of Japaneseness", "theories of Japanese culture", etc.), much of which theorise on such putative features as determined by one or more of a range of macro structures such as Japan's geo-climatic circumstances, the residual "feudal" social structure, the vertical quasi-familial organisation of social groups, etc. Moreover, as noted by critics of this genre, they often suffer from a heavy reliance on anecdotal evidence, a lack of rigorous methodology, and a culturally nationalistic stance (Mouer and Sugimoto

1986; Dale 1986). They have also been described as a source of myths and "anti-myths" concerning Japaneseness (Miller 1982). Such works leave unanswered questions concerning the detailed ways in which Japanese interaction takes place: e.g. does it differ in fundamental ways from Anglo-American interaction, or are the similarities simply being overlooked; are the Japanese as "harmonious" and group-oriented as frequently claimed, and if so, how is this interactionally accomplished; what concrete practices, if any, have given rise to the view of Japanese communicative conduct as ambiguous, indirect, illogical, or rambling; what lies at the root of the stereotype of the "enigmatic oriental smile" or the "myth of silence", etc.?

Nihonjinron literature has not only pervasively informed common perceptions of the Japanese and Japanese patterns of interpersonal interaction both at home and abroad, but has also set the tone for much subsequent research on comparisons of Japanese and non-Japanese cultures. Broadly speaking, claims for the distinctiveness of Japanese culture and interactional patterns have typically relied on holistic theoretical models, and on the group or consensus model in particular (Mouer and Sugimoto 1986). One consequence of this has been the static view of social action and interaction that it has generated, directing attention away from the creative and contingent nature of human interaction, and giving rise to certain stereotypical images of the Japanese as well as of "westerners". A brief survey of some representative works within this body of writings provides an indication of the impact it has had on vernacular conceptions (as well as scholarly works) on Japanese patterns of social interaction.

Ruth Benedict's *The Chrysanthemum and the Sword* (1954) is frequently referred to as a point of departure for comparative studies of Japanese and western cultures following the Second World War (e.g. Soeda 1993; Aoki 1990). Benedict describes Japan in part as a "shame" culture and western cultures as founded on the notion of "sin". Accordingly, she argues that westerners think and act within the framework of an antagonistic relationship between God and mortals, and an individual's conscience dictates his/her conduct based on absolute moral standards. In contrast, the thought and behaviour of the Japanese are claimed to be shaped by the assessment of other members of society and one's relative station or status *vis-à-vis* others, where the sense of public shame provides a sanctioning mechanism. Benedict's study was guided by the analytic framework of "cultural patterns" which attempted to categorise cultures into various types. Her work bequeathed to later Japanologists the dual themes of "culture of shame" and "collectivism" (though she did not use this particular word), and set a trend in the employment of holistic or structural approaches to understanding Japanese society and culture (Aoki 1990: 30–52).

The *Nihonjinron* of the immediate post-war years resonates with the perceived need to reconsider the past and to redefine Japan's national identity within the newly coalescing domestic and world order. The lack of popular resistance to the excesses of the totalitarian regime of the pre-war years, for instance, was blamed on the nature of the pervasive hierarchical relations in Japan, characterised by *onjō* (benevolence) and *shihai* (authority) on the part of the superior, *vis-à-vis kyōjun*, the unquestioning subservience and loyalty of the inferior, which bound together members of a group through relations of *wa*—archetypal human relations embodied in the pre-war *ie* (familial) ideology (e.g. Maruyama 1952; Kawashima 1948). According to such views, the euphemistic notion of *wa* (harmony) masked the inability of the individual—caught up in the social nexus of the collectivity—freely to articulate inner wishes, personal opinions and criticisms of others within one's group, or to communicate effectively with those outside the group. In sum, social interaction was seen to be severely restricted by the vestiges of feudalistic structures within Japanese society.

As Japan entered the era of high economic growth in the 1960s, however, the tone of discourses on Japaneseness began a subtle transformation from negative to distinctly positive (Aoki 1990: 81–82). Consensus theorists stormed onto the centre stage of the *Nihonjinron* debates, taking the very same themes mentioned above, but rendering them with a positive gloss. For instance, collectivism began to be characterised as one of the "unique" societal features that was integral to Japan's economic success (e.g. Odaka 1965).

In an influential work of this period, *Japanese Society* (1973), Nakane Chie undertakes a comparison of the principles of social organisation in Japan and the west. She presents two distinct criteria which bind people into a group: (1) sharing common "attributes", and (2) according to situational positions within a particular "frame". Attributes include ascribed characteristics, such as being a member of a class or descent group, as well as achieved characteristics such as level of education and type of occupation. Nakane claims that this criterion defines the formation of groups in terms of characteristics of individuals which distinguish them from those outside the group. On the other hand, the criterion of frame is an organising principle contingent on the members' situation or position in a given collectivity such as "a member of Company X", rather than based on their birth or merit. Nakane argues that the criterion of group formation in Japan is predominantly of the frame variety, which is ordered along the vertical social axis of relationships between superiors and subordinates. For this reason, she concludes that the behaviour of the Japanese is overwhelmingly shaped within the context of the hierarchical structure of the collectivity to which an individual belongs, making it difficult for them to interact on a horizontal level, said to be characteristic of the organising principle of groups in the west.

Another work which had a major impact on subsequent *Nihonjinron* writing was Doi Takeo's *Anatomy of Dependence* (1971). Doi singles out *amae*—variously translated as dependence, interdependence, presuming on others' indulgence, fawning, and mollycoddling—as an instinctive emotion which permeates human relations among the Japanese. *Amae* is said to occur naturally and in its unadulterated form in the primordial mother-child relationship, characterised by intimacy, lack of separation, mutual *sasshi* or *ishin-denshin* (telepathic communication; ability to anticipate others' wishes), and *omoiyari* (the ability to take the point of view or wishes of others into consideration). This type of relationship is also seen to be reproduced pervasively in adulthood in the quasi-familial relations of *oyabun-kobun* (leader-follower), the building blocks of Japan's "vertical" society. Doi regards the affirmation of the desire for *amae* not only as a distinguishing feature of Japanese social relations, but also to be of critical importance for the psychological well-being of the individual. In *Anatomy of Self* (1988) Doi goes even further, to claim that the systematic repression of the "hidden *amae*" (for instance in the USA) can lead to excesses, violent tendencies, and distortions within society.

Countless other studies on the nature of Japanese society and explanations for cross-cultural differences (commonly contrasted with western societies) were generated during the roughly twenty years (from the mid 1960s) corresponding to the era of high and stable economic growth. Just three have been touched upon above, but we can discern a pattern. Although each work makes insightful contributions, they rely heavily on the author's sense of intuition, and present an essentially holistic and static view of the human actor and social interaction, determined by some overriding feature of the culture or social structure: Benedict regards the shame/sin pattern of culture to be of paramount importance in influencing behaviour; for Nakane, the vertically or horizontally organised dimensions of the social structure determine patterns of human interaction; Doi proposes *amae* as the key to unravelling Japanese psychosocial behaviour. In each of these works, structural explanations of Japanese society are employed to characterise relations among the Japanese in contrast to patterns of interaction in the west, conceived in monolithic terms. Broadly speaking, the models of the human actor portrayed in these theories bear a close resemblance to the Parsonian view of the social actor (Parsons 1937) unable to counteract the relentless and overarching force of socialisation. Moreover, once a particular structural explanation or dichotomy is set up, examples are often extracted from personal experience, literature, or anecdotes as evidence for the validity of a proposed causal account.

These works are also closely associated with ideologies of the Japanese language and language-use, which include a bewildering array of often conflicting theories and descriptions of Japanese thought and communicative behaviour. According to Loveday (1986: 19), cultural beliefs concerning the Japanese language also enter into the work of academics. We consider below two dominant themes of this ideology: collectivism and silence.

Collectivism is one of the central themes in the works of Benedict, Nakane, and

Doi. Theories of language-use draw heavily on the predominance of the group orientation, and describe Japanese interpersonal relations as essentially hierarchical, co-operative, non-confrontational, polite, and mutually dependent (e.g. Haga 1979a: 57; Shibagaki 1984). Many writers cite historical reasons for the evolution of a collectivist mentality among the Japanese. For instance, Haga claims that the "core personality" of the Japanese was largely formed early in Japanese history as far back as the Yayoi period (300 BC–300 AD), developing in parallel with the culture of wet-rice agriculture based on communitarian values (Haga 1979b: 41).[1] Moreover, the Japanese are regarded as a relatively homogeneous race of people, sharing similar outlooks on life, value systems, and ways of thinking (T. Suzuki 1975: 189; Ito 1989). Of these, the maintenance of *wa* (harmony) is seen to be one of the prime group values to have been traditionally fostered in Japanese society (Hirokawa 1987: 140; Ito 1989: 117). Inherent in the concept of harmony is a hierarchically ordered society where everyone is expected to know where s/he belongs within the social milieu. Midooka, for instance, argues that this social organisation affects communicative behaviour in several ways:

1. people often make strong self-claims or self-expressions toward those in equivalent or lower ranks. But people seldom do so toward superiors;
2. people usually do not strongly oppose a superior's opinions, or disobey his or her orders even when they think that the superior is wrong. This is because they think disobedience is impolite as well as disadvantageous, and also because they trust and rely on the superior's rich experiences;
3. when people talk to their superiors, they use *Keigo* (honorifics), a language different from that which they use to communicate with those in equivalent or lower ranks. (Midooka 1990: 483)

Not only is sensitivity to social hierarchy cited as a major constraint on free expression, but interactional styles are believed to be dictated by particular communicative settings. In particular, formal and official events are described as occasions accompanied by a pronounced asymmetry in the speaking rights of superiors and inferiors, with the former typically dominating the floor, often engaging in a monologue (Nakane 1973; Kunihiro 1976: 274). Furthermore, the pressures of hierarchy and "harmonious" relations are claimed to be so overpowering that a dual communicative structure has arisen, where one adopts an attitude of *tatemae* (overt principles or diplomatic attitude) for formal and official occasions, and reveals one's *hon'ne* (real intentions) only in intimate settings (Doi 1988; Ito 1989: 117; Midooka 1990: 485). In various other ways, propriety, etiquette and politeness are regarded as the essential ingredients of social discretion in this purportedly homogeneous, hierarchical society.

Closely related to the collectivist position are views concerning the distrust of language and a corresponding stress on the virtues of silence. A historical source of

Japanese attitudes towards taciturnity is traced to the oppressive regime of the Edo period (1603–1867) which implemented strict regulation of speech (Tsujimura 1987: 120). Examples of proverbs such as "Least said, soonest mended" or "Out of the mouth comes evil" are cited as evidence that loquacity was regarded as politically and socially hazardous (Tsujimura 1987: 120). Another major source of attitudes toward silence is said to be the extraordinary level of racial and linguistic homogeneity among the people (Kunihiro 1976: 270; Tsujimura 1987: 119; Ito 1989: 194). Ito (1989) claims that homogeneous societies are akin to familial organisations, where explicit linguistic communication is unnecessary for mutual understanding. In order to preserve the sense of unity in society, language came to be regarded not only as woefully inadequate, but even deleterious to the tacit understanding and "harmony" prevailing within the community. As a consequence, the argument continues, the Japanese came to value indirectness, ambiguity, allusiveness, *ishin denshin* (empathetic or telepathic communication) and silence over persuasion, rhetoric, logic, and garrulity (see Shibagaki 1984: 109; Haga 1979b: 32–7; T. Suzuki 1975: 189–92; Okabe 1993: 75). According to Kunihiro (1976: 270), "Japanese tend to be taciturn, considering it a virtue to say little and rely on non-linguistic means to convey the rest. Verbal expression is often fragmentary and unsystematic, with emotional, communal patterns of communication." Lebra (1987) also analyses several dimensions of silence in Japanese society, noting that it is variously seen to be a sign of truthfulness, social discretion, modesty, and sensitivity to one's lack of speaking rights.

Furthermore, there is an implicit endorsement of silence, indirectness, and ambiguity as forms of expression. Not only is ambiguous communication considered adequate when much of the culture is shared, as is said to be the case in Japan (Ito 1989: 194), but on a practical level, ambiguity is seen to be beneficial in hierarchical settings to avoid loss of "face" (Hirokawa 1987: 147). Kunihiro also attributes the practice of ambiguous communication to the Japanese sense of aesthetics: "Japanese respect the feelings of others, and therefore prefer to surmise rather than to question them; open confrontation between opposing viewpoints is often considered offensive, disagreeable to our sense of beauty" (Kunihiro 1976: 272). Tsujimura likewise cites the virtues of indirectness epitomised as an art form in the traditional *waka* (poems consisting of thirty-one syllables) which were exchanged by courtesans in the Heian period (794–1185) as an oblique expression of affection in place of the overt declaration of love (Tsujimura 1987).

On the other side of this coin lies a devaluation of logic or rationality. Kunihiro characterises Japanese communicative behaviour as antithetical to western dialectics and "Cartesian tension-filled dualism"; instead, communication involves "leaps in logic" or an "all-or-nothing" logic, which might be called a "logic of nonlogic" (Kunihiro 1976). Some go so far as to attribute the allegedly illogical nature of the

Japanese to the Japanese language, which is claimed to be inimical to analytical reasoning (Shibagaki 1984: 148; Tsunoda 1978). Although there appears to be some consensus that the cultural climate has not been conducive to the development of rationality, this view is contradicted by others who claim that the Japanese language is, in fact, quite logical and efficient with respect to word order (e.g. Haruhiko, Kindaichi 1981: 194–203) or morphology (T. Suzuki 1975: 86), and may be even more suited for logical expression than European languages (Haga 1979a: 64). For instance, the existence of certain grammatical particles (*ga* and *wa*) in Japanese is claimed to permit a logical distinction to be made between the subject and topic, a differentiation which reportedly cannot be made in English or other European languages (Haga 1979a: 63–5).

Due in part to the prevalence of ambiguous and non-logical communication, the Japanese are said to have acquired particular forms of intuitive communication, such as *haragei* (belly art) or *ishin-denshin* (implicit or telepathic communication), which compensate for the impoverishment of language and further uphold the Japanese aesthetic ideal (Kunihiro 1976: 272). This is said to be a way of communicating which relies on subtle cues and intuition in displaying and surmising internal feelings (Lebra 1987: 352). Included in the art of *haragei* is the ability to read the prevailing *kūki* or atmosphere of the setting, and to act accordingly (Ito 1989: 117). The importance of implicit understanding is also reflected in the ethics of *omoiyari* or the ability to empathise and infer others' wishes and feelings without resorting to explicit language, which in turn is seen to be a key to maintaining harmonious relations within a collectivity.

Much of the *Nihonjinron* literature cited above draws heavily on intuition and invented or decontexualised examples. Thus, even though these perspectives provide insights into possible generalised normative rules and values of the Japanese, they fail to offer concrete, defensible explanations for the ways in which such rules may be employed and implemented in actual interpersonal contact. Further, the static model of social action, on which a majority of the theories are based, has produced idealised images of the Japanese as culturally distinctive, group-oriented, harmonious, homogeneous, and favouring emotion over logic, ambiguity over explicitness, telepathy or non-verbal communication over verbalisation, silence, and reticence over verbosity. One of the consequences of theorising on Japaneseness using this loaded vocabulary is that these cultural associations have become reified, and have engendered a deterministic view of human conduct. Although these descriptions—perhaps in a rather vague way—may be pointing to cultural resources shared by the Japanese which participants orient towards, exhibit consideration of, and are constrained by, the structural theorists seem to overlook the possibility that participants are nevertheless free to align with, disregard, or countervail accepted social norms for the accomplishment of particular social actions. In other words, these holistic explanations do not address the process through which members of a culture contingently invoke cultural norms and other communicative resources, and the consequent infinite possibilities for human conduct. Furthermore, a preoccupation with cultural specificity has led to an exaggerated or selective emphasis on cross-cultural differences, and a corresponding disregard for potentially shared features.

The intention here is neither to uphold nor to refute such *Nihonjinron* theories, but to begin to throw some light on aspects of Japanese interactional organisation which may lie at the root of such images, through a more satisfactory, empirically grounded approach to communicative phenomena. While examining the diverse resources utilised in the moment-to-moment production of naturally occurring talk, this study attempts to explore the types of communicative practices which are facilitated or impeded by Japanese grammatical structures and turn-taking organisation, and whether they might lend themselves to usages which merit descriptions such as illogical, ambiguous, indirect, etc. What is clear, however, is that a far more cautious and systematic approach than is employed in many of the *Nihonjinron* writings is necessary before we can begin to comprehend the dynamic and complex interrelation between socio-cultural norms and patterns of social interaction. The next section briefly reviews some research strategies of CA, which address the contingent nature of talk-in-interaction.

1.3. Methodological strategies of conversation analysis

Holistic "cultural" explanations of behaviour have fallen short of providing an empirical warrant for a linkage between alleged macroscopic features such as national character, homogeneity and collectivism on the one hand, and situated interaction on the other. Several deep-seated issues have been pointed out in the attempt to establish the relevance of generalised structural descriptions in particular instances of interaction: i.e. the need to verify that the participants actually orient to such contextual features and the difficulty of ascertaining the "procedural consequentiality" and interactional salience of such features (Schegloff 1987a).

Schegloff cites three potential sources of "tension" inherent in investigations into the relation between social structure and interactional organisation. The first is the concern with foreclosing possibilities for making discoveries about conversational or sequential organisation. When subsuming a particular sequential organisation as a feature of a certain social structure, one may potentially overlook the general applicability of the sequential organisation in question to a variety of other contexts. A second way in which excessive concern with the social structure can mask our understanding of interaction is that a kind of analytic complacency may set in, once the task of showing the relevance of context and its procedural consequentiality has been established in some instance. Schegloff spells out the need to engage in a continuing dialectic of analysing the displayed orientations in relation to the constant renewal of the context, rather than to remain content with an original formulation of the social structure. A third problem is the risk of trading attention to features of the interactional organisation for attention to aspects of the social structure. Two pitfalls are identified: an excessive focus on the implications of social structure on talk can potentially draw attention away from interesting conversational structures; also, it may be difficult to ascertain whether some aspect of talk should be attributed to features of the social structure or to conversational organisation. In order to overcome some of these issues, Schegloff recommends the strategy of treating the talk itself as part of the context, rather than as a separate dimension to be linked together (Schegloff 1987a).

The questions one asks in conducting analysis of talk are sociological rather than psychological, and a great deal of descriptive analysis is involved in identifying the structural and sequential organisation of social interaction. In particular, the analysis is directed towards unravelling the normative orientations underlying the production and recognition of intelligible social interaction which are "internal" to the interaction itself, rather than making conjectures on the intentions or motivations behind particular actions (see Heritage 1990/91; Edwards 1996). It is often necessary to collect a large volume of data and conduct major reviews of it in order to delve beneath surface phenomena to delineate microscopic differences. Heritage notes that "Conversation analysts have generally pursued their objectives by showing regular forms of organization in a large variety of interactional materials produced by different speakers" (1984b: 244).

Tentativeness is also as an inherent feature of the attitude towards research; the process of coding is an ongoing task, not a distinct phase of research (Hopper 1989). The actual research activity involves alternating between listening/transcribing and analysing/coding. Thus, "coding in CA is a prelude to description of instances. A coded instance in CA is not a fact, but a gesture toward some paths for analysis, an invitation to dialectic." (Hopper 1989: 57)

An integral part of this dialectic is the process of attending to the sequential interlocking of utterances in "real time" as a resource for analysis, as a direct application of Garfinkel's insights on the documentary method of interpretation and the "doubly constitutive" nature of normative orientations (Heritage 1984b). "A central assumption of interactional sequencing is that, unless otherwise signalled, each turn is addressed to the matters raised by the turn preceding it" (Heritage 1988: 129). Thus, a turn can be interpreted as a display of the speaker's understanding of a previous turn, while that same turn forms the context for the next turn. The analysis centres on how participants exploit their knowledge of conversational sequencing in order to comprehend what is going on, to produce their own turns, to make normatively accountable the actions of others, as well as to gain a sense of how one's turn has been understood by others.

Several concrete techniques have been identified in the CA literature for conducting interaction analysis, including establishing a pattern, deviant-case analysis and single-case analysis (see e.g. Heritage 1984b, 1988, 1995; Schegloff 1988; Levinson 1983: 326; Drew and Heritage 1992), though these strategies are mutually interlinked and not strictly separable. More recently, explorations have been made toward quantification of interactional phenomena (Schegloff 1993; Heritage and Roth 1995; Heritage 1995; Ford and Thompson 1996).

Specifically, the three basic techniques or steps below are recommended for conducting analysis:

> (a) collecting recurrent patterns in the data and hypothesizing sequential expectations based on these; (b) showing that such sequential expectations actually are oriented to by participants; and (c) showing that, as a consequence of such expectations, while some organizational problems are resolved, others are actually created, for which further organizations will be required. (Levinson 1983: 326)

The first point, (a), refers to the essentially inductive process of examining conversational data to identify interactive practices or structures. This process may either have originated from a "hunch" about a recurrent pattern of interaction as a competent language-user (Heritage 1995: 399) or, alternatively, it may be used to form hypotheses about phenomena under investigation. In order to show that participants actually orient to a phenomenon in a certain way, (b), one searches for evidence of displays of some orientation in the data. This is not a straightforward process, since not all the detail is available from every recording. Fragments instantiating a phenomenon and the displays of orientations are collected to describe and explicate a class of occurrences. One way to proceed in this direction is to demonstrate the existence of a norm by looking for requests and offerings of explanations and accounts where a projected or expected normative behaviour does not happen (Heritage 1988: 132). The third point, (c), is a warning against dismissing exceptional or marginal cases of a recurrent pattern as a "one-off" deviant or residual case. Rather, such instances may provide an opportunity to discover a different order of generality that would account for the exception. This technique is normally referred to as "deviant-case analysis" (e.g. Schegloff 1968, 1996b: 192–9; Heritage 1984b: 248–53, 1995: 399–402). Heritage notes that it is often the deviant cases which paradoxically "provides the strongest evidence for the normative character" of certain orientations or structures (1984b: 248–9).

As mentioned above, another technique which is sometimes employed in CA work is "single-case analysis". This strategy is based on the idea that single instances of interaction can be an illuminating locus of social activity:

> the analytic machinery which we develop, intended as it is to explicate the orderly procedures of the participants in interaction (conversational or otherwise), should be able to deal in an illuminating manner with single episodes of talk taken from "the real world." There is a constitutive order to singular occasions of interaction and to the organization of action within them. This is the bedrock of social life--what I called earlier the primordial site of sociality. And social science theorizing, both sociological and linguistic, must be answerable to it. Whatever concerns for macro-social issues we entertain, our ways of dealing with them will in the end have to be compatible with a capacity to address the details of single episodes of action through talking in interaction. (Schegloff 1988: 137)

The focus here differs from the other approaches listed, in that it draws on past research findings in CA to describe and explicate a single extract of an audio/video recording (see Schegloff 1987c, 1988: 137). Tracking the interactive work accomplished by participants in a single episode of talk can reveal the development of the flow of a conversation over a stretch of talk or the significance of an utterance in a larger context. For instance, a speaker's repeated attempts to pursue a recipient's affiliation over the course of a telephone conversation has been conducted by means of a case study by Jefferson, Sacks, and Schegloff (1987). In another study Schenkein (1972) examines an extended fragment of a therapy session to explore what a participant was trying to accomplish by a laughter token 'heheh'.

Finally, at the very forefront of methodological debates is the place of quantification in the analysis of social interaction (e.g. Schegloff 1993; Heritage 1995; Heritage and Roth 1995). It is reported that although informal quantification through the employment of terms such as "overwhelmingly", "massively", "regularly", and "typically" has been a feature of CA writings from its outset, it is only fairly recently that formal quantification has even been considered, apart from a handful of workers concerned with gender differences (e.g. Zimmerman and West 1975; West and Zimmerman 1987). According to Schegloff (1993), past reluctance to quantify reflects not so much a rejection of quantitative methods *per se* as that CA had not yet developed to an extent that it can reap the full benefits of such analyses. For quantitative analysis to be meaningful, what is minimally required are analytically defensible notions of "denominator", "numerator", and "domain or universe being categorised": where by "denominator" is meant "environments of possible *relevant* occurrence" of a phenomenon; "numerator" stands for "the set of types of occurrences whose presence should count as events", and "whose non-occurrence should count as absences"; and where "domain" refers to "a warranted conception of analytically coherent universes that it is relevant for a statistic to refer to" by virtue of their relevance as domains of activity for the participants themselves (Schegloff 1993). It should be clear even from this cursory summary of Schegloff's concerns that a prerequisite of quantification is a fine-grained analysis of a phenomenon being investigated on a case-by-case basis. Thus, "We can be led seriously astray if we allow the possibility of quantitative analysis to free us from the need to demonstrate the operation of what we take to be going on in singular fragments of talk" (Schegloff 1993: 102–3).

Heritage (1995: 406) echoes Schegloff's cautionary stance, but cites an added danger that "quantitative studies inexorably draw the analyst into an "external" view of the data of interaction, draining away the conduct-evidenced local intelligibility of particular situated actions which is the ultimate source of security that the object under investigation is not a theoretical or statistical artefact". On a more optimistic note, however, Heritage recommends several ways in which statistics may be constructively put to use:

(1) As a means of isolating "interesting phenomena"
(2) As a means of consolidating intuitions in areas which are well defined but where the existence of a practice is difficult to secure without a large number of cases.
(3) Cases in which independent findings about a conversational practice can have indirect statistical support.
(4) In almost all cases where a claim is made that the use or outcome of a particular interactional practice is tied to particular social or psychological categories, such as gender, status etc., statistical support will be necessary. (Heritage 1995: 404–5, slightly edited)

An illuminating use of statistics of types (2) and (3) is exemplified by Heritage and Roth's (1995) analysis of questioning procedures by news interviewers. Quantification is also put into practice in Ford and Thompson's (1996) study of the management of syntactic, prosodic, and pragmatic resources in turn-taking. Based on this work, a parallel statistical investigation for Japanese is attempted in Chapter 3. As will be elaborated, the very process of operationalisation which is a prerequisite for quantification can serve as a useful exercise for discovering features which are relevant to the participants, and hence for the analysis. Furthermore, quantification is likely to be of value in a study of verbal formulations of gender, status, formality, and social identity in Japanese interaction, a type (4) employment of statistics.

1.4. Cross-cultural analysis of social interaction

Although past research in CA has been concentrated mainly on studies of Anglo-American English, the utility of employing CA to undertake cross-cultural analysis of talk is progressively beginning to be recognised. According to Moerman (1988: 187), there is some work on the Mayan languages including Quiche, Tzoltzil, and Tamil. Moerman (1988) himself has compared Thai and English conversational organisation and has shown remarkable structural similarity between the two. Hopper and Doany (1989) have compared telephone openings in English, French, and Arabic. Cross-linguistic studies of Japanese and English have been conducted by Ford and Mori (1994), Lerner and Takagi (to appear), Fox, Hayashi, and Jasperson (1996) and Hayashi (1997), among others.

If we remain faithful to CA's main objective, which is to describe and explicate indigenous procedures, practices, and orientations, then the study of the organization of interaction of any culture should first and foremost be informed by the members' own methods and categories, rather than through an imposition of external analytical categories. Of relevance here is the methodological concern that the analysis should be both "context-free" and "context-sensitive" (Sacks, Schegloff, and Jefferson 1974: 699), which has also been described as the requirement that "the theory would have to be neither so inflexible or rigid that it lacks any sensitivity to the potentially infinite range of contextual variation in the world, nor so flexible or loose that nothing at all is held to be general across different contexts" (Atkinson and Drew 1979: 20). It is precisely the data-driven and naturalistic stance of CA which I believe renders it applicable in principle to the investigation of any system of conversational interaction irrespective of the language used or cultural domain.

Although the attempt to achieve context-sensitivity and context-neutrality may make CA eminently suited to a study of "exotic" cultures, a number of difficulties may be foreseen in conducting cross-cultural studies of interactional structures in diverse language environments. First, in contrast to the *Nihonjinron* studies examined above which emphasise cultural specificity, CA may perhaps have been biased towards the investigation of universal features of interaction, partly as a reaction to theories which emphasise differences, but also because of its central concern with primordial aspects of the generic organisation of conversation. Secondly, "there is a risk that the pre-existing knowledge of the structures of one language, i.e. English, might cause a bias towards certain findings and cloud analysts' sensitivity to subtle differences in achieving an interactional task in other languages" (Mori 1996b: 14). Thirdly, unlike intra-cultural differences such as those between "preferred" and "dispreferred" turns which are systematically designed as "alternative" and different choices, "it is important to remember that most [cross-]cultural difference is not produced for the most part as difference, but as separate features of their own cultural milieu" (Lerner and Takagi, to appear). Among other complications this creates, the task of comparison requires an understanding of the respective linguistic and cultural contexts in which particular differences are embedded. The same case can be made for similarities. Prima-facie similarities between aspects of language use or interactional organisation may, on closer analysis, turn out to be rather superficial if not to mask more significant structural differences. An example may be afforded by the ostensible similarity of the syntactic units which may be employed to construct turns in English and Japanese (see Chapter 2). A fourth major hurdle confronting comparative studies is the difficulty of operationalising equivalent cross-linguistic concepts that can form the basis of a comparison (see Chapter 3).

In spite of these potential obstacles, cross-cultural studies provide a unique angle for investigating taken-for-granted assumptions about our own cultures. The ways in which members negotiate encounters in a familiar environment largely lie in the region of common-sense reasoning, and form a part of the "background expectancies" which normally go unnoticed (Garfinkel 1967). Moreover, "For these background expectancies to come into view one must be a stranger to the 'life as usual' character of everyday scenes, or become estranged from them" (Garfinkel 1967: 37). The researcher, *qua* member of a culture, operates to a degree under similar restrictions. Cross-cultural CA work, however, involves a deliberate attempt to bring into relief—through the sheer force of comparison—the relative contours of these very expectancies, thereby rendering mundane conduct more readily discernible and hence accessible for examination. In this sense, cross-cultural analysis promises to be not only a powerful method for the co-investigation of different cultures, but also a way to heighten sensitivity to aspects of one's own culture which may elude a mono-cultural analysis.

Furthermore, comparative analysis seems particularly useful for generating research questions. For instance, if a phenomenon is shown to be organised in a particular way in one language or culture, we can ask whether a similar structure also obtains in the other. If not, a further line of enquiry might proceed through an investigation into whether this lack may be compensated for through the enlisting of other resources. The dialectic of comparison can therefore be a valuable heuristic for exploring how certain linguistic and cultural features may account for a different realisation of a similar action. One of the ultimate aims of this book will be to work towards devising techniques and methods for carrying out cross-cultural CA analysis, while at the same time maintaining an awareness of the pitfalls of comparative methods.

1.5. The data

The primary data collected for this book have been limited to Japanese. All the English data consist of recordings and transcriptions which are widely available, either through networks of conversation analysts or through published works.

The Japanese data set for this book comprises roughly 60 hours of recorded, naturally occurring interaction as noted below:

1. The Shakujii corpus: about two hours of telephone conversations taken over two days at a home, conducted in the Tokyo dialect; mostly transcribed.
2. The Tokyo corpus: approximately 50 hours of video-recordings of interaction in a non-profit-making organisation in Tokyo; half of which are informal multi-party conversations among staff members, clients, and friends of members of the organisation, and the other half of which are informal staff meetings and seminars. Most of the participants speak the Tokyo dialect, and about two hours of the entire collection of tapes have been transcribed.
3. The Ishiodai corpus: roughly ten hours of video-recordings taken over several weeks in a home in Nagoya; minimally transcribed. Most speakers also use the Tokyo dialect.
4. The RKK corpus: a video-recording of a 30-minute conversation among three participants, two of whom speak the Tokyo dialect, and one of whom speaks a dialect of an unidentified variety; transcribed.
5. The IMD corpus: an 18-minute telephone conversation in the Kansai dialect, transcribed.
6. The OBS corpus: a video-recording of a seven-minute multi-party conversation among four speakers of the Tokyo dialect; transcribed.[2]

The data corpora consist mainly of interaction by speakers of the Tokyo dialect (sometimes referred to as "standard" Japanese). The findings of this book will therefore necessarily reflect the nature of the data.

As indicated above, the recordings include telephone conversations, multi-party conversations and informal meetings. Only about five hours of the recordings have been transcribed, but have been selected to represent these three types of setting. The transcriptions were initially made for the purpose of unmotivated listening, but have subsequently been used to conduct detailed analysis of specific phenomena. However, untranscribed parts of the corpora were reviewed in order to verify the initial analyses, and selected portions were transcribed as necessary. The latter procedure was necessitated by the dearth of transcribed Japanese data in circulation, and also enabled a consideration of a larger volume of data beyond the portions originally transcribed.

1.6. Conversational grammar

This section briefly introduces some rudimentary aspects of Japanese conversational grammar which will form a foundation for the discussion in this book, and some relevant terminology.

The word order of a language is one of the "syntactic practices" (Fox, Hayashi, and Jasperson 1996: 191) that participants may invoke for engaging in turn-taking operations (see Chapter 4). Although the word order found in Japanese utterances is varied (e.g. Hinds 1982; Ono and Suzuki 1992; Simon 1989), the "canonical" or "standard" word order is characterised by a predicate-final structure: e.g. Subject-Object-Verb or Object-Subject-Verb (Kuno 1973). Conversational data indicates that a turn is typically treated as nearing completion when a final predicate is heard, although this need not be the case, for instance (1) when multiple turns have already been projected (as in the telling of a longer story), (2) where a speaker continues contiguously after a final predicate (see Chapter 4; Hayashi, Mori, and Takagi, to appear), or (3) when a syntactically incomplete turn is used to perform a complete action (see Chapters 3, 5, and 6). The following are some illustrations. (Note that unexpressed elements are furnished in the English gloss enclosed in double parentheses.)

An example of a Subject-Object-Verb structure:

(1) [Tokyo10#2, p. 2] informal meeting

G: → *Hi: Hirano san ga himoron kaita n jyanai?*
Mr Hirano NOM gigolo theory wrote VN not?
[subject] [object] [verb]
'Wasn't it Mr Hirano who wrote about the gigolo theory?'

An utterance with a post-predicate component:

(2) [Shakujii 1A(#6), p. 3] telephone conversation

B is reporting to F about his wife Yōko who went to a beach the previous day.

B: → *Mata jyūni ji goro kara itta ttsu no ne:=*
again 12 o'clock about from went say FP FP
[verb]
'((She)) says ((she)) went out again from about 12 o'clock'

[*Yōko ga* (.) *'N*
[((name)) NOM yeah
['Yōko did, yeah'
post-predicate addition [subject]
=[
F: [*'N* ( )
[yeah
['Yeah...'

In the following fragment, lines 2 and 3 do not have any expressed predicate:

(3) [Shakujii 1A (#1), p.2] telephone conversation

In this fragment, A inquires whether Y is coming back to see A.

1 A: ***Modoru***?
returning?
'((Are you)) coming back?'

2 → Y: ***Mada***
'Not yet'

3 → A: ((laughing)) ***Ma: (h)da(h)*** hm=
not yet
'Not yet? hm'

A second important feature of Japanese noted in the literature is that it is a *postpositional language* in contrast to English, which is predominantly a prepositional language. Notably, Japanese employs postpositional "particles" instead of prepositions. Grammatically, "particles are used not only to represent case relationships, or to represent the functions that are covered in English by prepositions and conjunctions, but also after sentence-final verbs to represent the speaker's attitude toward the content of the sentences" (Kuno 1973: 4–5).

The postpositional attachment of particles and other grammatical elements can result in an incremental construction and recognition of an emerging utterance. This may mean, for instance, that a noun (or even a verb) can become recognisable as a subject, object, indirect object, etc. by virtue of some particle which is produced as the final component of the phrase containing the item, or that an utterance ostensibly being constructed as a main clause can be transformed into a subordinate clause (e.g. by appending a conjunctive particle) before the turn reaches a possible completion. Some examples are given below.

The case particle *ga* marks the prior as a subject:

(4) [OBS: 1]

C: *Iron'na shuri* ***ga*** *aru n da.*
various types NOM exist VN COP
'Various types exist'

The locative case particle *ni* marks 'Sochira' as the indirect object:

(5) [Shakujii 1A #7: 1] simplified

Y: *Sochira* ***ni*** *mukatteru to omou n desu kedo*
over there LOC: to heading QUOT think VN COP CONJ
'((I)) think ((he)) is heading over there'

The conjunctive particle *tara* renders what precedes it into a subordinate clause:

(6) [Shakujii 1A #4: 19]

Y: *De mata:: gen'ki ni nat* ***tara*** *asoberu mon ne*
and again well P become CONJ play VN FP
'And, when ((she)) gets well again, ((you)) can have fun, ((you)) know'

Due to the postpositional placement of particles, the type of a syntactic unit within the overarching structure of a turn may remain tentative and revisable as a turn unfolds. Such possibilities are bound to have important implications for projectability. These points are addressed in detail in Chapters 4 to 6.

Third, in spite of the existence of particles such as those dealt with above, there are several reasons for avoiding an excessive concern with the specification of grammatical types (e.g. lexical, phrasal, clausal, and sentential) as the building blocks of turns. An aspect of conversational grammar (in both languages, but more so in Japanese) which makes the task of identifying spates of talk in terms of grammatical types rather counterproductive is the prevalence of unexpressed elements in talk, a phenomenon usually referred to as "ellipsis" in the linguistics literature. Ellipsis is defined as "the suppression of words or phrases presumably intended by the speaker and understood by the listener" (Martin 1975: 28). As Maynard notes, "Japanese is well known for its frequent ellipsis of verbal and nominal phrases as well as ellipsis of particles" in which various parts of speech which are essential to the construction of phrases, clauses, and sentences in English can be absent, and "are to be interpreted by incorporating grammatical, contextual, presuppositional and socio-cultural information that is recoverable or identifiable" (1989: 32–3). For an example of an unexpressed subject, refer to fragment (3) above. The fragment below illustrates how participants may also construct turns without the explicit use of any particles:

(7) [Shakujii 2A(#5): 2] telephone conversation

K: *Bentō*?
takeaway lunch
'((Do you want)) a takeaway lunch?'

N: *Bentō MA::ru.*
takeaway lunch MA::ru
'((For)) takeaway lunch, ((I'd like)) a MA::ru'

It is therefore not always possible to identify a syntactic unit simply by examining its external grammatical structure. Instead, the analyst must resort to "covert" members' knowledge to supply the "missing" but "recoverable" elements. In particular, participants' treatment of ellipsis is often understandable only in the sequential and pragmatic context in which it occurs. Moreover, since it is likely that there will be more than one way to furnish the unexpressed elements, one can at most hope to identify a kind of "equivalence class" of possible items which may have been unexpressed in a particular instance.

Although "ellipsis" will be used here in the sense generally found in the linguistics literature, it is important to note that this term is an "analytical" category which does not necessarily reflect participant orientation that something has been left out. Hayashi, Mori, and Takagi (to appear), for instance, remark that "In Japanese conversation, unexpressed referents are massively *not* treated as 'absent' or 'omitted'." Furthermore, they show that ellipsis may be exploited by coparticipants in the joint construction of a meaning of an emergent utterance, especially when they become problematised by a participant.

In this connection, a preoccupation with extrinsic syntactic categories such as phrases, clauses, and sentences can deflect attention away from aspects of talk which are relevant and meaningful for the participants themselves in recognising, managing, and producing turns at talk. Reflecting these concerns, this study will predominantly centre around how specific grammatical resources are employed rather than on the identification of the variety of unit-types employed to construct turns.

The reader is also referred to Fox, Hayashi, and Jasperson (1996) for a discussion of the implications of grammar on repair in Japanese and English. For more detailed treatments of Japanese grammar, please refer to Shibatani (1990), Kuno (1973), and Martin (1975).

1.7. Organisation of the chapters

The second chapter begins the exploration into the workings of turn-taking in Japanese by examining the applicability to Japanese of the turn-taking system proposed by Sacks, Schegloff, and Jefferson (1974)—demonstrated to be compatible with turn-taking in English. It emerges that there is a general commonality on the basic level of the gross rules operative in the construction and allocation of turns, which suggests that turn-taking is also geared toward solving similar interactional problems in Japanese as in English. It is shown that the resources provided by the host language are mobilised by the turn-taking mechanism for the construction and projection of the shape of a turn-in-progress, and that turn-taking is ultimately directed towards the performance of social actions. Moreover, methods for allocating turns identified by Sacks, Schegloff, and Jefferson (1974) are also found in Japanese, and appear to be organised along a similar ordering of priorities. On this fundamental level, then, the components and rules of turn-taking in Japanese are found to be essentially the same as in English.

Despite the basic similarity exhibited by the turn-taking "rules" in Japanese and English, however, the locally available linguistic and other resources to implement these shared rules may result in some differences in the concrete realisations of the basic operations. Chapters 3 to 6 are devoted to cross-linguistic comparisons of aspects of "projectability", which is a key notion in Sacks *et al.*'s (1974) systematics. There are two ways in which the notion of projectability may be relevant to turn-taking. First, participants in conversational interaction need to be able to anticipate possible turn-transition points, or the likely places where a current turn may become recognisably complete. Secondly, certain features of turns may permit participants to anticipate how it might develop. Chapter 3 employs a quantitative method for characterising the projectable termination of turns, whereas Chapters 4 to 6 are devoted to detailed sequential analyses of the two aspects of projectability.

More specifically, a statistical approach is taken in Chapter 3 to investigate the distribution of grammatical, intonational, and pragmatic resources in the localisation of turn-transition points, through a comparison with a similar study conducted for English by Ford and Thompson (1996). Remarkable cross-cultural differences in participant orientations to syntactic resources are observed: first, Japanese utterances pass through relatively few points of syntactic completion in comparison to English; secondly, whereas turn-transition points in English almost always coincide with points in talk which are syntactically complete, it is shown that this is not always the case in Japanese. An examination of the Japanese data indicates that there is a small but non-negligible class of complete turns which are syntactically incomplete but are treated as relevant for turn-transition. In contrast to syntactically complete turns, this class of syntactically incomplete turns can leave implicit (or unstated) the performance of some social action. Moreover, it is also shown that turn-endings in Japanese exhibit a high degree of "orderliness", and can be roughly classified into four different types, depending on their terminal designs.

In the fourth chapter, attention is directed towards the major differences that grammar can make to the way participants construct turns as well as to project turn-shapes and turn-transition points (or transition-relevance places) in English and Japanese. The relatively rigid word order and the canonical Subject-Verb-Object structure in English permit participants from an early stage in the production of a turn to project the likely shape of a turn, what activity a turn may be occupied with, and the probable point at which it may reach completion. On the other hand, the grammatical features of Japanese, including the variability of word order, the predicate-final orientation, and the use of various postpositional particles (for which there are no clear equivalents in English) allow the speaker constantly to modify many aspects of the turn as it progresses. These properties of turns in Japanese make it more difficult (in comparison to English) for participants to anticipate how a turn may be developing, or the point at which it may reach termination. However,

Japanese participants have at their disposal two devices, specific grammatical turn-ending elements and marked prosodic features, which they can use to signal the arrival of a turn-ending shortly before or just as it is due. It is concluded that Japanese talk is characterised by the "incremental transformability" of turn-shapes and a relatively "delayed projectability" of turn-transition points (in comparison with English).

Chapters 5 and 6 pursue further the findings of earlier chapters through the investigation of the specific role grammatical particles play in the projection of turns in Japanese. Chapter 5 explores the use of case and adverbial particles for the incremental construction and projection of the trajectory of talk in Japanese. Chapter 6 considers the consequences of grammar on the different projectability properties of the "compound turn-constructional unit" in Japanese and English. This grammatical form—which is realised through pre-emptive procedures in English and through postpositional conjunctive particles in Japanese—provides a prime example of the relatively early projectability of turn-shapes in English, whereas its capacity to project further units is delayed and more equivocal in Japanese. Particles are therefore shown to be important resources used pervasively by Japanese participants in the construction, recognition, and projection of turns.

Notes

1. However, this argument has been disputed in recent scholarship by historians such as Amino (1993).
2. I am extremely grateful to Makoto Hayashi for sharing with me the carefully rendered transcripts noted under 4–6.

Chapter 2

Basic organisation of turn-taking

2.1. Introduction

This chapter represents a formative endeavour to disentangle potentially universal from linguistically and culturally relative features of turn-taking with reference to Japanese and Anglo-American English. It begins with an overview of Sacks, Schegloff, and Jefferson's (1974) model of turn-taking (henceforth referred to as SSJ) and briefly touches upon other major approaches, followed by a discussion of how SSJ's systematics may be incorporated in strategies for discovering generalisable versus culturally specific features of turn-taking. Secondly, the rudimentary components of turns and the gross "rules" for the management of turns in Japanese are examined, with a view to investigating whether the turn-taking organisation in Japanese is fundamentally compatible with SSJ's model, which has been demonstrated to accommodate idiosyncrasies in English conversation. It is concluded that the turn-taking system on the basic level of the rules identified by SSJ is also applicable to Japanese.

The work begun in this chapter will be continued in Chapter 3, which undertakes a quantitative study of cross-linguistic similarities and differences in the use of grammatical, prosodic, and pragmatic resources for the management of turns; Chapter 4, which deals with possible differences in the way turn-projection is accomplished in Japanese and Anglo-American English; and extended further in Chapters 5 and 6 relating to the projectability of certain particles in Japanese.

2.2. Sacks, Schegloff, and Jefferson's (1974) Model of Turn-Taking

This section summarises the key features of SSJ's model of turn-taking for ordinary conversation, which forms the point of departure for a conceptualisation of the notions of "projectability", "turn construction" and "turn allocation" in Japanese for this book. SSJ represents one of several current approaches for characterising the mechanism of turn-taking in talk-in-interaction. Other major attempts to describe the exchange of turns include the signalling and the stochastic approaches. However SSJ provides by far the most useful starting point for gaining an understanding of the organisation and operations involved in turn-taking (Goodwin 1979a), and will thus be treated in some detail. I start by briefly mentioning some features of the other two approaches, and proceed to discuss important implications of SSJ's model, particularly with respect to its possible cross-cultural applicability.

The stochastic approach (Jaffe and Feldstein 1970 and Cappella 1979, 1980) treats turn-transition as a probabilistic process, in which the probability of speaker change is calculated for specific interactional events such as silence or syntactic completion. A general weakness of the stochastic approach is said to be its inability to describe how participants actually orient to conversational phenomena since it mainly deals with probabilities (Wilson, Wiemann, and Zimmerman 1984). Nevertheless a statistical approach itself can to be useful for gaining a sense for the relative distribution of events which are associated with occurrences of turn-completion, as demonstrated in Ford and Thompson's (1996) study and Chapter 3 below.

The signalling approach (Duncan and Fiske 1977) regards turn-taking as regulated and determined through the use of vocal and gesticulation signals or "cues" by speakers to yield or suppress turn-transition, which are monitored by auditors. This approach has been criticised for its limited generalisability across cultures and languages (Wilson, Wiemann, and Zimmerman1984) as well as its lack of predictive power and analytic detail (Goodwin 1979a). Indeed by emphasising cues and conventions, which apply to specific turn-taking systems, it suffers from the problem of the infinite extendibility of description. More importantly it fails to address the socially organised features of turn-taking—as a normatively accountable structure of social interaction (see Goodwin 1979a). Duncan and Fiske's (1977, 1985) signalling approach has informed the fairly extensive treatment of Japanese turn-taking and other aspects of conversation by Maynard (1989). Her exposition combines a mixture of methodologies and approaches: specifically a statistical and rule-based view of turn-taking, which is claimed to be a synthesis of Duncan and Fiske (1977, 1985) and ethnomethodology. Although her work will be referred to in passing, the present book attempts to adhere to a more strictly CA-inspired approach.

In contrast to the probabilistic or deterministic approaches touched upon above, SSJ conceptualise turn-taking as organised on a sequential, turn-by-turn basis, operating globally through cumulative serial application. Drawing from the analogy of game-playing, turn-taking is characterised as an "economy" to co-ordinate and allocate a scarce resource which, in this case, is a turn-at-talk or control of the floor. The model is proposed as a generic one for "any conversation", involving any number of participants in a small-group situation, accommodating variations in the particular identities of the parties, setting, or context of conversation. While reporting on the model's consistency across an indeterminate number of languages, the authors note that cross-cultural applicability can only be verified directly through an empirical examination of conversational material from different languages (SSJ: 700). Since the Japanese language is linguistically and historically unrelated to English,[1] demonstrating the model's applicability to Japanese would contribute considerably towards enhancing the case for the proposed universality of this model. Before addressing the issue of generalisability, the main features of this model are outlined below.

The turn-taking system first of all involves the definition of minimal units out of which a turn can be formed, referred to as *turn-constructional units* (TCUs). An important characteristic of the units is their *projectability* as a unit, i.e. that there are features of the unit which allow participants to anticipate or predict where an instance of the unit will come to an end. For English they can vary syntactically over anything from sentences, clauses, phrases, to lexical items, but the construction of such units is also determined in the course of production by other factors such as context and intonation, so that "(i)nstances of the unit-type so usable allow a projection of the unit-type under way, and what, roughly, it would take for an instance of that unit-type to be completed" (SSJ: 702). Whatever unit-type is selected by the speaker to start a turn, the speaker is initially entitled to one of these units.

The first possible point at which a turn-constructional unit is hearably complete is called a *transition-relevance place* (TRP). This is a juncture where turn-transfer or speaker-change may potentially occur, though it need not necessarily take place at the first transition-relevance place.

Two *turn-allocation techniques* co-ordinate the transfer of speakership from the current speaker to the next. One is the current speaker inviting or selecting a coparticipant to speak next by means of a range of methods, such as employing the first part of an "adjacency pair",[2] using address terms, or simply by gazing at someone at the end of a turn. A second technique is for a coparticipant to appropriate the next turn by self-selection.

The following is a set of rules which operate over the transition-relevance places (TRPs) of turn-constructional units on a turn-by-turn basis to co-ordinate the allocation of turns. (C stands for the current speaker and N for the next speaker.)

1. Supposing that C has initiated a current turn, the following rules apply at the initial turn-constructional unit's first TRP, consecutively in the order listed:
   (a) If C selects N in the current turn, then N has sole rights and obligations to

speak next, transfer occurring at the first TRP after N has been selected.
(b) If (a) has not been applied, i.e. C has not selected N in the current turn, then any other party may or may not self-select, with the first starter gaining rights to a turn, transfer occurring at that place.
(c) If neither (a) C selects N nor (b) another party has self-selected, then C may, but need not, continue, thereby claiming rights to another turn-constructional unit.

2. At the initial turn-constructional unit's first TRP, if rules (1a) and (1b) have not operated, and (1c) has been applied, then at the next TRP, rules (1a–c) reapply, and recursively at each subsequent TRP, until speaker-change occurs.
(SSJ: 702–4; Levinson 1983: 297–8)

As an additional feature of the rule-set above, although the application of the rules is relatively ordered, the higher-ranking rules are constrained by the existence of the lower-ranking ones. Thus for instance, in order to methodically ensure that rule (1a) is applied (i.e. if C intends a particular N to have the next turn), C should select N before the end of the initial TRP, lest another party self-select through the application of rule (1b). Likewise, even though (1b) has priority over (1c), the former is nevertheless constrained by the presence in the rule set of (1c) (SSJ: 704–5).

The authors characterise the model along three dimensions: that it is locally managed, party-administered, and interactionally managed (SSJ: 724–7). First the model is a locally managed system in terms of turn order and turn size. The rule-set operates only on one transition at a time: from the current turn to the next turn around the next TRP. Further, turn-size is determined and managed locally, in the course of the production of a turn. However, through serial application, the system is said to operate globally, regulating transition of speakership throughout the course of a conversation. Secondly closely connected with the idea of the locally managed operation of turn-order and size is the characteristic of the model as a party-administered system rather than a predetermined turn-allocation system. By involving the cyclically applicable options provided by the ordered set of rules, and in particular, by means of the locally managed transition of one speaker stopping and another starting, the system integrates the co-ordination of turn-order and turn-size, and places the management of the turn-taking machinery at the discretion of the parties. A third critical characteristic of the model is that the unit of a turn as well as the turn-size is not solely specified by the speaker while others monitor its development, but that it is interactionally-determined. When a current speaker projects a possible TRP, the other participants are free to pass up the talk, influence the course of the talk, join in the talk, or to take up the opportunity to do a next turn at the next TRP. Thus for instance, "displays indicating that a unit has come to a point of possible completion are subordinate to the alternative possibilities for action created at such a point by factors such as the use of different speaker allocation techniques" (Goodwin 1979a: 441). A turn is therefore regarded as a real time, joint construction of the participants of a conversation. The emphasis on the interactional and pragmatic dimensions of turn-taking is a major feature distinguishing this model from the other two considered earlier, which respectively regard speaker-transition as a statistical phenomenon (Jaffe and Feldstein 1970, etc.) or as achieved largely through the production and recognition of turn-transfer signals (Duncan and Fiske 1977).

Furthermore, the three features above characterise conversation as the most fundamental among the various speech-exchange systems. Although conversation can be seen as residing on the lower pole in a continuum ranging over degrees of preallocation of turns, with ceremony on the higher pole, it is nevertheless regarded as a generic speech-exchange system, with all others involving some transformation of its systematics. According to Heritage

> There is every reason to view ordinary conversation as the fundamental domain of interaction and indeed as a primordial form of human sociality. It is the predominant form of human interaction in the social world and the primary medium of communication to which the child is exposed and through which socialization proceeds . . . . Research is increasingly showing that communicative conduct in more specialized social institutions embodies task- or role oriented specializations and particularizations that generally involve a *narrowing of the range of conduct* that is generically found in ordinary conversation. (Heritage 1995: 394–5, italics added)

Thus, turn-taking for ordinary conversation should perhaps be viewed not as just one turn-taking system among many, but as the most rudimentary, of which others (such as turn-taking in institutional contexts) are derivations or modifications. The primary focus on investigating conversational organisation in this book also reflects these considerations.

The authors show that the model described above is either compatible with or is derivative of the following list of gross facts which hold for any conversation:

7. Speaker-change recurs or at least occurs.
8. Overwhelmingly one party talks at a time.
9. Occurrences of more than one speaker at a time are common but brief.
10. Transitions (from one turn to a next) with no gap and no overlap are common. Together with transitions characterised by slight gap or slight overlap, they make up the vast majority of transitions.
11. Turn order is not fixed but varies.
12. Turn size is not fixed but varies.
13. Length of conversation is not specified in advance.

14. What parties say is not specified in advance.
15. Relative distribution of turns is not specified in advance.
16. Number of parties can vary.
17. Talk can be continuous or discontinuous.
18. Turn-allocation techniques are obviously used. A current speaker may select a next speaker (as when he addresses a question to another party); or parties may self-select in starting to talk.
19. Various "turn-constructional units" are employed; e.g. turns can be projectedly "one word long", or they can be sentential in length.
20. Repair mechanisms exist for dealing with turn-taking errors and violations; e.g. if two parties find themselves talking at the same time, one of them will stop prematurely, thus repairing the trouble.
(SSJ: 700–701, authors' cross-references omitted)

Some of these points will be examined in depth in this book.

To repeat, SSJ's model is proposed as a generic one for all conversations. It purports on the one hand to being *context-free* to accommodate variations over the number of participants, identities of the participants, the degree of familiarity between the participants, as well as being amenable to contextual changes, without altering the system *per se*. At the same time it is claimed to be *context-sensitive*, in other words, capable of being particularised to the specific local circumstances in the conversation it is meant to describe. The emphasis on this dual feature underlies the flexible design of the model to exclude reference to specific situations so as to allow variability across different sets of situations, identities of participants, or cultures (SSJ: 700–1). The case for the universal applicability of SSJ would be greatly strengthened if it can be shown to be sufficiently context-free to serve as a rough model for Japanese turn-taking organisation, while simultaneously exhibiting context-sensitivity (SSJ: 699) to enable specific application to a language as seemingly distinctive from English as Japanese.

In fact, this model has been widely viewed as a robust and comprehensive description of turn-taking which appears to operate irrespective of contextual, cultural, or grammatical differences. It has informed work on various aspects of social interaction: e.g. gaze (Goodwin 1981) gender (Zimmerman and West 1975; West 1979; West and Zimmerman 1983), dominance (Molotch and Boden 1985) silence (Wilson and Zimmerman 1986), classroom interaction (McHoul 1978), news interviews (Heritage and Greatbatch 1991), etc. Attempts to investigate the model's transferability to other languages include an early work on Thai by Moerman (1972), Boden's (1981) examination of conversation in Norwegian, Italian, and Farsi, and Ren's (1989) study of turn-taking in Mandarin Chinese. The reported research has thus far supported the postulated universal applicability of the model.

What appears to enhance the potential transferability of SSJ to other sociolinguistic contexts may lie in its primary focus on the underlying structural and sequential organisation of turn-taking rather than on their realisations as idiosyncrasies of "practices in" conversation which are likely to depend on the locally-available cultural and linguistic resources (cf. Heritage 1995: 394, n. 8). Thus a direction in which to proceed for discovering possibly *universal features* of turn-taking would be to focus on basic interactional tasks that turn-taking is used to accomplish. One might ask for instance, whether projectability is also a feature of turn-construction in Japanese; if the turn-taking system is geared towards the performance of social actions; whether similar basic turn-allocation techniques apply, and if so, whether they exhibit a similar organisation.

An examination of the possible convergence of diverse resources on the resolution of potentially shared structural problems may lead to the identification of universal features of turn-taking. Furthermore an attempt to differentiate the structural universals from the resources employed to enact them would make it possible to go beyond the process of simply enumerating differences in the culturally-specific cues or signals which, for instance, announce an imminent transition-relevance place, as has been pointed out as a weakness of the signalling approach (Wilson, Wiemann, and Zimmerman 1984: 166).

On the other hand, cross-cultural differences in turn-taking are likely to be associated with particularities of the host culture and the language in which interaction takes place. One prominent feature of a language which cannot be overlooked is its grammatical or syntactic organisation. In speaking of syntax however, it is important to differentiate syntax as traditionally defined by linguists for an idealised written form of discourse from syntax which is relevant to conversationalists: what Schegloff (1979) coined as "syntax-in-conversation" or what will be referred to here as "conversational syntax" (see Chapter 3 for a fuller discussion). Conversational syntax is seen to have organisational features which set it apart from the requirements of other types of discourse such as written language. For instance it is replete with "disfluencies", "hitches", "gaps", etc., which nevertheless manifest orderly properties. Furthermore conversational syntax is co-organised with other normative orientations of participants, such as repair and turn-taking (Schegloff 1979).

Thus, if conversational syntax is regarded as a resource or constraint in the production and recognition of "coherent" conversation (i.e. coherent to the participants), it can be expected to have a limiting as well as facilitating effect on the performance of operations involved in turn-taking, such as the construction of turns and the projection or anticipation of possible turn-completion points or transition-relevance places. It is difficult to conceive of such all-pervasive systems of conversational organisation as conversational syntax and turn-taking not being dynamically interrelated in actual practice. Moreover in view of its linguistic- or culturally specific nature, conversational syntax can be expected to be linked to possible idiosyncrasies in turn-taking operations of a language.

SSJ go as far as to imply that syntax and turn-taking operations interact in such a way that particular features of syntactical organisation are not only compatible with, but are moreover, built in as features of the turn-taking design in a particular language:

> (w)hile the rule-set itself appears to treat as central only the "projectable completion" features of its host's language materials, it seems productive to assume that, given conversation as a major, if not THE major, locus of a language's use, other aspects of language structure will be designed for conversational use, and, pari passu, turn-taking contingencies. (SSJ: 722)

Furthermore,

> "turns" are at least partially organized via language-specific constructional formats, e.g., syntactic construction (of which sentential construction is a most important and familiar, but not sole, instance). (SSJ: 730)

In a more recent work, Schegloff underscores the need to examine the interpenetration of grammar and turn-taking:

> From the point of view of the organization of talk-in-interaction, one of the main jobs grammar or syntax does is to provide potential construction- and recognition-guides for the realization of the possible completion points of TCUs, and potentially of turns. (Schegloff 1996a: 87)

Whether it is conversational syntax or turn-taking which has primacy over the other is immaterial to our present concerns. What will be the focus of interest here are the concrete ways in which conversational syntax and turn-taking may be interrelated and interlocked.

In addition to syntax, an entire constellation of other resources may be employed for turn-taking purposes: e.g. sequential organisation, gaze, timing or rhythm, intonation, prosody, and bodily conduct. The specific ways in which such resources are enlisted for turn-construction and turn-allocation are likely to be intimately linked to the local socio-cultural orientations or to the language used. The process of teasing out the concrete ways in which such resources can introduce variations in the accomplishment of interactional tasks could direct us to discoveries of possible cross-cultural differences. At the same time, we should not lose sight of the possibility that interactional concerns may well over-ride constraints inherent in locally specific designs of turn construction.

With the above considerations in mind, I embark on a study of Japanese turn-taking by employing SSJ as a starting point for an analysis of the basic operations involved in turn construction and allocation. The main aim of this chapter is to verify whether there is a mustering of the available interactive resources in Japanese towards the implementation of the rudimentary turn-taking operations identified in the model. On the other hand, Chapters 3–6 will examine closely the salience of the locally available syntactic and other socio-linguistic resources on turn-taking practices. Extricating the similarities from the differences, however, is neither a straightforward nor a clean process, since similarities and differences often consist of two sides of the same coin. For instance, it is conceivable that the very same phenomenon may appear either similar or variant depending on the order of generality in which it is considered (e.g. basic level of rules or how the rules are realised grammatically). Indeed it will be argued that while the general application of turn-taking rules may be shared on a gross level, their concrete manifestations in the two languages may take on quite divergent forms.

2.3. Projectability

This section begins to explore possible similarities in the fundamental organisation of turn-taking in Japanese and Anglo-American conversation. The intent is to examine if features which permit projectability of TRPs are incorporated into the construction and recognition of turns, and whether turns in Japanese also admit at least a partial characterisation in terms of syntactic categories. Section 2.4 investigates whether turn-allocation techniques are shared across the two domains of comparison and if the operation of the techniques is constrained by a similar structure of priorities.

2.3.1. *Mobilisation of resources for projectability*

As a prelude to the analysis in subsequent chapters, it may be useful to gain some sense for whether there is a general mobilisation of locally-available linguistic and sequential resources enabling participants to project the unfolding of a turn and the projection of turn-completion. The aim here is simply to see if the interplay of various communicative practices are directed towards turn-taking ends, and for projectability in particular. Even a preliminary analysis of *how* projectability may actually be accomplished must await an in-depth examination of the structure of Japanese turns in Chapters 4 and 5. For illustration, consider the following sequence involving an exchange of turns with no gap or overlap. To exclude possible gestural and visual resources, the excerpt has been selected from a telephone conversation.

H telephones her neighbour Y to find out whether the latter has any eggs that she can spare. To this, Y first checks on the number of eggs needed (line 1), and subsequently offers to deliver the eggs to H's house (line 5). Recall that unexpressed (elliptical) elements are noted in double parentheses in the English gloss in the third line.

(8) [Shakujii 1B#1–2] telephone conversation

1 Y: =*Futatsu mittsu de ii n de↑sho*=
two three P good N COP
'Two or three would do, right?'

2 H: =*Sō na no*=
SO COP FP
'That's right'

3 Y: =↑*Ne*=
FP
'Isn't it?'

4 H: ='*N*=
'Yeah'

5 Y: =*Jyā ima motte iku wa yo*=
then now bring over FP FP
'Then ((I))'ll bring it right over'

6 H: =*Sō↑o*=
'Really?'

7 Y: ='*N*=
'Yeah'

What is immediately recognisable about line 1 is its grammatical completeness as a sentential unit. Moreover it is hearable as a question by virtue of the rising intonation of the final word *de↑sho*. Without this intonational contour, line 1 would permit an alternative gloss as an assertion: '((I)) imagine that two or three would do', since *desho* employed without a rising intonation may in specific contexts be glossed as '((I)) imagine that . . .' What appears to render this line unambiguously complete as a turn is a combination of its grammatical completeness and sequential implication of the adjacency pair organisation involving a question which makes an answer due immediately upon its production: i.e. that after a question has been produced, the producer of the question should stop speaking, and allow the second speaker to provide an answer. Indeed the second speaker H starts up immediately with the answer *Sō na no* '((That))'s right' in line 2. This turn is another sentential unit, which incorporates further syntactic resources—a copula *na* and a final particle *no*—which are regularly used to announce the completion of a turn, to be discussed in detail in Chapter 4.

Y's next turn (line 3) follows without any pause, constructed as a lexical unit, consisting simply of the final particle ↑*Ne* 'Isn't it?' which serves to solicit reconfirmation of H's answer at line 2, i.e. whether two or three eggs will *really* be enough (see Tanaka to appear-c). Note that *ne* is referred to as a "final" particle, but it can perform a complete conversational action even when occurring alone as in this example, and represents a highly elliptical sentence. This particle is also delivered with a rising intonation, again consisting of the first part of an adjacency pair, soliciting reconfirmation.

H's answer *'N* 'Yeah' which follows contiguously in line 4 is hearable as an expected second part of this adjacency pair. The brevity of this turn renders it a reconfirmation of the answer given earlier in line 2, since further elaboration here could implicate some difficulty in producing a reconfirmation. As a second part of an adjacency pair, this turn is recognisably complete.

That Y ratifies line 4 as a positive confirmation of her understanding that 'Two or three would do' (line 1) is also revealed by Y's next turn in line 5: *Jyā ima motte-iku wa yo* 'Then ((I))'ll bring it right over'. The social action performed by this turn alone may have rendered it hearably complete, but its syntactic completeness and the employment of the two final particles *wa* and *yo* serve as additional grammatical devices to reinforce the recognisable completeness of this turn, thereby marking a possible TRP (more on these turn-ending devices in Chapter 4).

The fragment above suggests that a wide range of resources may be directed towards localising possible TRPs, permitting next speakers to judge when to begin speaking: e.g. syntax, grammatical particles, intonation, and the adjacency pair structure. The next task is to investigate whether, as in the model proposed by SSJ, speakers are initially entitled to one TCU, and if TRPs are treated as "appropriate" places for the current speaker to stop and for others to begin speaking. To see whether turn-transfers are indeed co-ordinated around possible TRPs, the following "deviant case" is examined. In this extract the current speaker attempts talking beyond an initial TRP (line 3) without taking pre-emptive measures to suspend its relevance.

The fragment is from an earlier part of the same transcript shown above. From the context of the conversation it is clear that H usually obtains her eggs through Y. In the portion shown below H asks Y (line 1) whether she intends to go to the supplier to get some eggs on that day. To this, Y replies that she is planning on going the next day (line 2). Again elliptical elements are supplied in double parentheses.

(9) [Shakujii 1B (#1), p. 1] telephone conversation

1 H: *Tamago*: *mada kyō wa*
eggs not yet today TOP
'((You haven't collected)) the eggs yet today?'

2 Y: *Ah- ashita iku no*
oh- tomorrow go FP
'Oh-((I))'m going tomorrow'

3→ H: *Sō deshō ne* [*kyō mata*
SO COP FP [today again
'That's what ((I)) thought' ['as for today, again'
[
4→ Y: [*Sō na no*
[SO COP FP
['Yes that's right'

In line 3, H reaches a possible initial TRP after producing a sentential unit, 'That's what ((I)) thought', ending with a copula *deshō* and a final particle *ne* which potentially mark turn-endings (Chapter 4). But it happens that H continues by beginning another TCU: *kyō mata* 'as for today, again'. However Y starts up (line 4) at H's initial possible TRP, thereby overlapping H's continuing turn. The precise placement of Y's entry at the initial TRP displays an orientation that a speaker is entitled to one TCU in the first instance, and that speaking beyond an initial TRP is vulnerable to overlap by another speaker.

The brief description above provides just a glimpse of the profusion of devices which may be put in motion for projecting the completion of turns. No doubt face-to-face interaction would have enlisted an even wider range of interactional resources such as gaze, posture, head, and hand movements. It appears that for any turn, multiple resources are co-ordinated for the localisation of a possible TRP. For instance, syntactic completion is just one of many ways through which projectability can be accomplished. Other grammatical resources, such as the use of copulas and final particles, may serve as devices to mark a possible turn-completion. A final intonation may contribute to indicating a possible TRP. Also sequential organisation, such as the achievement of an action which is conditionally relevant given a prior action, is a vital resource allowing participants to anticipate possible turn-completions. Thus the projection of TRPs can be regarded as an ongoing collaborative activity which also plays a crucial part in turn-taking in Japanese.

Moreover, as in English, there is a motivated reason for exploiting whatever resources are available to localise turn-endings:

> Turn taking is potentially problematic for those engaged in interaction when there is no prior arrangement providing for the order, lengths, or contents of turns . . . . In the absence of such arrangements, the participants must manage turn taking themselves in the course of the interaction and consequently require some mechanism to accomplish the exchange of turns in an orderly manner. (Wilson and Zimmerman 1986: 376)

This problem is arguably inherent in conversation regardless of the linguistic medium. What apparently remains invariant is that the projection of turn-completion is a universal problem that needs to be resolved in locally-occasioned ways through turn-taking. However, given the potentially great differences in grammar and cultural orientations of the socio-linguistic environments under comparison, at least some of the resources employed for turn-taking operations in Japanese may be culture- or language-specific, and hence unavailable in English (and also vice versa). Chapter 4 inspects some resources and practices which are employed in Japanese for turn-projection, and the resultant differences in the concrete methods by which similar turn-taking operations are actualised in the two languages.

2.3.2. *Turns as social actions*

Fragment 8 above exemplified a point of similarity between English and Japanese: the possibility of little gap or overlap through the employment of multiple resources for the production and recognition of possible TRPs. However, interactive resources available to Anglo-American speakers also permit the possibility of coparticipants beginning a next turn before the completion of a current turn, through "motivated" overlaps (see Jefferson 1983a, 1983b, to appear), collaborative and anticipatory completions and terminal-item completions (Lerner 1987, 1989, 1991, 1996), or alternatively, for passing over TRPs through the use of action projections such as "pre-pres" and the temporary relaxation of turn-taking rules through story-projections (e.g. Levinson 1983: 345–364).

As in English, Japanese participants also orient to features other than just the monitoring of an upcoming TRP to co-ordinate entry into talk. A striking cross-cultural similarity is observed in the kinds of instances where interactional considerations may be prioritised over displays which can mark turn-completion. This point is consistent with the key emphasis in SSJ on the locally and interactionally managed character of the turn-taking system, which is ultimately directed towards the accomplishment of situated social activities. What follows is a small selection of cases demonstrating this feature of interaction, though only fragments in Japanese are given in the interests of space.

Display of recognition

Recipients may display recognition through the use of the "change-of-state token"

Ah, which is crudely equivalent to 'Oh' in English (see Heritage 1984a) as well as a strategic placement of entry immediately after the point where the recognition takes place:

(10) [Tokyo 7 p. 23] multi-party conversation; slightly simplified

Before W arrived at this setting, the participants (including K) had been talking about Akutagawa's novel describing a Japanese woman displaying her grief not through facial expressions, but through a subtle wringing of her handkerchief. Immediately before the extract shown below, two participants M and K raise this topic again, describing a coparticipant H (who is not overtly expressive) as a member of the 'handkerchief team'. In line 1, W asks what is meant by this term. (Please refer to fragment (23) for a longer extract.)

1 W: *Ne*: *hankachi gumi tte nan na no*?
FP handkerchief team QUOT what COP FP
'Hey what's a handkerchief team?'

2 K: *Ano*:: (.) *Nihon no* [↑*ne*
uhm Japan GEN [FP
'Uhm, (.) you know the Japanese . . .'
[
3→ W: [*A- sō ka- ano-* . .
[oh so QP uhm
['Oh- right, uhm . . .'

W initiates repair in line 1, requesting clarification concerning what K is referring to by 'handkerchief team'. K responds in line 2 by embarking on an explanation: that it is a Japanese 'something'. But before K finishes her turn (i.e. before the onset of a TRP), W produces the interjection *A*-, the Japanese equivalent of an 'oh'-receipt in line 3. Indeed the part of K's talk shown in line 2 projects further talk to come, through the employment of the genitive particle *no* (see Chapter 5) as well as through the soliciting of an acknowledgement through the particle *ne* delivered with a rising intonation in this position (Tanaka to appear-c). W's turn-beginning in line 3 is therefore an "early" start before K's turn has reached an initial TRP. Nevertheless, by beginning early, W appears to be proposing that she now understands what is meant by the term in question. According to Heritage, "(t)he particle 'oh' is a major resource for the achievement of this proposal which, in turn, permits a mutually ratified exit from repair sequences" (1984a: 318). This fragment incidentally illustrates a similarity in participants' orientation to the token *A* (or *Ah*) in Japanese and 'Oh' in English, as well as the type of sequential environment in which the tokens may be employed in the respective languages.

Opportunistic completion

"Opportunistic completion" is a term employed by Lerner (1996) to describe a practice identified in English, whereby the "impedance of progressivity" of a turn provides a resource for coparticipants to make an early entry to complete a TCU-in-progress at "unprojected opportunities". The progress of a current turn may be retarded by various means such as laugh tokens, pauses, word searches, cut-offs, etc. That such locations in Japanese are likewise taken as opportunities by the next speaker to begin a turn is illustrated by the following fragment. W is describing a *kabuki* play Kanjinchō, which she saw as a child. She engages in a word-search for the name of the actors who appeared in the play. Terms appearing in line 2 refer to a naming practice whereby an actor inherits the name of his master (often his father) over generations, with a dynastic suffix such as *Godaime* 'the fifth' or *Rokudaime* 'the sixth'.

(11) [Tokyo 7 p. 31] multi-party conversation, slightly simplified

1	W:	*Kanjinchō ga at te*	
		((name of play)) NOM exist and	
		'They were doing Kanjinchō and'	
2		*·hhh u::: Godaime no ·hhh jyanai Rokudai::*	[*me jyanai- roku*
		the fifth GEN not the six::	[th not six
		'·hhh u::: the fifth, no ((I)) mean the six::'	['th, no, the six'
			[
3→	H:		[*Rokudaime desho*?
			[the sixth COP
			['The sixth, right?'

In line 2 W begins to search for the name of an actor who appeared in the play Kanjinchō, first proposing *Godaime* 'the fifth', then cancelling this with *jyanai* 'not'. Then W goes on to name the next possible candidate, *Rokudai*:: 'six::', using a sound stretch which indicates further problems in recalling the actor in question. Before W finishes stating the suffix *Rokudaime* 'sixth' in its entirety, H comes in with his suggestion 'The sixth, right?' in line 3. (Refer to Hayashi 1997 for a more extensive discussion of opportunistic completion in Japanese.)

Pre-empting a possible apology

Discussed below is an instance where grammatical resources permit a recipient to anticipate an upcoming apology, thereby providing an opportunity to pre-empt the apology before it is produced in full. A "compound TCU" format—e.g. syntactic forms such as *since X–therefore Y* or *if X–then Y* analysed by Lerner (1987, 1991)—and an adverb in the current speaker's turn project what type of turn is being produced, enabling the recipient to engage in an early performance of a "preferred" course of action (see Chapter 6).

Y had previously promised K to run an errand for her by stopping over at the house of a neighbour to make a payment on K's behalf. Prior to the segment shown below, Y has telephoned K to apologise for not having carried out the errand yet, stating that she had been rather busy. In line 1, Y goes on to reassure K that she intends to do it the following Monday:

(12) [Shakujii 1A (#4) p. 3] telephone conversation

1 Y: >*Getsuyōbi ni wa ikeru to omou n da yo*=
Monday P TOP can go QUOT think VN COP FP
'((I)) think ((I)) can go on Monday'

2 =*kokontokoro chotto sa* [*dearuiteta* [*mon de sa*:-
these days little bit FP [going out [VN since FP
'but since ((I))'ve been running around a bit these days'

[[
3 K: ['*N* ['*N*
['Yeah' ['Yeah'

4 Y: ***nakanaka*** [*yorenakute*<]
rather [can't stop by]
'It's been rather difficult to stop by'

[
5→ K: [*Warui ne*]
[bad FP
['Sorry for the trouble']

6 Y: Uun
'Not at all'

Line 5 is a case of an early start of a next turn before the arrival of a projected end of a turn-constructional unit. Y's utterance 'but since I've been running around a bit these days' in line 2 can be heard as the first part of an emerging compound TCU: *since X–therefore Y*. Further, the beginning of the formulaic adverb *nakanaka* 'rather' in line 4 hints that Y is about to report a difficulty which had prevented her from carrying out the errand. Indeed *nakanaka* normally precedes either a statement of inability such as *nakanaka umaku ikanai* (meaning 'even after repeated attempts, something cannot be done well') or alternatively, as a device for intensifying a positive description, such as *nakanaka subarashii* 'truly superb'.

Given that Y had already mentioned at the outset of the call that she had been unable to make the payment as promised, *nakanaka* can be heard as projecting a re-articulation of the inability to carry out this task. The production of *nakanaka*, then, provides a resource for K to anticipate that Y is about to reiterate the problem, which may even be followed by a further apology by Y of the said failure. By immediately launching into the next turn, *Warui ne* 'Sorry for the trouble' in line 5, K is able to pre-empt the projected reiteration of the trouble (as evidenced by the overlap) and an apology by Y. K may have been motivated to take an earliest possible opportunity to start to talk, not only to forestall Y's potential apology, but also to show affiliation by counterbalancing Y's report of failure through a display of contrition for the effort required by Y and to indicate that K is not treating Y's failure as blameworthy. Further, Y responds to K's intersected talk in line 6, by denying that it is any trouble: 'Not at all', which effectively reverses the prior position of apology-giver and apology-receiver. Thus K's early entry into Y's ongoing turn-space before the completion of the second component of a projected compound TCU displays an orientation to an early performance of a "preferred" action. To wait until Y repeats her report of failure may have been seen as confirming Y's conduct as reproachable.

The examples above illustrate just a few of the contingent ways in which delicate interactional work may be accomplished through a calculated placement of next-turn beginnings before a possible TRP. As in English therefore, participants do not simply wait for the production of potential "cues" such as syntactic completion and final intonation, which may mark a possible completion of a turn, but may strategically begin a next turn prior to a projected completion (see Ford and Thompson 1996). The positioning of talk then, not only displays sensitivity to the projectability of TRPs, but is also closely aligned with the expectable kind of social action it is performing on a particular occasion.

The next section examines the ostensible similarity observable with respect to the types of units which are employed for turn-construction.

2.3.3. *Unit-types*

As outlined in Section 2.2, SSJ identify turn-constructional units for English in syntactical terms as lexical, phrasal, clausal, or sentential constructions, such that their possible completion points are projectable for the type of construction they are. In other words, recipients do not start up a next turn at any arbitrary point, but discretely over the course of a turn at possible completion points of one-word constructions, phrases, clauses, sentences, or multiples of such units (p. 721).

To begin with, it is useful to see whether the termination of unit-types in Japanese are also oriented to as possible TRPs. The fragments below have been listed merely to illustrate that one-word constructions, phrases, clauses, and sentences also appear to be admissible as turn-constructional units in Japanese. The possibility of the next speaker starting up with no gap or overlap suggests that participants are likewise able to project the completion of such units. Suffice it for now to simply note some superficial similarities in the types of syntactical units, which are recognisable in their immediate sequential contexts as constituting turns. Rather than delving into an extended discussion of these fragments here, an in-depth analysis of turn-construction is left for Chapter 4.

2.3.3.1. *Lexical units*

Each of the turn-units below is a lexical construction. In this telephone conversation, a mother A and daughter Y exchange minimal turns in the course of attempting to arrange a meeting. A asks Y if she intends to return (to where A is calling from) through the use of the verb construction: *Modoru*? '((Are you)) coming back?', to which Y produces a highly elliptical response (with unexpressed subject, verb and object) consisting solely of the adverb: *Mada* 'Not yet'. A then recycles the same adverb, this time as a request for confirmation: *Ma*: (*h*)*da*(*h*) hm 'Not yet? hm'. Finally Y produces another adverbial lexical turn *Muri* 'Impossible' with an unexpressed subject and verb.

(13) [Shakujii 1A (#1), p. 2] telephone conversation

→ A: *Modoru*?
returning
'((Are you)) coming back?'

→ Y: *Mada*
'Not yet'

→ A: ((laughing)) *Ma*: (*h*)*da*(*h*) *hm*=
not yet
'Not yet? hm'

→ Y: =*Muri*=
'Impossible'

2.3.3.2. *Phrasal construction*

In this fragment, H rings Y to find out when Y's husband is coming to visit. H asks Y whether her husband had indicated that he was heading towards H's house (line 1). Y responds in the affirmative (line 2), to which H replies, 'Oh really' (line 3). Y then adds *Ano*: *betto tori ni* 'Uhm to get the bed', a phrasal construction (line 4).

(14) [Shakujii 1A (#7), pp. 1–2] telephone conversation

1 H: . . . *ah- uchi kuru tte itte mashita*?=
oh ((*my*)) house come QUOT say SFX
'. . . oh did ((he)) say ((he)) was coming to ((my)) house?'

2 Y: =*Eh::* =
'Yeah'

3 H: =*Ah-* (*honto*)
oh (really)
'Oh (really)'
[
4→ Y: [*Ano*: *betto tori ni*=
[uhm bed get P
['Uhm to get the bed'

5 H: =*Ah*: *sō sō sono koto de d(h)enw(h)a shit(h)a n(h) d(h)a*
oh: right right that matter P telephone did VN COP
'Oh: right right, that's what ((I)) telephoned about'

2.3.3.3. *Clausal unit*

Turns may also be constructed as a clausal unit, as in the following example from a telephone conversation in which A informs Y that she is visiting *kocchi* 'over here'. In constructing her utterance, A attaches a conjunctive particle *kara*: 'because at the end of a sentential unit *Kocchi kiteru* '((I))'m over here', transforming the sentence into a clause. It will be argued in Chapters 3 and 6 that ending a turn with a conjunctive particle can result in a turn which leaves unstated some consequence of an action, e.g. in this case, the implications of the fact that A is 'over here'.

(15) [Shakujii 2A(#4) p. 3] telephone conversation

→ A: *Kocchi kiteru kara*:=
over here have come because
'Because ((I))'m over here'

Y: ='*N wakatta*
yeah understood
'Yeah, ((I)) got you'

2.3.3.4. *Sentential unit*

The following is the same as fragment 8. The turns highlighted by the arrows are sentential.

(16) [Shakujii 1B#1–2] same as fragment (8)

1→Y: =*Futatsu mittsu de ii n de↑sho=*
two three P good N COP
'Two or three would do, right?'

2→H: =*Sō na no=*
SO COP FP
'That's right'

3 Y: =↑*Ne=*
FP
'Isn't it?'

4 H: ='*N=*
'Yeah'

5→Y: =*Jyā ima motte iku wa yo=*
then now bring over FP FP
'Then ((I))'ll bring it right over'

6 H: =*Sō↑o=*
'Really?'

7 Y: ='*N=*
'Yeah'

The arrowed lines represent "full sentences", but in fact, every line in the above fragment may be considered a sentential unit, if "elliptical" sentences are included (see Chapter 1).

From the examples above we can tentatively conclude that rough equivalents in Japanese of the syntactic units identified by SSJ can be used to construct turns, although other significant features of turn construction will be discussed in subsequent chapters. On first inspection these units seem to be employable in ways that allow participants to project when the instances will come to an end. Turn-transfers do not occur randomly as the turn unfolds, but at discrete points, which include completion points of syntactic units. Moreover the fact that next speakers may start up immediately after such units is in line with SSJ's "rule" that speakers are entitled to one such unit in the first instance.

The characterisation of turn-construction in terms of similar syntactic turn-units is in itself an interesting feature, but it gives us little idea of how projectability is oriented to by conversationalists in either language. Beyond noting that TCUs can be described partially in syntactical terms, SSJ go no further in specifying the concrete ways in which projectability is achieved:

> How projection of unit-types is accomplished, so as to allow such "no gap" starts by next speakers, is an important question on which linguists can make major contributions. Our characterisation in the rules, and in the subsequent discussion, leaves open the matter of how projection is done. (SSJ 1974: 703)

Indeed, the deceptive similarity of possible unit-types dealt with here will be shown subsequently to gloss over a host of differences in the grammatical realisations of the accomplishment of projectability in Japanese and Anglo-American English. For instance even the brief discussion in this section points to the potential importance in Japanese of what happens towards the end of a turn for gaining a sense that it may have come to a completion, particularly through the employment of elements such as final particles and copulas. On the other hand, the "canonical" Subject-Verb-Object structure of English grammar turns out to be consequential for rendering the beginning of a turn a key locus for projectability (see Schegloff 1987b). A more detailed treatment of such differences follows in Chapter 4. But for now, attention will be shifted to further cross-cultural similarities in the basic organisation of turn-taking, and in particular, to features relating to the second component of SSJ's model.

2.4. Turn-allocation

This section considers whether basic turn-allocation techniques are shared in the two socio-linguistic domains. Recall that for English, SSJ identify a set of turn-allocation techniques which operate recursively over successive possible TRPs in the following order of priority: the current speaker selects next, the next speaker self-selects, and the current continues or does not continue. The overall aim of this section is to investigate whether these fundamental types of turn-allocation techniques also exist in Japanese, and if their operation is crudely organised along the same order of priority.

2.4.1. *Current speaker selects next*

In SSJ the highest priority option operative in the allocation of turns is (1a): the current speaker selects the next. The selected coparticipant thereby gains exclusive rights and obligations to speak at the next possible TRP. Furthermore SSJ list a number of selection techniques employed in Anglo-American English conversation which permit current speakers to select next speaker(s), including (i) addressed questions or first parts of adjacency pairs used with address terms; (ii) repair techniques; (iii) tag questions; and (iv) incorporating the social identities of participants. Here the aim is to see if roughly similar procedures are also found in Japanese.

2.4.1.1. *Adjacency pairs*

SSJ note that an effective and perhaps most important technique for the current speaker to select the next is the use of first parts of adjacency pairs in conjunction with an addressing device (e.g. address terms, gaze, etc.). As noted earlier, an adjacency pair is an ordered pair of utterances or actions comprising of the association of a certain "first pair part" with a "second pair part" to form "pair types". The first pair part is produced with the expectation that the second part will be produced in the immediately following turn: i.e. in the adjacent turn. This property has been described by Schegloff (1972: 76) as *conditional relevance*, i.e. that the first action makes the production of a second action relevant, and its non-occurrence becomes a noticeable absence which is potentially sanctionable. Adjacency pairs then, are a powerful method to associate a first pair part with an "appropriate" second pair part. Adjacency pairs include question/answer, invitation/acceptance or declination, offer/acceptance or declination, complaint/denial, compliment/acceptance or rejection, and self-deprecation/denial, etc. (see Heritage 1984b: 269; Pomerantz 1978, 1984a).

Moreover, by incorporating an addressing device to a first pair part, the addressed person is selected as the second speaker who should then provide the second pair part, thereby doubly contributing to the selection and specification of the next speaker (SSJ: 717).

Examples may be found in the Japanese corpora which indicate that Japanese speakers also employ these generalised devices as next-speaker selection techniques. For instance in the following fragment, the participants have been talking about T's ability to operate a new personal computer without reading the accompanying instructions. M selects T as the next speaker, both through her gaze direction (addressing device) and by complimenting the latter on his superior sense of intuition (the first pair part of an adjacency pair, compliment/acceptance or rejection). T responds immediately, in this case by less favourably reformulating the activity referred to (see Pomerantz 1978).

(17) [NY3–2620] multi-party conversation
(M is marvelling at T's ability to begin using a new personal computer without first reading the instructions.)

M: ((looking at T) . . . *yappari kan ga ii n desu yo ne*::
after all intuition NOM good N COP FP FP
'. . . after all, ((you)) have a good sense of intuition'

minasan *no baai*
you ((plural)) P case
'in the case of people like you'

dakara (.) *.hh*
'therefore'

shize::n *ni wakatte* [*kite*
naturally P come to understand
'((it)) just comes naturally'
[
T: [*Iya mendokusai da- dake* (*hh*) *to* *iu* *oh*
[no bothersome DF only QUOT say DF
['No, it's just that ((I)) can't be bothered'

S: *hhh*

In fact, an address term may serve a dual purpose both to specify someone and as a summons of a summons/response adjacency pair. In the next fragment, H has been speaking on the telephone, and puts down the receiver to shout to Yōko chan who is in the same house to say that the call is for her, after which the latter picks up the receiver and starts to talk (not shown).

(18) [Shakujii 1B #2, p. 1] telephone conversation, simplified

H: *E::to* *Yōko* *chan* (.) *Nao*
uhm Yōko-((name suffix)) Nao
'Uhm, Yōko (.) ((It's)) Nao'

The fragments above illustrate that addressed first parts of adjacency pairs may also be employed by current speakers in Japanese as a technique to select the next speaker and attempt to bring about a turn-transfer.

2.4.1.2. *Repair initiators*

A variant of a question cited as a technique for selecting a next speaker without recourse to devices such as addressing is a "repair initiator" (Schegloff *et al.* 1977), as in "repetitions of parts of a prior utterance with 'question' intonation; a variety of 'one-word questions' such as *what*?, *who*?, etc.; and other 'repair techniques' " (SSJ: 717, citation omitted). There are parallels in Japanese conversation. The following instance of repair initiation involves a partial repetition of a prior utterance with a rising intonation:

(19) [Tokyo 10A: 11] informal meeting, simplified

S: . . . *matomete itadaku*: no dat ↑*tara ii to omou kedo*=
summarise to have VN if-then good QUOT think CONJ
'. . . although ((I)) think it would be alright if ((he)) were asked to do a summary'

= *ano*: *are jya nakute*
uhm that not
'uhm instead of that'

G:→ *Ah intabyū jya naku* [*te*?
oh interview not
'Oh, instead of the interviews?'

[

S: [>*Intabyū jya nakute*<
[interview not
['Instead of the interviews'

In the line highlighted above, the current speaker G selects S as the next speaker by doing a repair initiation of S's prior utterance: i.e. an "understanding check". As noted by SSJ, the selection of the next speaker is dependent on the turn-order bias introduced by the repair technique, which systematically singles out the speaker of the prior trouble-source turn. The above example in Japanese supports SSJ's claim that this technique is context-free and is identified solely in turn-taking terms (pp. 717–18).

2.4.1.3. *Tag questions*

Another technique for next-speaker selection identified in SSJ is the attachment of a tag question such as 'you know?' and 'isn't it?' to an utterance after the first transition relevance place which, in English, has the status of a "recompleter". As noted previously, this is a technique regularly realised in Japanese through the use of the final particle *ne*,though it may also be accomplished by other means. When employed in a turn-final position, this particle solicits some affiliative response from a coparticipant (see Tanaka to appear-c for a fuller discussion).

(20) [Tokyo 7(a): 30] multi-party conversation, simplified

→ W: . . . *āiuno ga* (0.8) *risō datta wake yo* ↑***ne***
that kind NOM ideal COP reason FP FP
'. . . that sort of thing (0.8) was ((my)) ideal, **you know**?'

→ G: *Ma:: mattaku gyaku desu mono* ↑***ne***:
well completely reverse COP thing FP
'Well, whereas it's just the reverse, **isn't it**?'

K: thh heh heh .hhh hhh [.hhhh hhh .hhh hhh
[
H: [*Honto ni sō na no*
[real P right COP FP
['That's truly the way it is'

The final particle *ne* may be attached at the end of an otherwise declarative format such as in the instances above—'. . . that sort of thing was ((my)) ideal' or 'whereas it's just the reverse'—and invite affiliation from coparticipant(s). This particle may thus be used to signal the end of a turn and select others as potential next speakers. In this sense *ne* can be utilised as "exit techniques" much like tag questions in English.[3] This device however, differs from other techniques mentioned above, since tags in themselves do not necessarily designate a particular next speaker, but may invite an unspecified coparticipant to take the next turn, whether in English or Japanese.

2.4.1.4. *Incorporation of participants' social identities*

SSJ demonstrate the existence of a further "current selects next" technique for English which operates through an incorporation of the social identities of the participants. As an example, when one partner of a couple asks someone to visit them, it is assumed by the participants that the partner is not one of those invited. Not surprisingly, such extra-linguistic techniques relying on shared social knowledge can also be observed in Japanese conversation.

In the following fragment, W's question recognisably selects her husband H as next speaker when she asks what would have happened if she were to be unfaithful and runs away with someone else. Note that since 'you' is unexpressed in W's turn, no linguistic device is used to specify the addressee of the question.

(21) [Tokyo 7: 16] multi-party conversation, simplified

W: → ( ) *moshi*( ) *watashi ga uwaki o ·hhh shi tara*
if I NOM affair ACC do if-then
'if I had an affair'

→ [*de dareka to* (.) *icchat tara dō shita*?
[and someone with ran away if-then what did
['and if ((I)) ran away with someone, what would ((you)) have done?'
[
( ): [( )

```
H:      Iya  [::::hijyo:::    ni nageki]  kanashinda kedomo            [.hh . . .
        well [   extremely P  wretched saddened       CONJ             [.hh
        'We::ll, ((I)) would have been wretched and saddened, but'     ['.hh . . .'
               [                          ]                            [
D:             [(                         )]                           ['N
                                                                       ['Yeah'
```

Independently of any other resources, reference to having 'an affair' may have been sufficient to pick out W's husband H as the next speaker.

The examples above indicate that certain generic structures of conversation (e.g. adjacency pairs, repair) as well as features of social organisation are enlisted by current speakers in both English and Japanese for the selection of the next speaker. Considered next is whether similar procedures can also be observed for self-selection in Japanese.

2.4.2. *Self-selection*

The basic technique for self-selection (rule (1b)) in English is said to be the "first starter goes", i.e. someone intending to speak should start as soon as possible at the next possible transition-relevance place. There appears to be a striking similarity in the operation of this technique in Japanese. Occurrences of simultaneous starts illustrate the independence for each participant of the determination of the timing of when to self-select in order to be assured of being the first one in:

(22) [Tokyo 7(a): 14] multi-party conversation, simplified

```
1 K:      . . . waku  no    sukima o    dete nai    to
                frame GEN   corner ACC  not go out  QUOT
          '. . . that ((it)) hasn't broken out of the pattern'
2         kōiu      koto  de  [shō
          this sort thing COP
          'is what it means, doesn't it?'
                              [
3 G:→                         [Daka ↑ra
                              ['Therefore'
                              [
4 W:→                         [Tsumari         sa: ·hh . . .
                              [in other words  FP
                              ['In other words ·hh . . .'
```

In the fragment above, G and W start up simultaneously in lines 3 and 4, illustrating the possibility of recognising an impending TRP, where a prospective self-selecting next speaker should start in order to claim the next turn. In Chapter 4, it will be shown that the onset of copulas such as *deshō* (as in this example) is contingently treated as signifying an imminent TRP.

In this connection, another point of similarity lies in the employment of appositional beginnings or "pre-starts" to embark on turns (or to claim the floor) without constraining what will follow or jeopardising the turn's analysability when subject to overlap with a preceding turn. For instance in lines 3 and 4 above, the speakers employ appositionals *dakara* 'therefore' or 'so' and *tsumari* 'in other words', which are connectives regularly latched onto a previous speaker's turn to link an utterance to a prior. Other commonly used appositionals include *ano* 'uhm', inhalations, and labial or "sibilant" sounds.

As in English, the rule that the first self-selector starts first does not imply that more than one participant regularly starts up of which the first one becomes the next speaker (SSJ: 718–19). Rather, only one party usually starts, since once the new speaker begins the turn, a second speaker would again have to wait until the next possible transition-relevance place to self-select. Overwhelmingly, there is a brief or no pause between the previous turn and next, or a short overlap.

Depending on the type of turn however, a second starter's talk may supersede the first starter's earlier start. SSJ claim that "when a self-selector's turn-beginning reveals his turn's talk to be prospectively addressed to a problem of understanding prior utterance, he may by virtue of that get the turn, even though at the turn-transfer another started before him, so that his start is second" (SSJ: 720). Again similarities can be observed in Japanese:

(23) [Tokyo 7(a): 24] multi-party conversation, slightly simplified; refer to fragment (10) for the background of this fragment

1 M: *Demo- Yoshida sensei mo=*
but Professor Yoshida also
'But Professor Yoshida is also'

2 *=ano hankachi no shh heh*
uhm handkerchief GEN
'uhm handkerchief's shh heh'

3 M [*heh ne::*
[heh FP
['heh ((you)) know'
[

4 K: [*Ne? hankachi gumi da mon ne?*
[FP handkerchief team COP N FP
['Isn't ((he))? ((he)))'s in the handkerchief team, isn't ((he))?'

5 H: *Sorya* [*sō ne*
that's [right FP
'That's [right, isn't it'
[
6 W:→ [*Ne: hankachi gumi tte nan na no?*
[FP handkerchief team QUOT what COP FP
['Hey, what's a handkerchief team?'

7 K: *Ano*:: (.) *Nihon no* [↑*ne*
uhm Japan GEN [FP
'Uhm, (.) the Japanese . . .'
[
8 W: [*A- sō ka- ano-* . . .
[oh so QP uhm
['Oh- right, uhm . . .'

In the fragment above K uses the term *hankachi gumi* ('handkerchief team') (line 4), characterising H as a member of the 'handkerchief team'. In line 5, H starts to respond, but is intercepted in line 6 by W's mention of a difficulty in understanding what is referred to by 'handkerchief team' in K's utterance in line 4. K begins to respond to this repair initiation in line 7 with a clarification. Thus, although W is the second starter (with H the first starter) in this instance, W is successful in getting the turn, as ratified by K's ensuing response which provides the explanation solicited by W.

It was argued above that the technique of starting first is a common way to self-select in the respective languages. While seemingly simple, this technique rests on precise timing to co-ordinate entry with reference to a prior talk's possible TRP or in the interests of performing an interactive task such as repair initiation. Further, turn openings regularly incorporate appositional turn-beginnings to enable an early entry while minimising possible loss of audibility through overlap with the prior turn or other contenders for the floor.

2.4.3. *The current continues*

Finally, the operation of rule (1c) will be investigated for Japanese: i.e. given the non-application of current selecting next (1a) and next self-selecting (1b), the current speaker may or may not continue. In the following telephone conversation, Y has just told A that she would not be able to go to see A until early evening (not shown). Then Y continues below (line 2) to provide an account that her baby is asleep. A short pause ensues, which may have been taken by Y as necessitating further explanation. Y continues elaborating on the account in line 4: that she cannot wake the baby up.

(24) [Shakujii 1A #1: 4] telephone conversation, simplified

1 A: [(   )
     [
2 Y: [*Ima ne- nechatteru n da*
     [now FP sleeping VN COP
     ['Right now, ((she))'s asleep'

3   (0.6)

4 Y: *chotto okosenai shi ne*
     a bit can't wake CONJ FP
     'and ((I)) can't wake ((her)) up, you know'

Y's turn (line 2) does not involve any technique to select a next speaker (non-application of (1a). Nor does A start the next turn through self-selection in the ensuing gap of 0.6 seconds in line 3 (non-application of rule (1b)). The duration of the gap represents a period when neither option (1b) or (1c) is taken until the silence is terminated in this instance through the selection of (1c) (see Wilson and Zimmerman 1986: 379). Y then continues in line 4 (i.e. invokes (1c)). This example illustrates that the technique of current continuing is also a turn-allocation option available to participants in Japanese.

2.4.4. *Ordering of the techniques*

What remains to be examined in relation to turn-allocation is whether the techniques considered above exhibit a ranking in Japanese congruent with that identified for English: i.e. that (1a) takes precedence over (1b), and (1c) is operative on the condition that (1a) and (1b) have not been selected.

We can readily find instances of the prioritising of rule (1a) current selects next over (1b) self-selection: i.e. that if the current speaker has selected the next speaker by some means, the latter has sole rights and obligations to speak; and in particular, these rights and obligations override attempts by others to self-select. Consider the following example involving an addressed question produced by M, which selects the next speaker T (through gaze direction and the content of the question):

(25) [NY3–805 4/1/89] multi-party conversation (slightly simplified)

M: ((gazing towards T)) *Ano omake ni* (.)
uhm extra P
'Uhm, on top of that,'

eiken ikkyū o otori ni natta n desho?
English proficiency test level one ACC obtained VN COP
'((you)) obtained the English proficiency test level one didn't ((you))?'

W: °*Ah*: [*sō*° ( )
'Oh [really ( )'
[
→T: [*Ha*: *muka:shi*: (*no*: *totta kinezuka tte*)
[* past P acquired skill QUOT
[*'(a skill acquired) in former times, one might say'

*This acknowledgement *Ha*: is difficult to translate, but it seems to display attentiveness to the prior talk, while not necessarily being an agreement. The place where it occurs is marked by * in the translations.

In the above fragment, M addresses a compliment to T designed as a question asking for confirmation that the latter had passed the English proficiency test level one (i.e. exercise of option (1a)). To this, W self-selects (rule (1b)), starting a turn with a news marker *Ah*: *sō* 'Oh really'. But T's subsequent start which responds to M's compliment overlays W's earlier start. This fragment exemplifies a selected next speaker exercising his sole rights to the next turn (rule (1a)).

The following is another example of a next-speaker selection via an addressed compliment:

(26) [Tokyo 28 2:09 (2)] multi-party conversation

1→ T: *Mō sensei tottemo happī sō de mō*: *oh heh heh heh*
very teacher very happy like P very
'((You)) seem so happy really oh heh heh heh'

2 [*heh heh* ((quiet laughter))
[
3→ M: [(*Ko*) *koko dake*(*ya*) *ne*. *Koko e kita toki dake yo ne*
[here only FP FP here to came time only FP FP
['Only here only when ((I))'ve come here'
[
4 H: [( )

5 G: *Iya iya*: [*doko e it temo*
no no [wherever to go even if
'No no: wherever ((you)) go'
[
6 T: [( )

In this instance, when T compliments M on seeming very contented, M and another speaker H respond simultaneously (lines 3 and 4). In the next turn (line 5), another coparticipant G addresses M's response, thereby ratifying M's claim to the prior turn. This fragment also exemplifies the priority of rule (1a) over (1b), while at the same time illustrating that the provision of rule (1a) is constrained by the possibility of (1b) being applied should (1a) not be chosen.

The next task is to investigate whether the invocation of rule (1c) is contingent on no-one resorting to the higher priority rule (1b). One situation which demonstrates this relative ordering of priorities is fragment (24) above, where the current speaker continues after a short gap during which no-one self-selects (i.e. (1c) operating after the non-application of (1b)).

The following is another type of sequential environment indicating the precedence of (1b) over (1c). In this fragment, a current speaker attempts to continue beyond an initial TRP (by applying rule (1c)), but stops talking when intersected by another speaker who starts near the TRP (invoking rule (1b)).

W and H have been describing what W's father was like when he was still alive. H has just mentioned that W's father was a very good person. W qualifies H's positive assessment by mentioning his neurosis in lines 1–4:

(27) [Tokyo 7: 34] multi-party conversation

1 W: *Dakedo hayaku shinkeishitsu de yoko ni nachat te*:=
but early neurotic P side P became and
'But ((he)) became neurotic at an early age and had to take to bed and'

2 H: =*'N*=
'Yeah'

3 W: =*tōisu ni hebaritsui te .hhh*
wicker chair on cling and
'clung to ((his)) wicker chair and .hhh'

4 *en nanimo i* [*wanaku nacchat*(*h*)*ta*(*h*) *ka*(*h*) [*ra*(*h*) *heh*
DF nothing say [not became CONJ
'became unable to s [ay a word' ((overlapping line 6))
[[
5 H: [*ah heh heh heh heh heh*

6 ( ): ['*N*: '*N*: '*N*:
['Mm Mm Mm'

7 W:→ ·*hhh* ·*hhh* [*s so*: *iu* ( )
[that say
['that kind of ( )'
[
8 K:→ [( ) *sō iu kachi handan no naka de sodate ba*
[( ) that kind value system GEN inside P grow up CONJ
['( ) if ((one)) grows up within that kind of value system,'

9 K: *ii kata wa sō nari(h) ma(h)su(h) ne*
good person TOP that way become SFX FP
'a good person is bound to turn out that way'

In lines 1, 3, and 4, W explains how her father became neurotic at an early age, and was unable to function socially. W reaches a possible TRP at the end of line 4, but starts to continue with her description in line 7 by invoking rule (1c). However when a new self-selecting speaker K begins to talk in line 8 overlapping W's continuing talk, W drops out. This instance exemplifies the precedence of (1b) over (1c).

A further illustration of the ordering of the techniques is afforded by the following "deviant case" where a speaker insistently talks beyond possible TRPs without obtaining prior ratification through devices such as pre-announcements. The current speaker K quickly passes over numerous TRPs, and finds herself in competition with another speaker G who makes repeated bids to self-select. Although the transcript does not adequately capture the prosodic qualities, the non-lexical sounds produced by G in lines 4, 6, and 8 can be heard as appositional beginnings prior to speaking rather than affiliative tokens. (The possible TRPs in K's talk are marked with asterisks*.)

(28) [Tokyo 7(a): 10] multi-party conversation: the English gloss has been provided separately below without quotation marks.

1 K: *.hhh Suto kanzen::: shugisha (desho)*=*
then perfectionist COP

2 = *tatoeba .hhh [ano kenkyūsha to shite mitomete [hoshii*=*
for instance [uhm scholar as accept [want
[[
3 H: [*eheh heh heh heh heh*
[
4 G: [*Hmm hmm*

5 K: [*tsuma to shite mitomete hoshii**=
[wife as accept want
=[
6 G: [*Hmm hmmm hmmm hmmmmmm*=

7 K: [*onna to shite mitomete hoshii* zenbu to.* ·hhh*
[woman as accept want all QUOT
=[
8 G: [*hmmm . . . hmmm*

9 K: [*de sakki- sakki-*] *no hanashi dato*=
[and the earlier- the earlier-] GEN talk if-then
[ ]
10 G: [(*Sakki*)]
[(the earlier)]

11 K: [( ) *uchi no* ↑*ne uchi no* [↑*ne*
[( ) my FP my [FP
=[[
12 G: [*sanyonin datte* [*'N::: ((trailing off))*
[three or four even if [Mmmm

13 K: *ano: shujin nanka dattara . . .*
uhm: husband for instance if-then

Gloss (X is an elliptical referent in the Japanese original, referring to W):

1 K: .hhh Then that makes X a perfectionist (doesn't it)*=

2 =for instance .hhh [X wants to be accepted as a scholar*=
[[
3 H: [eheh heh heh heh heh
4 G: [Hmm hmm

5 K: [X wants to be accepted as a wife*=
=[
6 G: [hmm hmmm hmmm hmmmmmm=

7 K: [X wants to be accepted as a woman,* wants it all.* ·hhh
=[
8 G: [hmm . . . hmmm

9 K: [and the earlier the earlier] as mentioned before=
[ ]

10 G: [(The earlier]
11 K: [( )my you know my [you know
=[[
12 G: [Even if there were three or four [Mmmm ((trailing off))
13 K: uhm: in the case of ((my)) husband, . . .

K employs the "latching" technique (denoted by '=') at the occurrence of possible TRPs in lines 1, 2, and 5. Indeed at the TRP in line 1, there is no pause before K launches into the next turn unit with *tatoeba* 'for instance . . .'. K speaks very rapidly, and leaves no pause at the possible TRP in line 2. Overlaying the end of K's second TCU (line 2), G attempts to self-select with a pre-start *Hmm* (line 4), which K over-rides by successively claiming further TCUs (lines 5 and 7). G starts up at the beginning of line 10, this time through verbalisation instead of non-lexical pre-starts. But again G's entry is overlapped by K competing to claim yet more TCUs by speeding up, speaking more loudly, and recycling parts of her utterance overlapped by G. Eventually G drops out, and K comes out in the clear (line 13). However K's repeated exploitation of the latching technique coupled with the massive resistance met by K to maintain speakership beyond possible TRPs in competition with G's attempts to self-select at successive TRPs paradoxically points to the precedence of technique (1b) over (1c).

> a speaker can talk in such a way as to permit projection of possible completion to be made from his talk, from its start, allowing others to use its transition places to start talk, to pass up talk, to affect directions of talk, etc.; and that their starting to talk, if properly placed, can determine where he ought to stop talk. That is, the turn as a unit is interactively determined. (SSJ: 727)

Thus although K has in effect "succeeded" in the competition for the floor, the outcome has by no means been positively sanctioned by other participants. (An additional method that K employs to compete for the floor in this fragment is discussed in Tanaka to appear-c).

The preliminary analysis above indicates that there is a basic structural similarity in the ordering of the turn-allocation techniques in Japanese and English.

2.5. Closing comments

In the foregoing, a striking similarity was observed with respect to the types of gross structural problems that turn-taking is catered towards resolving in Japanese and Anglo-American conversation, on the general level addressed by SSJ. The presence of multiple resources to enable participants to judge the onset of TRPs implies that projectability is also an integral feature of Japanese turn-construction. Similar turn-allocation techniques were identified for Japanese conversation, and were shown to share much of the same organisation as in English. Moreover turn-taking in Japanese was also seen to be interactionally managed: first and foremost directed towards the accomplishment of social activities. However different the local linguistic or cultural differences may be between Anglo-American and Japanese conversation, the basic workings of the turn-taking rules remains essentially the same.

It has been shown that many resources (e.g. syntax, sequential organisation, intonation, gesture, gaze, social knowledge) are implicated in turn-taking operations. However, this does not necessarily mean that the individual resources are shared cross-culturally or that the *concrete ways* in which they may be mobilised are the same. What needs to be underscored is the distinction between the gross level of turn-taking rules which have been described so far and the possibly disparate ways in which they may be implemented through the specific resources provided by the host language and culture.[4] Thus, although the discussion in this chapter has demonstrated the cross-cultural commonality of the turn-taking system on the most rudimentary level of turn construction and allocation, this is not to say that the available resources (such as grammar) cannot introduce major differences in the ways the rules are realised. The next chapter undertakes a statistical comparison of the mobilisation of grammatical, intonational, and pragmatic resources for the localisation of possible TRPs in the respective languages.

Notes

1. According to Shibatani, "Japanese is the only major world language whose genetic affiliation to other languages or language families has not been conclusively proven" (Shibatani 1990: 94). However, Japanese has been shown to share selected features with Korean, Altaic, Malayo-Polynesian, Tibeto-Burmese and, Dravidian (Loveday 1986: 3).
2. An *adjacency pair* is an ordered pair of utterances or actions composed of two parts, the initial and latter parts, produced by two different speakers, called respectively the "first pair part" and the "second pair part". The pairings are typed so that first pair parts are associated with certain second pair parts to form "pair types". The first part is produced with the expectation that the second part will be produced in the immediately following turn: i.e. in the adjacent turn. The first and second parts are relatively ordered with the first part preceding the second part—which cannot be any second part but one of the same pair type that the first part belongs to. Furthermore, there is a "rule" which operates on the production of adjacency pairs: "given the recognizable production of a first pair part, on its first possible completion its speaker should stop and a next speaker should start and produce a second pair part from the pair type the first is recognizably a member of" (Schegloff and Sacks 1974: 239).

3. However, it should be noted that a structural difference exists between turns ending with tag questions in English and final particles in Japanese. SSJ refer to tag questions as *recompleters* or (1c–1a)s (i.e., where rule (1a) is applied following the non-application of (1b) in the first instance). In other words, tag questions are appended following an initial transition-relevance place, in the second cycle of the operation of the rule-set. It is thus possible to distinguish the sequential structure of tag questions from addressed questions which involve the application of rule (1a) from the outset. Such a distinction cannot necessarily be made in Japanese, since, as discussed previously, final particles such as *ne* and *sa* may be appended to the ending of an utterance without passing through a transition-relevance place.
4. Having said this, it has nevertheless been shown that at least some of these resources are partially shared, and can be employed in roughly similar ways to accomplish similar ends (e.g. adjacency pairs and repair initiation to select next speaker; certain intonational contours; use of addressing devices like gaze).

Chapter 3

Syntactic, intonational, and pragmatic resources in turn-taking

3.1. Introduction

In a recent contribution to investigations into the interpenetration of grammar and social interaction (Ochs, Schegloff, and Thompson 1996), Ford and Thompson (1996) break new ground in research on turn-taking by pursuing further the work begun by Sacks, Schegloff, and Jefferson (1974), which characterised transition-relevance places (TRPs) primarily with reference to syntactic unit types (see Chapter 2 for a summary). Incorporating a statistical approach, and building on previous research into the role of syntax, intonation, and interaction for the localisation of TRPs (e.g. Oreström 1983; Wilson and Zimmerman 1986; Wilson, Wiemann, and Zimmerman 1984), Ford and Thompson extend the notion of TRPs in English by explicitly proposing that they are managed not only by syntactic, but also pragmatic and intonational resources.[1] The authors conclude that although "syntactic completion points alone are the least reliable indicators of any other sort of completion", the convergence of syntactic, intonational, and pragmatic completion points—coined "complex transition-relevance places" or CTRPs—are oriented to by participants as expectable places for speaker-change (Ford and Thompson 1996: 155–6).

The present chapter is a preliminary study to reflect this and other contemporary research to gain an overall distributional sense of how syntactic, intonational, and pragmatic resources are mobilised for localising TRPs in Japanese conversation through a comparison with Anglo-American English. First, a statistical comparison is made between the analysis of some Japanese data with Ford and Thompson's (hereafter F&T) results. Secondly, the Japanese data are further analysed in this chapter, with a view towards categorising the variety of types of turn-endings which are associated with speaker-change (possible TRPs). This exercise provides a rough indication of the available types of turn-ending designs which are typically used to produce, locate, and recognise TRPs in Japanese.

Specifically, this study addresses whether participants in Japanese also orient to CTRPs, or possibly other types of completion points as locations for turn-transfer. To give a preview of what is to follow, the statistical results first indicate that, of the various types of completions, pragmatic completions in general—and not just CTRPs—have a high correlation with instances of speaker-change in Japanese.[2] It is therefore concluded that all points of pragmatic completion (i.e. whether or not they are CTRPs) are candidates for TRPs in Japanese. Secondly, it emerges that syntactic completion points occur relatively less frequently in Japanese than in English. These differences raise the possibility that an important socio-linguistic difference may exist in orientations to syntax.[3] The results of this study suggest that Japanese conversationalists *do* rely on syntactic, intonational, and pragmatic resources in projecting TRPs, but that ultimately, the most important feature of conversation that has a bearing on the localisation of TRPs is whether or not a complete conversational action (i.e. pragmatic completion) has been accomplished.

However, as there are major limitations in the degree to which participants' indigenous orientations may be accessible through a statistical study (see Chapter 1), the findings of this chapter will be subject to more detailed sequential analyses in the remainder of this book.

Moreover, as Lerner and Takagi (to appear) point out, comparison of interactional organisation in two apparently divergent languages such as English and Japanese can be difficult, as details of interactive practices are deeply embedded in the particulars of their respective local social, cultural, and grammatical contexts. This point is felt most keenly in the present chapter. The danger that some ostensible cross-linguistic similarity or difference may be produced as an artefact of a particular research design is a real one indeed. Accordingly, two alternative approaches to the operationalisation of syntactic completion points (in Japanese) are considered to illustrate potential differences in results.

As touched upon in Chapter 1, the "operationalisation" and "quantification" of participants' orientations are controversial ideas in CA. It may be argued, for instance, that a preoccupation with achieving analytical comparability across cultures and languages can detract from the investigation of the situated character of interaction by masking more important issues. Moreover, it may simply not be feasible to formulate comparable operationalisations of phenomena to be measured due to linguistic differences, or because a phenomenon may not be well-defined (e.g. Heritage and Roth 1995; Schegloff 1993). On the other hand, the process of trial and error involved in an attempt to arrive at comparable criteria may itself prove to be a fruitful heuristic for improving visibility of interactive practices, by drawing attention to features which may not have easily identifiable equivalents in the respective languages under comparison. As an initial endeavor to come to terms with these research problems, no definitive claim of strict comparability of data or particular phenomena under scrutiny can be made at this stage, but will be regarded as an ongoing project.[4] Instead, one of the main aims of this chapter is to highlight some research issues which can emerge through the exercise of applying a particular method for studying interaction (such as the statistical calculations undertaken in F&T) in one socio-linguistic domain to another.

3.2. Operationalisation of syntactic, intonational, and pragmatic completion points in Japanese

3.2.1. *The data*

F&T use as their database audio-recordings of two multiparty conversations among middle class native speakers of American English, totalling approximately 20 minutes. The data used to conduct a corresponding numerical analysis for Japanese similarly consists of audio-recordings[5] of two multiparty conversations among middle-class native speakers of Japanese (of the Tokyo dialect), also lasting approximately 20 minutes, which will be referred to in this chapter as the "Tokyo" data. In one of the conversations, the participants comprise of six speakers, including an elderly married couple H and W. The talk centres around W's relationship with her husband H, concerning which W voices dissatisfaction, and other interlocutors (G, K, T, and M) offer their views. The other conversation also involves six participants, but is largely occupied by the talk of two of the participants K and S (both women) who are discussing the point that men can enjoy "quality time" with their children after work in a concentrated form, whereas wives are faced with the double burden of work and their children's day-to-day care.

While the equivalent duration of the respective data sets provides a comparable starting point for engaging in a statistical analysis, it should also be kept in mind that the Tokyo data and F&T's data may not necessarily represent "typical" conversations in the respective languages. Strict comparability is difficult to achieve since features of conversation can vary from one to the next, even within a particular language community. The observation that conversation is "interactionally-managed" (Sacks, Schegloff, and Jefferson 1974) is relevant here, since it is quite possible, for instance, that one or more speakers may "dominate" a conversation by telling extended "stories", so long as they have the ratification of other parties. In such a case, the relevance of a TRP may be suspended for the duration of the stories. The proportion of time taken up by such activities within conversations is bound to be variable, and have an effect on statistical results pertaining to the occurrences of TRPs. It would therefore be well to exercise caution in attributing undue significance to the absolute numbers of completion points which are calculated. On the other hand, it can also be argued that if major cross-linguistic differences do exist in participants' orientations to the resources under investigation, such features are likely to appear in some form in almost any sample of conversation of substantial length.

The Japanese audio recordings mentioned above are used as the basis for the statistical compilation in the interest of achieving some comparability with the data used in F&T. However, in Section 3.4, other data (as described in Chapter 1) have also been cited to illustrate points emanating from the statistical analysis.

3.2.2. *Issues in operationalisation*

F&T's formulations of syntactic, intonational, and pragmatic completions for English served as the point of departure for operationalising the three types of completions in the context of Japanese conversation. Their strategy of defining possible syntactic, intonational, and pragmatic completions independently of one another was initially considered, but a number of modifications have been introduced where believed appropriate in view of features of Japanese conversation. In aiming for a formulation of these measures in Japanese, it seemed reasonable to give thought to at least several questions:

1. Is it necessary to introduce a different mode of operationalisation due to sociogrammatical differences in English and Japanese?
2. What does the formulation measure?
3. Is the formulation relevant to the participants themselves?
4. If not, does it make any difference to the end statistical results?
5. Also, how would it be possible to alter the formulation to reflect endogenous understandings?

Discussed below are some issues which F&T's mode of operationalisation raises in the context of comparisons with Japanese, with a view towards discovering appropriate concepts for Japanese. With respect to the Japanese data, significant modifications of F&T's criteria for operationalisation of syntactic completion points have been made in light of point 1 above. Furthermore, two methods for calculating the number of syntactic completion points are initially considered, respectively based on an analytical criterion and one which approximates endogenous orientations (relevant to points 2–5 above).[6] However, the operationalisation of intonational and pragmatic completions broadly follow those employed in F&T's study. Ultimately, this exercise is a provisional attempt to formulate operational concepts which are most useful for illuminating the process through which participants parse talk to arrive at possible TRPs.[7]

3.2.3. *Syntactic completion*

F&T base their operationalisation of syntactic completion on the clausal unit, and judge an utterance to be syntactically complete "if in its discourse context, it could be interpreted as a complete clause, that is, with an overt or directly recoverable predicate, without considering intonation or interactional import" (p. 143).[8] Furthermore, syntactic completion is judged to occur incrementally in relation to prior talk, as in the following, where syntactic completion is marked by a slash:

(29) (K67) from F&T, p. 144

V: And his knee was being worn/- okay/wait./
It was bent/[a] that way/[b]

Thus, a slash indicates that the talk up to that point constitues a syntactically complete utterance, but not necessarily the portion of an utterance intervening between two slashes such as between [a] and [b] above.

In devising a workable operationalisation of syntactic completeness in Japanese, an initial problem is that the very concept of "clause" is somewhat contentious in Japanese (Fox, Hayashi, and Jasperson 1996: 209–13). More generally, taking even further F&T's expressed uneasiness about relying on established notions of "well-formedness" (p. 143–4), a case can be made for avoiding where possible, any reference to analytical syntactic categories such as clause, sentence, etc. Reflecting these concerns, syntactic completion will be defined in this study as *a point in a turn where no further talk is syntactically projected when considered within its prior context*, to be described in detail below. This definition would include minimal acknowledgements ("backchannels") proffered by those taking primarily a recipient role, and can also include lexical and phrasal units within their sequential contexts (as demonstrated in Sacks, Schegloff, and Jefferson 1974), as well as "collaborative completions" (Lerner 1987, 1991). However, in accordance with F&T, this definition does not "include a notion of the completion of a sequentially relevant conversational action" (p. 144). Thus, for instance, the pragmatic projection of further stories will not form a part of the notion of syntactic completion.

The first point to underscore is that the notion of "within its prior context" in the definition above is not totally independent of pragmatic and intonational features. Indeed, it can be argued that some accounting of pragmatic and intonational features—as explained below—would be necessary in order to identify points of syntactic completion which are relevant for the participants. First, the following extract illustrates how an utterance which is ostensibly syntactically incomplete in isolation can be recast as a complete syntactic unit when heard in the context of preceding talk, and further, how a determination of the utterance's relation to prior talk may be dependent, at least partially, on intonational factors.

In fragment (30) below, H (husband) and W (wife) have been talking about their marriage. In the section before the portion shown, H has remarked that even though his wife insists he would be happier with a *sewa-nyōbō* (trial translation: 'a traditional motherly wife'), he didn't want such a wife in the first place, implying that he is quite content about being married to W. To this, W provides a cynical interpretation that her husband must feel that way because it is convenient to have a wife who can assist him (professionally). The turn in question is line 10 below. Borrowing F&T's notation, syntactic completion points are denoted by a slash '/'.

(30) [Tokyo 7, p. 4 middle] (slightly simplified)

1 W: *atashi wa ·hh tokidoki ijinowarui kimochi ni naru tok ya,*
I TOP sometimes unkind feeling P become when TOP
'when I sometimes feel like being unkind,'

2 W: *·hhh sor ya: benri dakara desho*
that TOP convenient because COP
'·hhh "isn't it because it's convenient?"'

3 *tte ii taku naru koto an no yo ↑ne/=*
QUOT want to say become VN exist FP FP FP
'that's what ((I)) feel like saying ((to him/you)) sometimes, ((you)) know?'

4 H: *=Sore wa sō ne/*
that TOP SO FP
'That's right, isn't it'

5 (1.2)

6 H: *tto iu kara ikenai no/*
QUOT say because wrong FP
'that ((I)) say things like that is what's wrong with ((me))'

7 (1.4)

8 ( ): *'N/*
'Yeah'

9 M: *Nanka,=*
AP
'Sort of'

10 W:→ ***=atashi ga ire ba./***
I NOM exist CONJ: if
'if I am around'

11 M: *E*: ./
Yeah

In the extract above, W's utterance in line 10 'if I am around' regarded independently is not syntactically complete, since the conjunctive particle *ba* 'if' can project further talk (see Lerner 1991; Lerner and Takagi, to appear; Hayashi 1997). But when heard in the context of preceding talk, line 10 can be linked to W's prior talk in lines 1–3, i.e. that it is convenient (for H) if W is around. This phenomenon has also been described by Schegloff as "skip-tying" where "a speaker links a next utterance to their own prior, skipping over the intervening talk by another" (Schegloff 1996a: 96). W, in effect, disattends the intervening talk, and produces line 10 as a post-predicate addition (a recompleter) to lines 1–3: i.e. a subordinate clause to the main sentence in lines 1–3. The incorporation of context in the process of operationalisation, however, invariably implies that certain pragmatic features can be critical in the determination of syntactic completion points.

Notice that the intonational delivery of W's talk in line 10 'if I am around' can also play a part in the determination of line 10 as syntactically complete. In other words, it is also by virtue of the tone of "finality" hearable in the prosodic delivery of line 10 which can doubly reinforce the perception that line 10 might be a recompleter to W's prior talk in lines 1–3, as is ratified by M's acknowledgement in line 11. If instead, W had employed a continuing intonation at the end of line 10, it may have been heard as a preliminary part of an emerging "compound TCU" (Lerner 1987, 1991) with the form *if X* which projects a *then Y* format to follow, irrespective of the possibility of it being linked syntactically to lines 1–3 (see Chapter 6 for more on this point). Thus, the judgement as to whether a bit of talk is syntactically attached to prior talk or projects further syntactic units is partly informed by intonation, thereby suggesting that the perception of syntactic completion may on occasion be dependent also on intonational features.

Another crucial consideration in operationalising the notion of syntactic completion in Japanese—or for that matter in any language—is the possibility of parsing data in terms of at least two (or more, for making finer distinctions) different categories. Of salience is the distinction between (1) *conversational syntax*, i.e. syntax as oriented to by participants in conversation "based on the analysis of action and interaction and focused on the real time utterance as its unit" from what will be called here (2) *analytical syntax*, i.e. "the received version, based on the analysis of written texts and with a focus on the sentence" (John Heritage, personal communication; see also Schegloff 1979). What is notable about Japanese is the striking difference which is generally observed between spoken interaction and the written narrative (Shibatani 1990: 357–71; Clancy 1982).[9]

It is not possible within this chapter to deal extensively with the various distinguishing characteristics of these two types of discourse. But to note a few differences, a prominent syntactic feature of conversation which is systematically absent in written discourse is the use utterance-internal and final particles such as *ne*, *sa*, *yo*, *wa*, *no*, etc. (Shibatani 1990: 360; Clancy 1982). These particles are used in part for turn-taking purposes such as for eliciting acknowledgements, self-selection, and marking TRPs depending on the particle (see Tanaka to appear-c; Squires 1994; Maynard 1993; R. Suzuki 1990; Cook 1992). On the other hand, ellipsis of nominal forms, certain case particles, and the topic particle *wa* is said to be more prevalent in conversation than in writing (Shibatani 1990: 360–8). Moreover, in conversation, participants orient to interactional and contextual features which may be relevant for a determination of conversational syntactic completion points. As another contrast, prosodic features are obviously absent in analytic syntax (although it may be presumed that the reader will supply the "appropriate" prosodic gloss), whereas prosody and intonational features can be critical for a judgement of possible conversational syntactic completions, (as will be demonstrated in fragment (31) below).

Specifically, a difference which can be relevant for the way parties process talk is the phenomenon of *agglutination*. Whereas languages such as English and French are classified as the "isolating type", i.e. "all the words are invariable" (Crystal 1985: 166),[10] some other languages including Japanese and Turkish are known as the "agglutinative type", partially characterised by the "(a)bundance of affixes attached to a word base" (Sgall 1995: 54–6). Shibatani remarks that "Japanese is not as highly agglutinative as Turkish, especially in the domain of nominal constituents", but "in the realm of verbal constituents, Japanese shows a high degree of agglutination involving a fair number of suffixes in a row" (1990: 306). The following is "a typical order" of a predicate phrase given by Shibatani (1990: 307), in which suffixes are attached grammatically to a verb stem (see Chapter 4):

Vstem–causative–passive–aspect–desiderative–negative–tense

Furthermore, it has been reported that agglutination in Japanese applies not only to grammatical but also to phonemic construction. Neustupný notes that agglutination is consequential for how a series of units in talk gets segmented, and that there is an indeterminacy of phonemic segmentation which extends over the entire system (Neustupný 1978: 139). Following F&T in regarding an "intonation unit" as "a stretch of speech uttered under a single coherent intonation contour" (Du Bois *et al.* 1993), it is thus doubly unlikely that a point which occurs in the middle of an agglutinated segment produced within a single intonation unit would be heard as a point of syntactic completion in conversation. On the other hand, such considerations would not enter into an analytical definition of syntactic completion.

The parsing of syntactic completion points can therefore vary significantly depending on whether a conversational criterion (which would need to reflect participants' treatment of features such as agglutination and intonation) or an analytic criterion (independent of prosodic features) is used. This difference is illustrated by the following example in which candidates for analytical syntactic completion have been marked by #, and conversational syntactic completion by a slash /. The boundaries of the intonational units have been noted by the symbol ||.

(31) [Tokyo 7 p. 9, mid] slightly simplified

1 K: . . . *ano*:|| *Yoshiko sensei ni totte mireba*: ||
uhm name teacher P for

2 *tabun* ||
probably

3 *soko no bubun ga*
that GEN part NOM

4→ *chittomo kaishō* ***saretenai# mitaina*** *omoi ga*
not at all not resolved sort of feeling NOM

5 *oarininaru*# *n jyanai*# *desu ka* #/ ||
have VN not COP QP

6 W: *Ari masu*# *ne*: .#/ ||
exist SFX FP
'Indeed'

Gloss of lines 1–5: 'Uhm, for ((title of respect)) Yoshiko, isn't it the case that ((you)) have the sort of feeling that that part is not at all resolved?'

Analytical syntactic completion points may be deemed to occur at places in the talk where an utterance being produced, considered independently of prosodic features, does not syntactically project further units. Thus, analytic completion points (hash marks) can occur in the middle of an agglutinated segment. As parties in conversation parse talk in real time, however, analytic syntactic completion points such as those occurring between *saretenai* and *mitaina* (line 4) are likely to be passed up as irrelevant for conversational syntactic completion, unless of course, there is a prosodic marking or break of some kind at this point. But since *saretenai# mitaina* is not only fused morphologically through agglutination, but also produced as part of a continuous intonation unit in the data, the hash mark occurring after *saretenai* would most certainly not be considered as a candidate for conversational syntactic completion. A similar argument applies to the analytic completion points after *oarininaru* (line 5), *jyanai* (line 5), and *masu* (line 6). Thus, syntactic completion points which are identified on the basis of a formal analytical category can be out of alignment with participants' processing of the delivery of talk, which is to some extent informed by its prosodic and intonational delivery.

The foregoing discussion therefore implies that in Japanese, the recognition of conversational syntactic completion points, among other features, is likely to be informed by a consideration of syntax, pragmatic factors (to the extent they are consequential for how an utterance may be syntactically linked to prior or subsequent talk), and the delivery of an intonation unit: something that cannot be fully addressed here. On the other hand, analytic syntactic completion points would include conversational syntactic completion points, but also select other junctures in the talk where the utterance-so-far could be "imagined" as conversationally syntactically complete if the reader were to deliberately supply a final intonational contour.

To summarise, a conversational syntactic completion point satisfies Conditions 1 and 2 below; whereas an analytical syntactic completion point would only need to satisfy Condition 1:

1. within its prior context, no further talk is syntactically projected.
2. intonation is taken into account to exclude points which fall within agglutinated expressions, unless there is a prosodic break of some kind at that point.

In the case of F&T's treatment of English, the criterion for judging syntactic completion points appears to depend solely on grammatical structure to the exclusion of prosodic features. In this sense, an analytical criterion seems to be chosen. Although speculative, we also need to take account of possible cross-linguistic differences which might render the contrast between analytic syntax and conversation syntax in English (in the sense dealt with above) relatively insignificant in comparison to Japanese: e.g. structural[11] as well as lexical differences between the two versions of syntax in English are less apparent than for Japanese (e.g. there is no immediate equivalent of final particles; and agglutination is much more limited in English).[12] These considerations may make the distinction between the two forms of syntax more tenuous for English.[13] Thus, it may not be as unreasonable to use an analytical category for locating syntactic completion points in English, in the hope that their intersection with intonational and pragmatic completion points would in any event select the conversational syntactic points out of the analytic ones. For Japanese, however, it may be difficult to even identify possible conversational syntactic completion points unless morphological and prosodic features are taken into account.[14]

For the purposes of the statistical analysis which follows, syntactic completion in Japanese will be operationalised through conversational syntax, but the number of analytic syntactic completion points has also been supplied in one of the tables presented below to demonstrate the significance of the criterion chosen for calculating the number of syntactic completion points.

3.2.4. *Intonational completion*

F&T define intonational completion as "a point at which a *clear final intonation*, indicated by a period or question mark, could be heard" (p. 147, emphasis added). Thus, intonational completion is dealt with by F&T "only in terms of the binary distinction between 'final' versus 'non-final'", without considering syntactic boundaries (p. 146).

Specifically, F&T's basis for operationalising intonational completion is the "intonation unit", which it can be recalled is defined as "a stretch of speech uttered under a single coherent intonation contour" (Du Bois *et al.* 1993). Treating intonation as a "perceptual" or "auditory" phenomenon, intonation units were first classified as to whether or not they ended with a final intonational contour. Furthermore, in line with the transcription conventions already employed in Sacks, Schegloff, and Jefferson (1974), units ending with clear falling intonation were marked with a full-stop '.' and those terminating with a clear rising intonation were denoted by a question mark '?'. (F&T)

The same method for operationalising intonational completion points is employed here for the Japanese data for the purposes of this study. It should be noted, however, that the determination of final intonational contours necessitates further investigation and refinement in the future. On the one hand, the claim that "consistent and reliable judgements can be made as to intonation unit boundaries by trained analysts who have never heard the language being analyzed" (F&T: 146) suggests that F&T's method of identifying intonation units has some cross-linguistic applicability. On the other hand, recent studies on prosody and syntax suggest that a simple categorisation into clear rising pitch or clear falling pitch is far from straightforward (Couper-Kuhlen and Selting 1996). Previous research, moreover, indicates some differences in the structures of intonation units in Japanese and English (Clancy 1982; Maynard 1989: 21–3; Iwasaki 1993). These works report that intonation units tend to be longer and frequently have a clausal structure in English. In Japanese conversation, although intonation units are sometimes clausal (Iwasaki 1993), they are more often shorter and fragmented, consisting just of "(t)emporal, locative, and adverbial phrases, arguments of the predicate, modifiers, verbal complements, conjunctions, and even hesitations" (Clancy 1982: 73). In the scope of this chapter, it will not be possible to examine the implications of such differences for the auditory perception of intonational boundaries.

However, let me take a moment to explore some environments where a clear rising intonation was found. A total of 95 cases were identified in the Japanese data, of which 61 coincided with syntactic completion points—interrogatives or syntactically complete utterances ending with a final particle. A further 34 cases did not correspond to syntactic completion points, but occurred at syntactically incomplete points where final particles *ne* or *sa* were used mid-turn to elicit acknowledgements from coparticipants. In short, the rising intonational contours of such a deployment of final particles were indistinguishable to the unaided ear from the rising intonational delivery occurring at syntactically-complete locations.[15] Some possible implications of the differential intonational structures for the statistical results will be touched upon later.

The following are examples demonstrating endings of intonation units where a clear rising and falling intonation are found, respectively marked '?' and '.'

(32) [Tokyo 7: 17] slightly simplified

K: *Sono toki wa honki desho***?/=***
that time TOP serious COP
'In that case ((you/she)) would be serious, right?'

G: =*Honki desu yo***/.****
serious COP FP
'((She)) would be serious'

*Rising final intonation at syntactic completion point: interrogative. ** Falling final intonation.

(33) [Tokyo 7: 8] slightly simplified

1 H: *De- desukara* ↑***ne*?***
DF therefore FP
'Therefore ((you)) know'

2 *'N jya: ·hhh a:no te- kochira no* =
AP then uhm DF this side GEN

3 =*bengo o be- N bengo o sure ba ne*: . . .
defence ACC DF DF defence ACC do if-then FP

Gloss of lines 2 and 3: 'then uh:m if ((I)) were to defend ((myself)), then . . .'

*Rising final intonation at a syntactically-incomplete location: at a final particle.

Incidentally, the aspect of the intonational delivery of an utterance bearing on the discussion of conversational syntactic completion points (Section 3.2.3) differs from what is referred to here. Whereas the former pertains to the intonational and morphological linkage within an intonation unit, intonational completion is judged solely on the basis of the intonational contour employed at the terminal boundary of an intonation unit.

3.2.5. *Pragmatic completion*

"Pragmatic completion" is operationalised in F&T as an intonationally complete utterance which is "interpretable as a complete conversational action within its specific sequential context" (p. 150). A vital point to bear in mind is that all pragmatic completions are by definition, also intonationally complete. The authors further differentiate two levels at which an utterance can be seen to be pragmatically complete: "local" pragmatic completion referring to "points at which the speaker is projecting more talk, but at which another speaker might reasonably take a minimal turn such as offering a continuer, display of interest, or claim of understanding", and "global" pragmatic completion points which are places where nothing is being projected "beyond itself in the way of a longer story, account, or other agenda" (p. 150).

For this chapter, the "global" rather than the "local" sense of pragmatic completion will be employed, since the former appears to capture more effectively the notion that no further talk (or action) is being sequentially projected. The "local" sense is more difficult to operationalise for Japanese at this stage. Indeed, a survey of the literature on "backchannels" in Japanese suggests that more research is needed before we can reliably identify points in a speaker's talk where a recipient might proffer a minimal turn such as acknowledgements (e.g. Saft 1996; Maynard 1986, 1989, 1990; White 1989; Clancy *et al.* 1996).

Following F&T, a greater than symbol '>' is used to denote pragmatic completion points, as in the ensuing example:

(34) [Tokyo 7, p. 17, mid] simplified

K: *Sono toki wa honki desho*?/>=
that time TOP serious COP
'In that case ((you/she)) would be serious, right?'

G: =*Honki desu yo*./>
serious COP FP
'((She)) would be serious'

As described above, both the formulation of pragmatic completion and intonational completion for Japanese essentially follow the operational definitions proposed in F&T, whereas syntactic completion was operationalised in a radically different manner. Relevant to the coding of these completion points is that their identification involves an interpretive process on the part of the analyst (Paul ten Have, personal communication). Whether or not an intonation unit is perceived as final or non-final, for instance, can be disputable in certain instances. Likewise, the judgement of pragmatic completion can be open to different interpretations, as would be the case even for participants in conversation. In other words, the inherent "fuzziness" of the phenomena being measured is likely to introduce a degree of equivocality in the results obtained.

3.2.6. *Speaker change*

F&T calculated points at which speaker change occurred in order to study the association between the occurrences of the three types of completion points and speaker change. In judging and marking speaker change in the Japanese transcript, the following aspects of F&T's method were adopted, with minor modifications:

1. "Speaker change was judged to have occurred at any point where another speaker took a recognizable turn" (p. 152)—whether a "full turn" or an "acknowledgement" (including laughter). In slight contrast to F&T's specification, however, the category "acknowledgements" for Japanese will not include items such as "collaborative finishes" and "help with word searches", but only minimal acknowledgement tokens such as '*N*, *Mm*, *Nn*, *E*: , and *Hai* (equivalent to items such as 'Mm', 'Uh huh', 'Yeah', and 'Yes'). All other types of turns will be considered "full turns".
2. "Speaker change was marked at the completion point in the on-going turn which was closest to the beginning of the next speaker's utterance" (p. 152), which could be any of syntactic, intonational, or pragmatic completion point(s).

However, several major changes to F&T's criteria have been incorporated, as noted below:

3. In the case of overlap, F&T "judged a speaker change to have occurred at the closest completion point within two syllables to where the overlapping speaker started" (p. 152). For the Japanese data, it was considered inappropriate to limit the allowable span for speaker change to "within two syllables" of a completion point in view of (1) the possibility of participants operating according to mutually different metrics and (2) the doubtful equivalence of "syllables" in the two languages. Thus, the judgement of speaker change was based on whether or not a coparticipant started to talk "in the vicinity" of one of the possible completion points of full turns, basing the determination of the notion of "vicinity" on the analysts' familiarity with Japanese.[16] However, if the next speaker did not start a turn in the vicinity of any completion point, the overlap was marked at the precise location where it occurred as in F&T.
4. A noticeable silence following a turn of approximately one second or more before the onset of the next speaker's turn was marked as a "gap" instead of as an instance of speaker change—even if a speaker change subsequently took place—since an occurrence of silence indicates that, for whatever reason, an

opportunity to speak at a possible TRP was not taken. The choice of the one-second duration is derived from Jefferson's well-known research indicating that an interval of "more or less one second" is the threshold level beyond which conversationalists systematically treat a silence as somehow problematic (Jefferson 1989).

5. As will be elaborated below, in tabulating instances of speaker change for the completion points (see Table 2, page 83), the two types of turns—"full turns" and acknowledgements—were differentiated. To repeat, a "full turn" refers to any turn which is not a minimal acknowledgement token such as *'N* or *Hai*. Moreover, speaker change was counted only as a percentage of full turns: in view of (i) the possibly distinctive interactional work done by the two types of turns (F&T, p. 152), and (ii) since acknowledgements frequently occur in overlap with ongoing talk as in the proffering of *'N* 'Yeah' in lines 3 and 4 of the following example:

(35) [Tokyo 7: 14] multiparty conversation

The participants have been discussing W's marriage problems. In the part shown below, G is suggesting that W (who is being referred to as *sensei* 'teacher') need not have been so worried about being faithful to her husband.

1 G: . . . *sensei ga dareka sukina hito ga*
teacher NOM someone like person NOM

2 *dekita [ra dekita tte yo [katta jyanai ka to*: .>
had [if-then had even-if al [right not QP QUOT
[[

3→ ( ): [*'N*./>
['Yeah'

4→ ( ): [*'N*:: ./>
['Yeah'

5 ( ): *'N*: : ./>
'Yeah'

6 G: *Dakara* . . .
'Therefore . . .'

Gloss of lines 1–2: '. . . if (teacher) had fallen in love with someone, then that would have been all right too, it would seem'.

The production of the acknowledgement token *'N* in lines 3 and 4 above does not result in speaker change, as the speaker G is already talking when the acknowledgements are issued. The prevalence of this phenomena indicates that acknowledgements (at least in Japanese) are not necessarily oriented to as places for speaker change, although they may in particular instances. Another important consideration for the statistical analysis is that the inclusion of the number of speaker changes at occurrences of acknowledgements in the total number of speaker change points can obscure the determination of the frequency of speaker change points in relation to full turns.

3.3. Results of comparison

Table 1 (and Figure 1) is a compilation of the numbers of the various completion points for the Japanese data based on the mode of operationalisation formulated

Table 1. *Completion points in the English and Japanese data (based on conversational syntactic completion for Japanese)*

	Notation	English	Japanese
Total intonational completion	i	433	411
Total pragmatic completion	p	422	347
Total syntactic completion	s	**798**	**422**
Intonational and syntactic	i&s	428	347
Intonational and syntactic and pragmatic	i&p&s	417	325
Total analytic syntactic completion			877

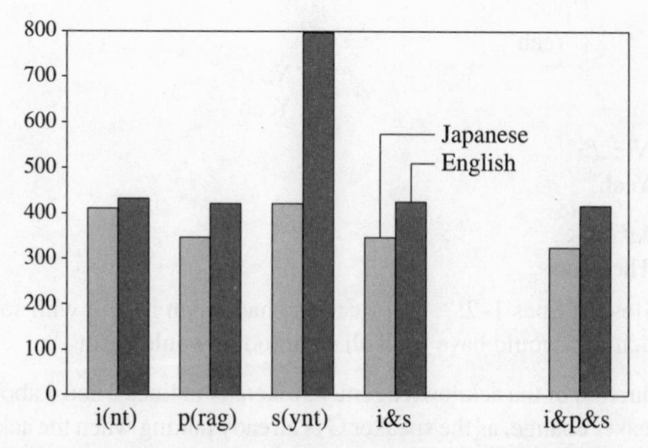

Figure 1. *Number of completion points by type (Japanese vs. English; partially derived from F&T)*

above in comparison with F&T's findings for English. A discussion of these results follows.

3.3.1. *Many more syntactic completion points in English in comparison to Japanese*

F&T found that the number of the co-occurrence of intonational, syntactic, and pragmatic completions (i&p&s) roughly coincided with both the numbers of intonational completions (i) and pragmatic completions (p). Moreover, while most of the intonational completion points and pragmatic completion points were also concurrently syntactic completions, the reverse did not hold. Indeed, only about half of syntactic completions were also intonational completions. In other words, syntactic completion points far outnumbered other types of completions.

A striking cross-linguistic contrast which is immediately obvious from Table 1 and Figure 1 is that for Japanese, the respective numbers of intonational (i), pragmatic (p), and syntactic completions (s), match more closely with the number of the coincidence of the three types of completions, i.e. the co-occurrence of syntactic, intonational, and pragmatic completion points (i&p&s), when compared with English. As indicated in Table 1, the respective numbers for Japanese are: 411 intonational completion points (i), 347 pragmatic completion points (p), 422 syntactic completion points (s), and 325 co-occurrences of the three types of completions (i&p&s). This difference can be largely attributed to the fact that syntactic completion points occur much less frequently and coincide to a greater extent with the other types of completions in Japanese in comparison to English.

Furthermore, for English, 98.8 per cent of intonational completion points were reported to be simultaneously syntactic completions (i&s). As for the Japanese data, a majority (84 per cent) of intonational completion points were also syntactic completions (i&s), even though this percentage is not as high as for English. These numbers are shown in Figures 2a and 2b, respectively. (The notation 'i¬s' refers to intonational completion points which were not syntactic completion points.)

The smaller percentage of intonational completion points which coincided with syntactic completion points in the Japanese data is partly explained by the fact that of the 64 (16 per cent) cases that were i¬s (i.e. intonational but not syntactic completion points), 34 occurred where final particles *ne* or *sa* were produced with a marked rising pitch at turn-internal positions to elicit acknowledgements from coparticipants (see Section 2.4). A further 22 cases of i¬s in Japanese overlap with the number of pragmatic completions which were syntactically incomplete (i&p¬s), as tabulated in Table 2 (p. 83) and discussed in Section 3.4.2 below.

Conversely, only 53.6 per cent of syntactic completion points were at the same time intonational completion points (i&s) in English, leaving 46.4 per cent of syntactic completions which did not coincide with intonational completion (s¬i), as shown in Figure 3a. As already noted above, this percentage presents a major divergence from the Japanese data, for which *a majority* (82 per cent) of syntactic

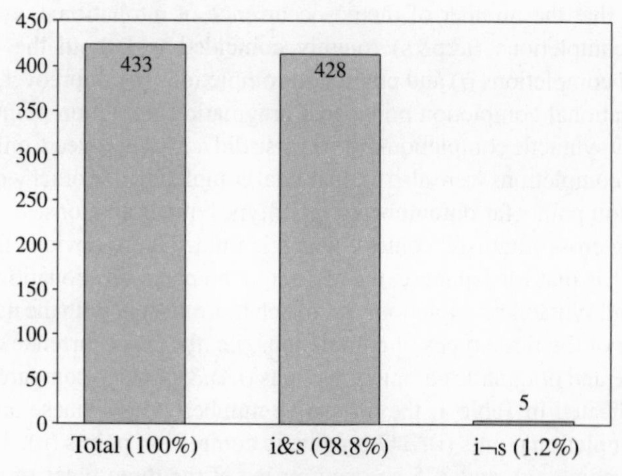

Figure 2a. *What percentage of intonational completions are also syntactic completions? (English; from F&T)*

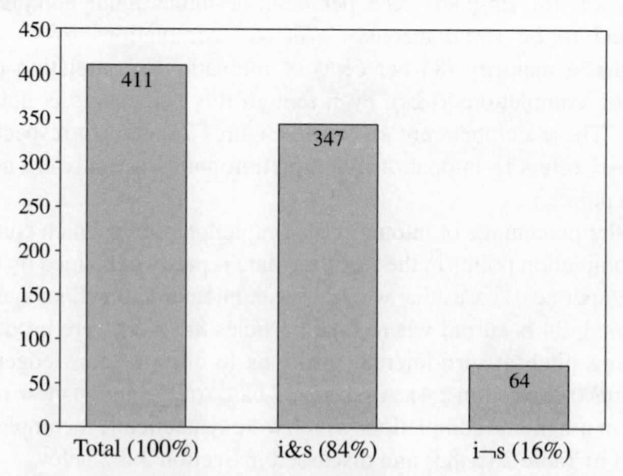

Figure 2b. *What percentage of intonational completions are also syntactic completions? (Japanese)*

completion points were also intonational completion points (i&s) as exhibited in Figure 3b.

In sum, although "syntactic completion points in English are *not* nearly always intonational and pragmatic completion points", and thus are "the least reliable indicators of any other sort of completion" (F&T: 154–5), syntactic completion points in Japanese coincide to a greater degree with all other types of completion. To reiterate, these results are related to the relatively smaller number of syntactic completion points in Japanese when compared with English. Perhaps this finding

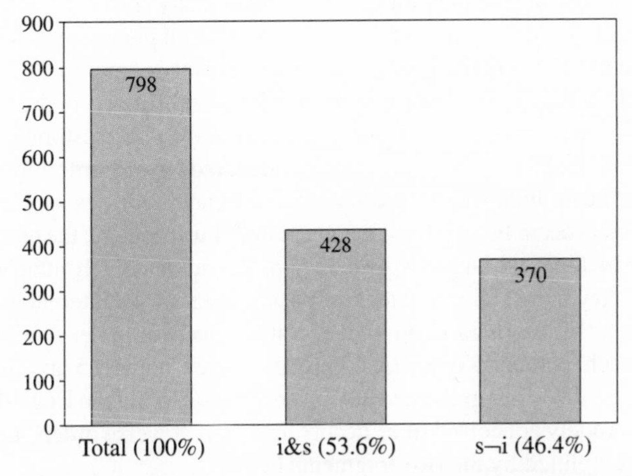

Figure 3a. *What percentage of syntactic completions are also intonational completions? (English; from F&T)*

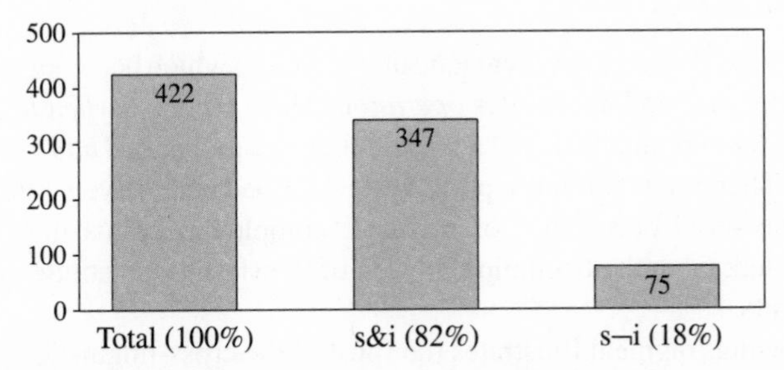

Figure 3b. *What percentage of syntactic completions are also intonational completions? (Japanese)*

is not as surprising as it may seem, however, given that the operationalisation of syntactic completion points in Japanese and English are based on different criteria.[17] Setting aside the differences in modes of operationalisation in the two languages for the moment, the relative infrequency of syntactic completion points in Japanese in comparison to English may also be due to major differences in the respective conversational grammatical structures, to be dealt with in subsequent chapters.

In this connection, it will be argued in Chapter 4 that the syntactic organisation of English typically permits an early projectability of the turn-design, whereas Japanese turns are overwhelmingly characterised by delayed projectability. In English, the main predicate often occurs early in the turn, with subordinate clauses and phrases regularly attached incrementally to syntactically complete utterances, as is suggested in F&T's description of syntactic completion points. This type of grammatical structure may inherently engender the occurrence of multiple syntactic completion points within a turn. On the other hand, several factors might contribute to the minimisation of syntactic completion points in Japanese. Postponing a detailed discussion for Chapter 4, the canonical or "standard" word ordering in Japanese favours a predicate-final structure where "subordinate" phrases such as the direct or indirect object occur before the main predicate.[18] Furthermore, the post-positional structure of the Japanese language (where particles are massively attached *after* the expressions they mark) allows extensive possibilities for an internal expansion of a turn through the use of case, quotative, conjunctive, and other particles without passing through a point of syntactic completion (see Chapters 5 and 6).

In a manner of speaking, then, syntactic completion points in English and Japanese can be crudely conceived of as occurring in the "reverse order" and "reverse time", as exemplified by the two fragments below:

(36) [(3) (K148) from F&T]

V: . . . made my Dad feel comfortable/. said that he's gonna have this/sa:me operation/when he's- in about (0.2) twenty years/cause he had bad knees/from football/n-in high school/

In this fragment, V starts a new syntactic unit with *said* which becomes syntactically complete after *this*, and again after *operation*. Then, a phrase *when he's- in about* (0.2) *twenty years* is attached, and a further clause *cause he had bad knees* is added after *years*. Thereafter, two more phrases are adjoined respectively after *knees* and *football*. The serial occurrence of syntactic completion points implies that the stretches of talk from the beginning to each of the slashes constitute syntactically complete units.

The following fragment illustrates the spirit of the cross-linguistic contrast. The reader is asked to engage in a kind of "mind-game" to highlight possible structural differences between English syntax and an example of the canonical word order in

Japanese. Temporally, only one conversational syntactic completion point occurs at the slash at the end of the turn (last line of the transcript). Curiously, however, each of the stretches of talk traced from a double slash to the single slash at the end of the turn also constitutes a syntactically complete unit. In other words, what makes this turn syntactically complete depends on what goes on towards the end of the utterance. (The background of the following fragment is provided with extract (30).)

(37) [Tokyo 7, p. 4, mid]	[gloss for each line]
W: *//Dakara sa:* therefore FP	'Therefore'
//atashi wa .hh I TOP	'as for me'
//tokidoki sometimes	'sometimes'
//ijinowarui kimochi ni naru tok ya unkind feeling P become when TOP	'when feeling unkind'
.hhh //sor ya: that TOP	'that is'
//benri dakara desho tte convenient because COP QUOT	'because it is convenient'
//ii taku naru koto* want to say become VN	'to want to say'
//an no yo ↑ne?/ exist FP FP FP	'there are times'

Gloss of turn as a whole: 'Therefore, there are times, you know, when I want to say ((to him)) that "isn't it because it's convenient" when ((I))'m feeling unkind sometimes'.

The structure of (37) is "anti-symmetric" to the English utterance) in the sense that many conversationally syntactically complete units are "embedded" in the single syntactically complete utterance above: i.e. the part of the utterance from each of the double slashes to the single slash at the end constitutes a syntactically complete unit. In this sense, syntactic completion points in Fragment (37) occur serially in Japanese when retroactively retraced from the end of the utterance in "reverse" order, in stark contrast to the points occurring forward in time in English (i.e. real time). Needless to say, however, the beginnings of these syntactically complete units for Japanese (marked by a double slash) are only available post-hoc to the researcher, and have no interactional significance for conversationalists. On the other hand, the "real time" imminent syntactic completion point for the Japanese fragment is only foreshadowed at the asterisk *, where the final verb component is beginning to be produced. The relatively delayed projectability of the syntactic shape of the turn means that the production of a syntactic completion point can also be deferred (but more on this in Chapter 4).

Finally, it should also be kept in mind that not all turns in Japanese have structures similar to this example, as multiple syntactic completion points may occur within one turn, for instance, when recompleters or post-predicate additions are employed to extend a prior turn (Section 3.4). It is also important to note that contextual and other features of the talk may allow coparticipants to anticipate a possible syntactic completion point even before the onset of a main predicate (see Chapters 5 and 6; Hayashi and Mori 1998; Hayashi 1997).

3.3.2. *Difference in coincidence with syntactic completion*

Another interesting result reported by F&T for English is that the numbers of intonational completion points (i), pragmatic completion points (p), the intersection of intonational completion points and syntactic completion points (i&s), and the coincidence of the three types of completion points (i&p&s) are almost identical. Indeed, 98.8 per cent of intonational completion points (i) and 98.8 per cent of pragmatic completion points (p) are also syntactic completion points (s). In other words, pragmatic, and intonational completion points are almost always simultaneously syntactic completion points. This, in turn, means that when an utterance is complete as a conversational action (i.e. pragmatically complete), it is almost always syntactically complete.

A somewhat different situation holds for Japanese. The Japanese data indicate that only 94 per cent of pragmatic completion points (p) and 84 per cent of intonational completion points (i) are simultaneously syntactic completion points. In particular, there is a total of 22 cases or 6 per cent of pragmatically complete utterances which, by definition, are complete as actions, but nevertheless incomplete in a syntactic sense.[19] Some implications of this difference will be touched upon subsequently in this chapter, and discussed in more detail in Chapter 6.

3.3.3. *The proportion of speaker change in Japanese is high for pragmatic completion points in general (i.e. both i&p&s and pragmatic completion points without syntactic completion, i&p¬s)*

Next, the incidence of speaker change at each of the possible combinations of completion points was computed for the Japanese data, in accordance with the procedure outlined in Section 3.2.6. The aim of this exercise was to discover which types of completion points have the highest correlation with speaker change. Recall that speaker change was calculated only as a percentage of full turns and not at completion points following acknowledgements, for reasons which have been stated in Section 3.2.6. The results are shown in Table 2.

F&T report that speaker change in the English data was most closely associated with the coincidence of intonational, pragmatic, and syntactic completion points (i&p&s), what they have called "complex transition-relevance places" or CTRPs. They thus conclude that intonation and pragmatics select from the many syntactic completion points, the ones which are oriented to by participants as relevant for speaker change. For this reason, i&p&s or CTRPs are seen to be equivalent to what Sacks, Schegloff, and Jefferson (1974) call "turns". The authors further note that even though a majority of speaker changes occurred at instances of i&p&s, only 47.5 per cent of i&p&s actually corresponded to speaker change points. This low percentage is attributed to "strategic and patterned interactional achievements", as dealt with in the CA literature (F&T: 157). One might also speculate that the relatively low correlation with speaker change may be due in part to the inclusion of acknowledgements in the total number of CTRPs for which speaker change was calculated for English, though this is something that cannot be verified without access to F&T's data.

As for Japanese, it can be seen from Table 2 that a high correlation with speaker change can be observed not only for the coincidence of the three types of completions (i&p&s), but in fact, for all pragmatically complete turns, i.e. the coincidence of the three completions (i&p&s) *as well as* for pragmatic completions not accompanied by syntactic completion (i&p¬s). First, speaker change was associated with 78 per cent of i&p&s (full turns) in Japanese. This percentage is remarkably high compared with only 47.5 per cent of i&p&s in English which

Table 2. *Speaker change (Japanese data)*

Type of completion point	Total no. of full turns	Speaker change (%)
i&p&s (int. and prag. and syntax)	149	**78**
i&p¬s (prag. and int./not syntax)	22	**73**
i¬p¬s (int. only/not prag. or syntax)	42	57
s¬p¬i (syntax only/not prag. or int.)	75	24
i&s¬p (int. and syntax/not prag.)	22	41
Analytic syntactic completion points (which were not simultaneously conversational syntactic completion points)	428	20

corresponded to instances of speaker change, as discussed above. Similarly, for pragmatic completion points which were not simultaneously syntactic completion points (i&p¬s), as many as 73 per cent were accompanied by speaker change in the Japanese data.

On the other hand, Table 2 also indicates that the coincidence with speaker change was significantly lower for all other combinations of completion points, though the samples are too small to draw any firm conclusions: speaker change at points which were only intonational and not syntactic or pragmatic (i¬p¬s) at 57 per cent;[20] only syntactic and not pragmatic or intonational (s¬p¬i) with 24 per cent; intonational and syntactic but not pragmatic (i&s¬p) with 41 per cent; for analytical syntactic completion points, excluding those which were simultaneously conversational syntactic completion points, the percentage of speaker change amounted to 20 per cent. These figures initially suggest that *pragmatic completion in general is most closely associated with speaker change in Japanese*. For this reason, it may be appropriate to use the terms "turn" or "TCU" (turn-constructional unit) to refer to all utterances ending with pragmatic completion in Japanese, rather than limiting it to only CTRPs (i.e. i&p&s) as in F&T's treatment of English.

Importantly, the low percentage of speaker change points (20 per cent) at analytic syntactic completion points (which were not simultaneously conversational syntactic completion points) is notable in connection to the earlier attempt to operationalise the notion of syntactic completion (see Section 3.2.3). Not only is this percentage considerably lower than the percentage of speaker changes at i&p&s (78 per cent) or at i&p¬s (73 per cent), but an inspection of the data also reveals that a majority of these speaker changes involved another participant proffering acknowledgements which display recipiency rather than turn-incumbency. Furthermore, none of these analytic syntactic completion points (which were not simultaneously conversational syntactic completions) coincided with either intonational or pragmatic completion points (by definition). These results show that the criterion of conversational syntax which was chosen for the statistical analysis has a significantly higher correlation with speaker change than the analytical variety.

As F&T discuss at length for English, participants in Japanese also strategically place speaker changes at junctures in ongoing talk other than at possible TRPs, and sometimes refrain from starting at possible TRPs. Such cases were briefly examined in Section 2.3.2. Here, it will simply be noted that: (i) there was a total of 168 instances where a speaker change occurred at points which were not in the vicinity of any of the three completion points; and (ii) of the 39 cases of all pragmatic completion points (i&p&s and i&p¬s) with no speaker change, 15 cases involved the current speaker continuing; in 9 cases, others were already talking; and in 15 cases there was a silence after a pragmatic completion point. A detailed study of cases similar to these has been undertaken for Japanese in Furo (1998, to appear).

3.4. Turn-endings

This section focuses on the structures of "full turns" in the Japanese data that are pragmatically complete—which were shown to correlate most highly with speaker change. As dealt with above, pragmatically complete turns in the Japanese data can be classified into two types: (a) those that are syntactically complete[21] (i&p&s) and (b) those which are syntactically incomplete (i&p¬s). In conducting the quantitative analysis, I was struck by the apparently extraordinary degree of "orderliness" which characterised the turn-endings of these pragmatically complete turns. As promised at the beginning of this chapter, the focus will now shift to an analysis of the grammatical and interactional features of the endings of these turns, in order to identify and tabulate some commonly observed forms and to assess their relative distribution within the Japanese corpus. To repeat, although the Tokyo data should not necessarily be taken to be typical of conversations in Japanese, this endeavour can be regarded as a preliminary attempt to gain a rough idea of possible turn-ending designs employed in Japanese and how they may be relatively distributed.

Recall that after excluding those turns which were minimal acknowledgements (e.g. *Hai*, *Ee*, *'N*, etc.), 171 "full turns" remained, further broken down into 149 turns which were syntactically complete (i&p&s), and 22 turns which were not syntactically complete (i&p¬s). Analysis of the endings of these turns reveal that they assume one of several generalised shapes, to be described below.

In the following discussion, the identification and statistical compilation of the turn-designs has been based strictly on the Tokyo data, but fragments from other corpora are also employed from time to time to shed light on particular phenomena which have been identified in the Tokyo data.

3.4.1. *Pragmatically complete turns which are syntactically complete (i&p&s)*

3.4.1.1. *Utterance-final elements*

First, turning our attention to i&p&s (characterised by syntactic, pragmatic, and intonational completion), syntactic completion massively, though not always, implies that a predicate component is produced, or is recoverable. Moreover, as will

Table 3. *Utterance-final elements (not exhaustive)*

(a) (SFX) final verb suffixes such as *masu*, *mashita*, *mashō*
(b) (COP) copulas such as *desu*, *deshō*, *da*, or *na*
(c) (FP) final particles such as *ne*, *yo*, *sa*, *ka*, *no*, *wa*, *zo*
(d) request or imperative: *kudasai*, *chōdai*, *nasai*
(e) others, including nominalisers: *wake*, *mono*, *mon*, *n*

be discussed in greater detail in Chapter 4, syntactic completion regularly involves the attachment at the terminal boundary of the turn, elements such as verb-following suffixes, copulas, and final particles: items which will henceforth be referred to as "utterance-final elements".

The following is an example in which points of syntactic, pragmatic, and intonational completion (i&p&s) are marked by utterance-final elements (highlighted in boldface.)

(38) [Tokyo 7 p. 28]

→ H: *Honto ni sō* ***na*** [***no.***/>
really P SO COP [FP
'((It))'s really so'
[
→ G: [*Sō* ***desu yo*** ↑***ne.***/>=
[SO COP FP FP
['((That))'s right, isn't ((it))?'
H: =*Sorekara*: . . .
'And also . . .'

In this fragment, H employs the copula *na* and final particle *no* marking the termination of his turn at the pragmatic completion, i&p&s. A speaker change occurs in the vicinity of this pragmatic completion. Likewise, H begins to speak immediately after G produces a pragmatically complete turn ending with a series of three utterance-final elements *desu yo* ↑*ne.*

In the Tokyo data, out of all instances of i&p&s, 71.8 per cent consisted of those ending with some form of utterance-final elements. Without going into any detail here, utterance-final elements seem to be directed towards at least three broad roles when occasioned in a turn-final position. First, they can contribute to the performance of turn-taking operations. The use of utterance-final elements for marking or announcing an imminent TRP when they are occasioned at the end of a syntactically complete unit will be examined in Chapter 4. Secondly, in addition to their use for essentially turn-taking purposes, utterance-final elements can be directed towards other activities. Indeed, a wide range of additional interactional work appears to be performed towards the end of the predicate component through a differential selection of particular utterance-final elements or a combination thereof. For instance the particle *ne* can be employed to solicit a supportive action from a coparticipant when employed turn-finally (Tanaka to appear-c). Thirdly, utterance-final elements seem to be mobilised for displaying the speaker's orientation to the context and as a social or relationship marking: e.g. displaying levels of "formality" to the occasion, "politeness" to addressee or referent, "deference" to addressee or referent, "coercion" to addressee, "intimacy" with referent or addressee, and the display of the speaker's "epistemic" relation to knowledge about something, to list a few possibilities (Tanaka 1996, to appear-b). Speakers select from among a range of possible utterance-final elements those which are fitted to the particular constellation of activities being performed and to the moment-to-moment way in which they constitute themselves vis à vis the interactional environment. This third potential use of utterance-final elements is somewhat conjectural at this stage, and very few studies from a conversation analytic perspective have been attempted to support these ideas (but see, for example, Maynard 1993; Kataoka 1995).

3.4.1.2. *Recompleters*

However, it is also the case that not all i&p&s completions end with utterance-final elements. The data reveals two generalised types of endings without utterance-final elements. One consists of "recompleters", i.e. turns that pass through a possible TRP, after which a further unit is adjoined which "recompletes" the turn under construction. There was a total of 18 occurrences of this shape (12.1 per cent of all instances of i&p&s). The recompleters can evidently assume almost any grammatical description, such as adverbial phrases, subject phrases, object phrases, clauses ending with conjunctive particles, etc. (see Ono and Suzuki 1992). The specific context in which such "additions" are produced and the final intonational contour can allow these instances to be heard as recompleters. Some examples are given below:

Adverbial phrase

(39) [Tokyo 7: p. 17] slightly simplified

A: → *Jya- honki dattara mitomerareru desho/=* ***kitto./>=***
then serious if-then can accept COP **most likely**
'Then, if ((she is/you are)) serious, then ((she/you)) can accept it, can't ((she/you)), most likely'

I: =*E*: *mitomerareru./>*
yeah can accept
'Yeah, ((she)) will be able to accept it'

Topic phrase

(40) [Tokyo 7: p. 22] slightly simplified

I: → *Yakimochi yaki masu yo*:: **./>** ***Sore [wa*:: *./>***
jealousy be jealous SFX FP that [TOP
'((He)) would be jealous as for that'
[

( ): ['*N*:: ./>
['Mmm'

W: *Yaka nai n jya nai ka to omou-*
get jealous not VN not QP QUOT think-
'((I)) don't think ((he)) would be jealous'

Subject phrase

(41) [Shakujii 1A(#6), p. 3] telephone conversation

B: *Mata jyūni-ji goro kara itta ttsu no ne*:=
again 12 o'clock about from went say FP FP
'((She)) says ((she)) went out again from about 12 o'clock'

→ [***Yōko ga*** (.) '*N*
[((name)) NOM Yeah
['Yōko did, Yeah'
=[

F: ['*N* ( )
['Yeah ( )'

Conjunctive particle

See fragment (30) above for an example of this type.

In the highlighted segments in each of the above fragments, a speaker first constructs a syntactically complete utterance which ends with utterance-final elements, and then goes on to append a further addition to the turn under way: an adverb, a topic phrase, or a subject phrase, respectively. These recompleters behave in much the same way as the incremental additions of further syntactic completion points in English discussed in F&T: i.e. the increment is not necessarily syntactically complete independently, but syntactic completion is calculated from the beginning of the turn to the end of the increment. Likewise, the recompleter portions above are not necessarily syntactically complete on their own, but only when considered as a continuation of the preceding syntactically complete portion. Interestingly, in each of the excerpts shown, the additions themselves do not have further utterance-final elements attached at their terminal boundaries. This appears to be a regular feature of the structure of recompleters, though there are exceptions. Indeed, in the Japanese data, there was only a single instance of a recompleter which terminated with any utterance-final elements (the particle *ne*).[22]

3.4.1.3. *The* iikiri *(truncated) form without utterance-final elements*

All the other cases of i&p&s which were not accompanied by utterance-final elements will be referred to here as the *iikiri* or "truncated" form. Note that this terminology is used for convenience to distinguish the remaining cases from the two types dealt with above, and is not intended to imply that the use of utterance-final elements is somehow the norm, nor that there may be something "lacking" when they do not appear turn-finally.

A total of 24 instances of the truncated variety was found in the data. Of this number, there were 19 cases in which a turn ended somewhat abruptly at the occurrence of a predicate, as in the fragments below:

(42) [Tokyo 7, p. 13] simplified

W is describing her husband below as someone who would have been fine as a friend, but not as a husband.

W: *Tsumari* *sa*: .*hh tomodachi dattara ii*:: *n dakedomo,*
in other words FP friend if-then good N even though
'In other words, ((it)) would have been fine if ((we)) had been friends, but'

→ *otto tte iu ki ga anmari* ***shina***[::*i*:./>
husband QUOT say feeling NOM very much does not
'((it)) doesn't feel as though ((he)) is ((my)) husband'
[
K: ['*N*::::./>
['Mm'

G: *Dakara*: . . .
'Therefore . . .'

In the above example, W's turn ends at *shina*::*i*:, which is the negative form of the verb *suru* 'do', without any utterance-final elements, but delivered with a final intonation. Another participant G starts up after this verb can be heard.

A recurrent sequential environment in which this format is found is "anticipatory completions", where a coparticipant completes a current speaker's turn-in-progress. Anticipatory completions have been analysed extensively for English (e.g. Lerner 1991, 1996) and also for Japanese (Lerner and Takagi, to appear; Hayashi and Mori 1998; Hayashi 1997). In particular, Hayashi and Mori (1998) demonstrate how participants in Japanese regularly furnish a verb or adjective to complete a speaker's turn-in-progress. The following is an example.

Just before the portion shown in the excerpt, H has mentioned that his wife (W) frequently suggests that he (H) must prefer a traditional motherly wife (instead of someone like herself). H continues below, indicating that he is going to refute this suggestion, as is foreshadowed by the adverb *zenzen* 'not at all', but pauses for a microsecond at the end of line 1. In line 2, another participant T produces a candidate predicate: *iya* 'don't like'. Notice that the participant T anticipates an upcoming predicate using the *iikiri* (truncated) form:

(43) [Tokyo 7: 4]

1 H: *Dakedo boku zenzen sewa (heh) nyōbō-* (.)
but I not at all traditional motherly wife

2 → T: *Iya.*/>=
don't like
'((is something you)) don't like'
[anticipated predicate]

3 H: =o hoshiku nai no yo./>
ACC don't want FP FP

Gloss of lines 1 and 3: 'But I don't want a traditional motherly wife at all'. It is difficult to provide a gloss of line 1 independently of line 3, since English does not normally permit the possibility of the object coming before a verb.

Though further investigation is required to probe into the interactional and contextual implications of truncated forms, this design can be massively occasioned in relatively "informal" or "intimate" talk.[23] Observe the following telephone conversation between a mother A and her daughter Y:

(44) [Shakujii 1A (#1), p. 5] telephone conversation

Y's daughter Yurika had previously been suffering from an upset stomach. A asks Y if Yurika has recovered.

1 A: *Yurika chan onaka no hō* ***daijō↑bu****?*/>
((name)) tummy GEN as for alright
'Is Yurika's tummy alright?'

2 Y: *'N daibun mata* ***naotte kita.***/>
yeah a lot again getting better
'Yeah ((it))'s getting a lot better again'

3 A: ↑*Ah* ↓***sō.***/>
oh right
'Oh, **is ((that)) right**'

Each of the turns in the above fragment terminate at a predicate without utterance-final elements, highlighted in boldface: line 1 ends at the predicate *daijō* ↑*bu* 'alright'; line 2 with *naotte kita* 'getting better'; line 3 with ↓*sō* 'is ((that)) right'.

Although the examples of the truncated form presented above conform to the predominant pattern of terminating at the occurrence of a predicate, it should be noted that this is not necessarily the case. Indeed, there were five other instances of the truncated form in the Tokyo data which consisted of lexical or phrasal turns. They included two instances of idiomatic expressions *naruhodo* 'indeed' and *dōmo* 'sorry', and three more cases which may fall into a kind of residual category: (i) a repair initiator, (ii) a combination of repair and acknowledgement, and (iii) a dramatic enactment of a greeting. Further analysis of the truncated form in relation to the localisation of TRPs follows in Chapter 4.

The results discussed in this section are summarised in Table 4.

Table 4. *Turn-endings of pragmatically complete turns which are also syntactically complete: i&p&s. (Full turns 149 = 100%)*

Turn designs	No. of cases	% of all i&p&s
Ending with utterance-finals	107	71.8
Not ending with utterance-finals: recompleter	18	12.1
Not ending with utterance-finals: truncated	24	16.1

3.4.2. *Pragmatically complete turns which are syntactically incomplete (i&p¬s)*

The range of turn-endings of pragmatically complete turns which are associated with syntactic completion in the Japanese data have been described above. To recapitulate, the computational work conducted in Section 3.3 pointed to a high correlation between speaker change and *all* pragmatic completion points—irrespective of whether they were syntactically complete or incomplete (see Table 2, page 83). Next, the structure of the endings of *pragmatically complete yet syntactically incomplete* turns (denoted i&p¬s in Table 2) will be investigated. Recall that as many as 73 per cent of these instances were accompanied by speaker change within the Tokyo data.

An examination of these turn designs reveals that they are not syntactically incomplete in an arbitrary way. Rather, the endings of this category of pragmatically complete turns are typically characterised by a relative dearth of items such as suffixes, copulas, and final particles (i.e. utterance-final elements). And in the very slots where utterance-final elements might otherwise appear in syntactically complete turns, are found particular types of grammatical constructions which syntactically project further talk by extending the TCU under way (items which will be called "extensions" as listed in Table 5). It will furthermore be suggested that these items can leave implicit entire projected clauses or other units of talk.

On first inspection, it may appear odd that grammatical constructions which syntactically project more to come should be treated as speaker change points. And indeed, it is also the case that the items listed in Table 5 are regularly employed mid-

Table 5. *Extensions (not exhaustive)*[24]

quotative particle *to* or *tte*
quotative particle *to* + *iu* 'say'
quotative particle *to* or *tte* + *iu* 'say' + question particle *ka*
conjunctive particle: e.g. *kedo*, *kedomo*, *te*, *kara*, *dakara*, *ba*
conjunctive particle (as above) + final particle *ne*

turn for projecting further syntactic units, thereby connecting a turn-in-progress with ensuing talk. A rather long fragment is employed below to illustrate these points.

Prior to the following excerpt, W has been complaining about her marriage, and the participants are theorising about a possible cause of the problem. In the extract shown, K proposes one of her first theories as to why the marriage has not been successful, by asking W if the latter blames the institution of marriage itself as being unjust (lines 1–5). W answers in the negative: that it is not the institution itself which is to be blamed, but it is (presumably) too late to do anything about her situation since she missed the opportunity (lines 6–27). Notice that many pauses, hesitations, rephrasings, and restarts are contained within W's emerging formulation of her position on the matter, which indicates that a disagreement is being produced. Through recourse to grammatical constructions like those listed in Table 5, W puts together her argument little by little, by incrementally extending her turn without passing through any syntactic completion points (until line 27):

(45) [Tokyo 7 p. 1] simplified

1 K: *Nantonaku rifujin na kanji ga shi masu?*/> (.)
somehow unjust feeling NOM do SFX
'Does ((it)) somehow seem unjust?'

2 *sono* (.)
'the (.)'

3 *kekkon seido sono mono tte iu ka*,=
institution of marriage itself QUOT say or
'should ((I)) say, the institution of marriage itself or'

4 =*ma*:: *nan te iu ka*,
AP what QUOT say or
'uhm what shall ((I)) say'

5 [( ) *dōkyo sono mono ga*./>
[living together itself NOM
['( ) living together itself'

[
6 W: [*Ss seido,*
[institution
['the institution'

7 (1.0)

8 ((slowly)) *ssseido sonomono* ***to*** ***iu*::**, ·*hhh* (1.3)
institution itself QUOT say
'((rather than?)) the institution itself ·hhh'

9 *datte ma*: ·*hhh*
because after all well
'because after all, well ·hhh'

10 *ssssss*: (.)

11 *seido no mondai yori* (.)
institution GEN problem more than
'more than ((it being)) a problem of the institution (.)'

12 *min'na ga kojin kojin no mondai* ***dakara*** [↑*ne*? ·*hhhh*
everyone NOM individual GEN problem because-so [FP
'because ((it))'s an individual problem for everyone, so you know ·hhhh'
[
13 K: [*Nnnnnnnnn./>*
['Mmmmmmm'

14 W: *kō ga yoi toka kō ga warui toka yuenai* ***kara,***
this NOM good e.g. this NOM bad e.g. can't say because-so
'because((one)) can't say if this way is good or that way is bad, so'

15 *atashi wa seido sono mono no mondai* ·*hhh*
I TOP institution itself GEN problem
'as for me, as for the problem of the institution of marriage itself ·hhh'

16 *mukashi wa* (.) <u>*atta*</u> ***kedomo*** [↑*ne*? (.7)
past TOP existed although-but [FP
'although ((I)) did have that problem in the past, but ((you)) know'
[
17 K: [((nodding))

18 W: *ima wa*, (3.0)
now TOP
'as for now'

19 *seido sonomono-* (.)
institution itself
'((as for)) the institution itself (.)'

20 (*ra*) *atakushi jishin to shite wa ima wa, ·hhh*
I myself QUOT do TOP now TOP
'as for me, at this point in time ·hhh'

21 *sss*: (.) *seido sono mono yorimo,*
institution itself more than
'more than the institution itself'

22 (1.0)

23 K: *Nnnn*
AP

24 (2.8)

25 W: ((looking at K)) *ma::: yappari ·hhhh* (.)
AP after all
'well after all ·hhhh (.)'

26 *oso sugita* ***to*** ***iu*** ***ka****, ·hhh*
too late QUOT say or
'that it was too late, should ((I)) say, or that ·hhh'

27 → *jiki o* [*shisshita* ***to*** ***iu*** ***ka*****.>** ((closes mouth))
timing ACC [missed QUOT say or
'the chance was [missed, should ((I)) say, or'
[
28 K: [((nodding)) '*N*:: / '*N*:: ./>
'Mm Mm'

29 K: *Osoku umareta hiai mitaina desu* ↑*ka*?/>
late born woe like COP QP
'Is it something like the woe of having been born late?'

The extensions listed in Table 5 which are featured turn-internally in W's talk in the above fragment include

(a) quotative particle + *to iu* 'say' (line 8)
(b) conjunctive particles:
dakara 'because-so' (line 12),
kara 'because-so' (line 14),
kedomo 'although-but' (line 16)

(c) quotative particle + *say* + conjunctive particle: *to iu ka*, which can be glossed as 'should I say, or . . .' (line 26)

Although the production of these forms can be followed by minimal acknowledgements (e.g. lines 12 and 16), coparticipants do not treat them as indicative of an imminent TRP (in this extract). The non-final intonation at each of the items coupled with their capacity to project further increments of talk render them useful devices for progressively building up an argument while circumventing a possible TRP where others may start up.

Interestingly, however, these grammatical items are also contingently employed and treated as signalling a TRP, as evidenced by the fact that speaker change took place in 73 per cent of the cases where items such as these occurred at the end of an utterance (see Table 2). For instance, in line 27 of the fragment above, W concludes her circuitous refutation of K's suggestion with the attributed construction, *to iu ka* (quotative particle + *say* + conjunctive particle) meaning 'should I say, or . . .', which is an ending vesting the turn with a degree of uncertainty while syntactically projecting more to come. (As mentioned above, this construction is also occasioned turn-internally in line 26). Although the exact same format is used in both instances, speaker change occurs in line 27 and not 26. There are two possible explanations for why the second instance (in line 27) is treated as appropriate for speaker change whereas the first invocation is not. First, the available Japanese conversational data suggest that the use of this form twice in succession may constitute something of a formulaic expression which is featured turn-finally to soften an assertion through a marker of uncertainty (see also lines 3 and 4 of K's turn above). Secondly, whereas the former instance is delivered with a continuing intonation, the latter ends with a final intonation. Incidentally, W closes her mouth at the end of this line, thereby providing a further display that she has finished speaking.

Similarly, slightly later in the same conversation, the participants have been discussing what would have happened if W had been unfaithful to her husband H and had run off with someone else. Before the excerpt reproduced below, H has just mentioned that he would have accepted it—albeit with a sense of sadness and resignation. To this, W responds in a humorous way as follows, employing a conjunctive particle *ba* at the end:

(46) [Tokyo 7, p. 18]

W: → *gg Motto hayaku itte* ***ku[re re ba.>***
more soon say if-then
'If ((you)) had told ((me)) sooner'
[
others: [((laughter))

W's talk is constructed as a syntactically incomplete turn, ending with the conjunctive particle *ba* 'if-then' which syntactically projects the second component of an *if X then Y* format (Lerner 1991; Lerner and Takagi, to appear). But as will be discussed in more detail in Chapter 6, the turn above terminates while leaving implicit the articulation of the second component Y. A possible implication of this utterance might be something like 'I may have run off with someone', but this is left unarticulated. By finishing with a conjunctive particle, then, the explicit performance of some action may be left as an innuendo.

Only a few instances of conjunctive particles have been dealt with here but work by other researchers also suggest how these particles may be employed for the accomplishment of delicate interactional tasks. For instance, Mori (1996b), who has done an extensive analysis of selected conjunctive particles (e.g. *dakara*, *-kara*, *kedo*) observes that they are used, among other ways, as part of delicate "opinion-negotiation sequences" for both agreements and disagreement turns. In disagreements, she reports that the particle *kara* can mark "the preceding clause as an account, creating an inference of unstated disagreement" (222); whereas the particle *kedo* can be used for "mitigating a disagreeing response, creating an inference of unstated partial agreement" (224). A systematic analysis of the interactional import of the employment of extensions in general deserves attention in its own right.

This section has been devoted to a preliminary description of the endings of turns which are pragmatically complete without simultaneously being syntactically complete (i&p¬s). It was first observed that the grammatical forms which are regularly employed in this type of completion are found both turn-internally and turn-finally. In addition to the sequential aspects of their employment, intonation appears to be a key feature which permits participants to differentiate between the two usages: turn-internal instances do not normally end with a final intonation, whereas their appearance in a turn-final position is regularly accompanied by a final falling intonation (see Chapter 6 for a detailed treatment). Though it has only been possible to deal briefly with the potential interactive consequences of the i&p¬s turn-design, the existence of a close relationship between syntax and social action has been hinted at: a turn constructed to be pragmatically complete yet syntactically incomplete can be employed for delicate tasks and can leave social actions tacit.

3.4.3. *Summary of turn-endings of pragmatically complete turns*

Finally, the incidence of the various types of grammatical constructions of turn-endings of pragmatically-complete turns in the Tokyo data have been recalculated as percentages of all pragmatic completions, and listed in Table 6.

This section has mapped out regularities in the terminal designs of pragmatically

Table 6. *Turn-endings of all pragmatically complete turns in the Japanese data (171 cases = 100%)*[25]

Turn-designs	No. of cases	% of all pragmatic completions
Syntactically complete turns (i&p&s) (149 cases = 87.1% of all prag. completions)		
1. Ending with utterance-finals	107	62.6
2. Not ending with utterance-finals: recompleters	18	10.5
3. Not ending with utterance-finals: truncated form	24	14.0
Syntactically incomplete turns (i&p¬s) (22 cases = 12.9% of all prag. completions)		
4. Extensions	20	11.7
5. Others[26]	2	1.2

complete turns in Japanese, which were shown earlier to be closely linked with speaker change. The orderliness of the types of endings should be clear from Table 6, which shows that all except approximately 1 per cent of the turn-endings (subsumed under "others") conformed to one of the four broad patterns identified: (i) turns ending with utterance-final elements; (ii) turns which do not end with utterance-final elements but terminate with recompleters; (iii) truncated turns which do not end with utterance-final elements; and (iv) turns ending with extensions of a TCU by items such as quotative or conjunctive particles. Although the relative distribution of these turn-endings may not be representative of all conversations in Japanese, Table 6 can be regarded as an initial attempt to identify typical (but not necessarily exhaustive) forms which are regularly employed to construct turns or TCUs in Japanese. A major finding of this exercise is the importance of what transpires at the end of an utterance for the determination of not just intonational and pragmatic completeness, but also for a judgement of syntactic completion in Japanese. The results of this chapter will form a foundation for the analysis of the projectability of TRPs in Japanese in the next chapter.

3.5. Summary and concluding comments

This chapter began with a discussion of how the very process of endeavouring to operationalise syntactic, intonational, and pragmatic completion in Japanese may provide important lessons for the conceptualisation and measurement of syntactic, intonational, and pragmatic phenomena in the divergent socio-linguistic domains.

Starting with F&T's formulations of these types of completions for English, it was observed that a simple transfer of their operational definitions into Japanese was fraught with potential cross-linguistic incompatibilites.

While definitions of intonational and pragmatic completions which were more or less similar to F&T's versions were adopted for Japanese, defining the notion of syntactic completion which reflected participant orientations to syntax turned out to be tricky. First, it was argued that intonational and pragmatic aspects of an utterance provide vital clues for determining how a particular bit of talk may be potentially tied to prior or projected talk. Secondly, it was found necessary to take account of agglutinative morphology in selecting a syntactic criterion which might be relevant to the parties themselves. As part of the attempt to arrive at a viable definition, however, two different criteria for syntactic completion were taken into consideration: conversational syntactic completion which approximated participants' parsing of syntactical units, and analytical syntactic completion which did not make allowances for the possible consequences of agglutination or prosody. It was shown subsequently that the correlation between speaker change and occurrences of analytic syntactic completion was much lower in comparison to conversational syntactic completion, thereby buttressing the case for choosing conversational over analytical syntactic completion for the purposes of this study. The analysis in the remainder of the chapter was therefore based on conversational syntax.

Employing the operational definitions of these completion points, two broad issues within the intersection of grammar and social interaction were addressed with respect to the Japanese data: (i) the statistical distribution of syntactic, pragmatic, and intonational completion points, and the occurrences of speaker change at various combinations of completion points; (ii) the identification of the grammatical designs of the endings of pragmatically complete turns in Japanese.

F&T has reported for English that syntactic completion occurs far more frequently than either pragmatic or intonational completion, and does not necessarily coincide with the latter two types of completion. When pragmatic or intonational completion does occur, however, it is almost invariably accompanied by syntactic completion. The authors moreover show that participants orient to the co-occurrence of syntactic, intonational, and pragmatic completions (i&p&s) as appropriate places for speaker change.

In Japanese, syntactic completion points were found to occur with far less frequency in comparison to English, partly due to the "anti-symmetric" structure of turns in the two languages. Syntactic completeness in English is to a considerable extent dependent on what goes on towards the beginning of a turn, as is borne out by the incremental occurrence of syntactic completion points which are progressively calculated in relation to the beginning of a turn. On the other hand, an utterance in Japanese is judged to be syntactically complete or incomplete, largely depending on what prevails at its terminal boundary, although recompleters provide exceptions to this pattern.

As a result of the relatively lower incidence of syntactic completions in Japanese, the differences between the numbers of the three types of completions were also less prominent than for English. Importantly, while i&p&s were also shown to have a high association with speaker change in Japanese, a class of pragmatic completions which did not co-occur with syntactic completions (i&p¬s) also turned out to have a high correlation with instances of speaker change.[27] The statistical results cumulatively suggested that pragmatic completion points on the whole—and not just the coincidence of the three completions i&p&s—are oriented to as possible TRPs in Japanese.

Furthermore, a high degree of orderliness was discovered in the structures of the turn-endings of pragmatically complete turns. It was demonstrated that the endings of pragmatically complete turns routinely assumed one of four generalised shapes. Those that were syntactically complete (i&p&s) terminated with (i) utterance-final elements, (ii) recompleters without utterance-final elements, or (iii) an *iikiri* (truncated) format without utterance-final elements. On the other hand, pragmatically complete turns which were not syntactically complete (i&p¬s) massively ended with (iv) grammatical items such as conjunctive particles and quotative particles which syntactically but not pragmatically extended the TCU in progress. It was also suggested that the latter turn-type may leave implicit further social actions, and is regularly occasioned in the performance of delicate interactional work. The analysis undertaken in this chapter suggests that the differential use of syntactic complete/incomplete turn designs in coordination with pragmatic and intonational features may serve as dynamic and versatile grammatical tools that participants can invoke in managing turn-taking and social interaction in Japanese. Equipped with some understanding of how syntactic, intonational, and pragmatic resources are implicated in the localisation of turn-endings in Japanese, Chapters 4 through 6 will take a more qualitative approach in investigating the role of these resources in the projection of TRPs and TCUs.

Notes

1. Sacks, Schegloff, and Jefferson (1974) do, in fact, allude to the significance of intonational and sequential features of talk in the management of TRPs, but do not go so far as to "operationalise" formulations of completion points in terms of these resources.
2. This is congruent with F&T's results. However, since there are apparently so few cases of pragmatic completions which are simultaneously not CTRPs in their data, the two categories are practically collapsible.

3. This claim is phrased in tentative terms since observation of differences depends on the mode of operationalisation employed for syntactic completion, as discussed below.
4. Accordingly, the statistical results reported here are very tentative. At the stage of submission of this manuscript, I am still in the process of refining methods of operationalising the phenomena under consideration.
5. Although the original Japanese data used for this investigation are video-recordings, only the audio track was employed for the statistical analysis, in order to achieve basic comparability with F&T's study.
6. This point is also aptly demonstrated by the quite different findings obtained by Furo (1998, to appear), who conducted studies of Japanese similar to the one undertaken in this chapter, but based on yet another criterion for operationalising syntactic completion.
7. In order to achieve greater comparability across the socio-linguistic domains, it would minimally be necessary to have access to the raw data used for the analysis of English and possibly to alter the operationalisation of measures employed for English in F&T as well as my attempt made here for Japanese, to strive for more "generalisable" or "universally-applicable" operational definitions which may simultaneously serve for both Japanese and English. This will be a task to be carried forward in a future study.
8. It is somewhat unclear to me why a clause has been selected as the unit on which to base the idea of syntactic completion, and in particular, whether it is claimed that the end of any "recoverable" clause is itself a completion, or alternatively, if the term "complete clause" is being used to mean a clause which does not syntactically project further talk. If the latter meaning is intended, then certain clauses would be excluded as candidates for syntactic completion. Indeed, participants can project compound TCUs through the employment of formats such as *if X–then Y* (Lerner 1987, 1991). Thus, the completion of a first clause beginning with *if* may only signal the end of the preliminary component, and not the entire compound TCU which has been projected. In other words, a clause which takes the form *if X*, even if classifiable as a complete clause, might project further talk in certain sequential contexts.
9. However, some question the view that spoken and written discursive styles can be effectively differentiated in terms of its affective dimension (Kataoka 1995: 427).
10. One of the features of isolating languages is that "(a)ffixes are absent, there are monosyllabic words, both lexical (autosemantic) and grammatical (function words, synsemantic)" (Sgall 1995: 56).
11. Of course there are major differences ensuing from the fact that conversational syntax reflects interactional concerns and is also characterised by the presence of disfluencies and repair, etc. But these features would apply equally to English and Japanese (see Schegloff, 1979).
12. However, in conversational English, agglutination does seem to occur to some extent, e.g. when the same consonant is used for the end of a word and beginning of next, such as 'went to' which may be produced as 'wen tuh'.
13. These are points for future investigation, which may usefully elucidate further syntactic differences between Japanese and English.
14. The discussion here may still raise questions as to why it was necessary to exclude ana-

lytic from conversational syntactic completion points from the outset, when the convergence of syntactic, intonational and pragmatic completion points is likely to yield conversational completion points, at any event. By including the analytic points among all the possible syntactic completions, however, it becomes difficult to determine which ones of the many analytic syntactic points may be relevant for speaker change, since they can on occasion occur very densely, particularly around a possible TRP.

15. Three types of places have been identified where a rising intonation occurs with regularity in the Japanese data: (i) interrogatives, (ii) syntactically complete utterances ending with a final particle such as *ne*, and (iii) elicitations of acknowledgements at syntactically incomplete points (via final particles *ne* or *sa*). Type (iii) is classifiable as simply "intonation only". Going on the basis of F&T's data, the fact that they have counted no completion points which are "intonation only" suggests that elicitations of acknowledgements rarely occur in syntactically incomplete junctures in English.
16. While acknowledging that this "impressionistic" method of locating speaker change points may be problematic from the point of view of "reliability", it was chosen as a tentative alternative to adopting an analytical measure which did not necessarily reflect indigenous orientations. F&T also voice their reservations about the criterion that they employ to determine where a speaker change occurred in overlapping talk (F&T: 175 n. 11).
17. As we saw above, however, the number of analytic syntactic completion points in Japanese amounts to 877, which is more than double the number of conversational syntactic completion points, i.e. 422. We obtain a much closer cross-linguistic match if analytical syntax is employed for operationalising syntactic completions in Japanese.
18. Of course this is not always the case, as participants—albeit relatively infrequently according to my data—employ a post-predicate addition, i.e. where items such as the subject, object, indirect object, or adverb occur *after* the main predicate (see also Ono and Suzuki 1992). In such cases, the utterance *will* pass through syntactic completion point(s) (see Chapter 4).
19. Again, slightly different results were obtained by Furo (1998), who has undertaken an investigation similar to the one in this chapter. In her study, all pragmatic completion points were found to be also syntactically complete.
20. Even though the percentage of 57 per cent is quite high, this category is not likely to be associated with TRPs since 34 out of the total 42 completions were shown to consist of final particles occurring at "acknowledgement-relevance places" (see Section 3.2.4).
21. Recall that the term "syntactic completion" is used here to denote "conversational syntactic completion".
22. This instance was categorised under the previous category of TCUs terminating with utterance-final elements (Section 3.4.1.1).
23. Most conversations of any length that I have examined involve some combination of turns ending with utterance-final elements as well as the *iikiri* form, whether or not they take place among intimates or non-intimates. A fuller investigation is needed to understand the selective deployment of these alternative turn-shapes depending on the type of interactional work they are engaged in.

24. Although not present in the Tokyo corpora, other data reveal that case or adverbial particles can also be employed at the end of a turn to construct pragmatically-complete yet syntactically incomplete turns, for instance in the formulation of questions (see Chapter 5, Section 5.7).
25. The statistical results presented in this table differs from that employed in Tanaka (1996), since the two tables are based on partially shared but different corpora of data and involve somewhat different categories of turn designs.
26. This category of "others" consists of cases of syntactically incomplete turns which had been brought to an "early" completion: in both instances after being overlapped by another speaker.
27. Although this may also hold for English, it is difficult to establish since there are apparently so few cases of pragmatic completions which are not syntactic completions in F&T's data.

Chapter 4

Turn-projection and construction

4.1. Introduction

This chapter examines ways in which grammar may be implicated in the construction of turns at speaking and in the projection of turn-endings in Japanese talk-in-interaction, in the light of reported conversation analytic findings on turn-taking for Anglo-American English. In a crude sense, the grammatical structures of Japanese and English can be regarded as polar opposites. This is reflected in dramatic differences in participant orientations to turn-construction and projection in the respective languages. Specifically, in contrast to English grammar which massively enables early projectability of the social action which might occupy a turn, the grammatical structure of Japanese permits the incremental transformation of a turn-in-progress, and overwhelmingly results in a later arrival of the point at which the emerging shape of a turn can be known. This delayed projectability in Japanese, however, is to a large extent compensated by a potentially greater degree of certitude with which participants can localise turn-endings through the use of devices which mark possible transition-relevance places.

It is fairly clear from the conversation analytic literature on Anglo-American English that there are ways in which grammar has a critical bearing on turn-taking in general and turn-projection in particular. The syntactic structure of English has been described as an important resource participants draw on to project a probable shape of an emerging turn[1] often well before the turn comes to a possible completion (Schegloff 1987b). The normative organisation of syntax also permits the projection of possible transition-relevance places or TRPs, i.e. the likely place where a turn may come to an end, within its immediate sequential environment (Sacks, Schegloff, and Jefferson 1974). The intimate relation between grammar and turn-taking in English is partly played out in the ways syntax has consequences for the projectability properties of turns.

On the other hand, much less is known about the implications of cross-linguistic variations in grammar for turn-taking operations in other languages such as Japanese. The Japanese linguistics literature suggests numerous differences between the grammatical structures of English and Japanese (e.g. Kuno 1973; Martin 1975; Shibatani 1990). The discrepant "standard" word order of the two languages is a case in point, as is the striking contrast in the employment of prepositions in English as opposed to postpositional particles in Japanese (see Chapter 1). Surely, the availability of such divergent syntactic resources can be expected to have profound ramifications on how participants go about building turns and where in the course of a turn a possible end of a turn can be anticipated.

Potential connections between turn-taking and the different "syntactic practices" between the two languages have been suggested in an illuminating study by Fox, Hayashi, and Jasperson (1996: 207–14), which already suggests many ideas broadly consonant with the findings of the present study. Whereas English syntax makes "early projection" relatively straightforward, the authors note that "the beginnings of TCUs in Japanese do not tend to have elements that *syntactically* project the possible organization of what is to follow", thereby impeding "early projection strategies". Instead, participants produce utterances "in small constituents", constructing them "bit by bit". As a consequence, recipients tend to "wait and see" the development of an utterance, "until they hear the last few syllables of the turn (which often contain such 'ending signals' as final particles or special completion-relevant verb forms) before starting their own utterance". The authors, however, remark that "at this stage of our research these suggestions on the organization of turn-taking in Japanese are merely speculations". Building on this and other previous research, the current study makes an attempt to provide an empirical basis for understanding the workings of turn-projection and to present a systematic overview of key features interlinking grammar and turn-projection in Japanese (in comparison to English).

The primary aim of this chapter is to explicate how the grammar (and to some extent prosodic features) of Japanese may be interactionally salient for turn-construction, and specifically for the projection of an emergent turn-shape and possible TRPs in Japanese conversation, in contrast to what is known for English. It begins by drawing attention to aspects of Japanese grammatical structure which are likely to be consequential for turn-construction and projection. In particular, the contrastive ordering of the two languages is examined for their implications for the location within a turn where projection becomes possible. Secondly, the normativity of the verb- (or predicate-) final orientation in Japanese conversation is investigated through (a) instances of overlaps and collaborative constructions of turns (e.g. Lerner 1987, 1991, 1996; Lerner and Takagi, to appear; Hayashi 1997; Hayashi and Mori 1998; Hayashi, Mori, and Takagi, to appear) and (b) "post-predicate additions". Third, the discussion delves into the "incremental transformability" of turn-shapes, an aspect of Japanese grammar which can render tentative and revisable the ultimate trajectory of a turn until it approaches its terminal boundary. These aspects of turn-organisation imply that, whether some item ultimately becomes recognisable as a predicate as a turn unfolds (which may be transition-relevant) *or* whether it might be reshaped into some other component such as a nominal unit (and therefore may project further talk) can be dependent on what follows the item. This feature massively results in "delayed projectability" of the possible turn-shape and the point at which a TRP may be imminent. However, fourth, it will be argued that the propensity for a later projectability of turn-shapes and turn-endings in Japanese does not present particular problems for parties to judge the onset of TRPs. Indeed, conversationalists in Japanese are overwhelmingly able to achieve smooth transitions from the current to the next with minimal gap or overlap. This is partly due to the existence in Japanese of two types of devices which can be deployed turn-finally to announce the imminent onset or arrival of a possible TRP: (i) utterance-final elements (such as copulas, final verb suffixes and final particles) or (ii) marked prosodic endings (as already introduced in Chapter 3). These devices compensate for the relative opaqueness and potential transformability of turn-trajectories, and enable a precise localisation of possible TRPs.

Needless to say, projectability in both English and Japanese is also heavily dependent on a number of other resources including sequential organisation, pragmatic features, and non-verbal conduct, as discussed in the CA literature (e.g. Goodwin 1979b, 1981; Lerner 1991, 1996; Ford, Fox, and Thompson 1996; Hayashi 1997; Hayashi, Mori, and Takagi, to appear; Hayashi and Mori 1998). But this chapter focuses primarily on the implications of grammar for turn-organisation.

4.2. Contrastive ordering

Before entering into a detailed study of turn-projection in Japanese, I will touch upon a feature of Japanese grammatical organisation which contrasts with English, to provide a "feel" for aspects of Japanese syntax which will prove to be particularly relevant for an analysis of turn-construction and projection in Japanese. As already hinted in Chapter 3, the structure of turns in English can crudely be seen as a mirror image of the turn-organisation in Japanese. Of note is the remarkable cross-linguistic difference in the position within a turn where the turn-shape begins to be made manifest. On the one hand, turn-beginnings in English have been described as critical locations for turn-projection (i.e. to anticipate how the turn might develop), and in particular for the initial projection of the shape a turn may take:

> One important feature of turn construction . . . and the units that turn construction employs (e.g. lexical, phrasal, clausal, sentential constructions) is that they project, *from their beginnings*, aspects of their planned shape and type . . . . There are other sorts of projection that are, or can be involved from the very beginning of a turn. For example, question projection . . . Or: beginnings can project "quotation formats" . . . Or: a beginning like 'I don't think' can project, in certain sequential environments, "disagreement" as a turn type for its turn . . . .Again: *turn-beginnings are important because they are an important place for turn projection*, and, given the importance of turn projection for turn taking, they are important structural places in conversation. (Schegloff 1987b: 71, italics added)

An early projection is facilitated in English, since the type of activity which might occupy a turn or the stance of the speaker is regularly made available towards the beginning of a turn (although of course, they may also be displayed at a later point). Furthermore, participants can massively project a possible point at which an initial TRP may arrive through anticipation of the progress of the "planned shape" or "format".

It is also the case that participants in Japanese can display what action a turn may be occupied with early in the turn through the use of adverbial phrases, turn-initial connectives, discourse markers, interjections, etc. (Mori 1994, 1996b; Hayashi and Mori 1998; Hayashi, personal communication). However, an examination of utterance-structure in Japanese suggests how the placement of grammatical constituents in Japanese which accomplish many types of interactional work (e.g. displaying a stand on something, indicating "disagreement", quotation formats, expressing a wish, etc.) are also concentrated towards the end of a turn. Some examples are shown below.

For fragments (47)–(49) below, the items in boldface correspond in the original Japanese transcript and the rough English gloss.

(47) [Shakujii 1A#4 p. 2] telephone conversation

Y: → >*Getsuyōbi ni wa ikeru to* ***omou n*** *da yo*
Monday on TOP can go QUOT think VN COP FP
'((I)) **think** ((I)) can go ((there)) on Monday'

The order of the appearance of information in this turn can be mapped out roughly as follows:

On Monday, can go ((there)), ((I)) think.

The positioning of the verb *omou* 'think' towards the end entails a later arrival of the point at which the action of a turn (e.g. the display of a stand) may be accomplished, in contrast to the claim for English noted above.

Likewise, the proximity of the end of a turn in Japanese is often a locus for displaying an assessment or sentiment pertaining to the substance of a turn:

(48) [Tokyo 10A p. 19] multi-party conversation; simplified
The final particle *na* is used to express an aspiration in the following instance, and is roughly equivalent to 'how'.

S: *Dakara . . . kigen no ( ) anzen o (hakatta) hō ga* ***ii na***
so deadline P safety ACC (aim for) direction NOM **better** FP
'So . . . how **much better** it would be (to aim to) meet the deadline'

The mapping of the order of appearance of the phrasal increments in this example is:

So, the deadline, meet, to aim for, would be much better, how

Again, the ordering of the constituents in the original Japanese utterance is roughly the opposite of what may be considered a "natural" ordering in English (compare with the English gloss). For instance, the final particle *na* 'how' here is employed to formulate the utterance as a wish or aspiration. Whereas corresponding markers such as 'how . . .' tend to occur at the beginning in English (as in the gloss), the sense of the Japanese utterance as a display of an aspiration is not available to parties until the terminal item *na* is produced.

Similarly, note that it is the turn-final verb-suffixes *te kudasai* 'please' in the following which formulates the entire utterance as a request:

(49) [Shakujii 1A #1, p. 2] telephone conversationY is talking to H a friend of her husband who is drinking at a bar with the latter.

Y: *Dewa*: *ano- nomisugi nai yō ni* ***yuttoite kudasai***
okay uhm- not to drink too much like P say please
'Okay, uhm **please tell ((him))** not to drink too much'

The action which occupies the above turn gradually crystallises as the turn progresses, and is only fully revealed through the production of *kudasai* 'please' at the terminal boundary of the turn.

In contrast to the projectability properties of turns in English alluded to above, then, some important displays revealing the type of action performed in a turn (e.g. display of one's thoughts, expression of an aspiration) as well as the shape or type of turn (e.g. exclamation, request, question, etc.) may not be available until near the end of a turn in Japanese. A major consequence of this organisation for turn-taking is that the projectability of the point at which the turn might come to a possible completion can be substantially delayed (in comparison to English).

It will be argued below that the divergence between an early or delayed projectability is partly due to differential normative orientations to word order in the two languages. According to Fox, Hayashi, and Jasperson (1996: 200), most English utterances they examined conformed to a relatively rigid S-V-O (i.e. Subject-Verb-Object) order, with prepositional phrases—where one or more are present—following the direct object. It may be speculated that the relatively stable word order in English can be exploited by conversationalists for projecting the trajectory of a turn as well as the possible point at which an initial transition-relevance place or TRP may arrive through anticipation of the progress of the "planned shape" or "format" as mentioned above (Schegloff 1987b: 71). On the other hand, the "canonical" or standard syntactical order for transitive Japanese sentences has been described as S-O-V (Subject-Object-Verb) and secondarily, O-S-V (Object-Subject-Verb), the common feature being their verb-final ordering.[2] To reiterate, the production of the verb towards the beginning of a turn in English can provide a strong indication for how the turn might evolve. In contrast, Japanese turns regularly have verb components placed towards the end of a turn-constructional unit.[3] Since the action which occupies a turn is regularly indicated by a verb or predicate component, the deferred production of such components can retard the point where the potential turn-shape or probable turn-ending becomes projectable. In sum, the syntactic structure of English can be said to be conducive to relatively early projectability, whereas Japanese syntax may have built-in features which delay the projectability of an emerging turn.

It has been suggested above that there is a fundamental asymmetry in the location within a turn where turn-projection is possible in the two languages, owing in part to (i) the early occurrence of the verb phrase in English and its delayed production in Japanese, and (ii) early indication of the action performed by a turn in English as opposed to the tentativeness of a conversational action in Japanese before the turn reaches completion. These points will form the foci of the discussion on the relevance of grammar for turn-projection in this chapter, outlined below.

Not withstanding the canonical S-O-V or O-S-V structure of Japanese sentences, it will first be shown in Section 4.3 that the order of appearance of the main constituents (subject, verb, object) within a turn is, in fact, extremely variable. For instance, a subject or object may be "inverted" to a position following the verb. Nonetheless, an analysis of the treatment of such apparent "violations" of verb-final turn shapes will provide robust evidence for the verb- or predicate-final orientation in Japanese. A later production of the verb (predicate) phrase in Japanese results in a postponement of the point at which one can project what a turn is recognisably doing and the probable point at which the turn may reach completion.

Furthermore, Japanese conversationalists employ postpositional particles for the incremental construction of turn-shapes (see Chapter 1) while typically reserving the production of the "thrust" of the turn for the end. Some consequences of this feature of Japanese grammar will be discussed in Section 4.4. Specifically, it will be shown that both the syntactic nature and the interactional import of an utterance can remain essentially indeterminate until the utterance approaches completion and can be modified retroactively even after the initial termination of the turn (see Section 4.6 below). As a consequence, the projectability of an emergent turn may be vastly limited prior to turn-completion.

Because of the delayed and limited projectability of the shapes of turns-in-progress, coparticipants hold off coming in, while awaiting a clear sign that no further transformations of the current turn are intended (Section 4.4.2). However, it will be demonstrated in Section 4.5 that speakers have at their disposal one of two types of turn-ending devices to forestall further transformations, thereby signalling a possible point of turn-completion: (i) certain grammatical elements or (ii) marked prosodic contours. Not surprisingly, the employment of these devices at the terminal boundary of TCUs is closely related to the predicate-final orientation in Japanese. In what follows, normative orientations to turn-construction and projection will be examined in some detail: a process which is intended to fill out the significance of grammar for turn-taking.

4.3. Predicate-final structure of turns

This section explores normative orientations to word ordering in Japanese by examining two types of turn-shapes: (i) turns ending with a predicate, and (ii) the so-called "inversion" of word order, i.e. the post-predicate occurrence of the subject, object and/or other components, where the term "predicate component" will be employed to refer to a verbal, adjectival, or nominal expression which modifies a subject. Whilst the superficial word order of turns is found to be extremely variegated, it will nevertheless be shown that a strong orientation exists that the verb or predicate component should occur as the last component of a turn-constructional unit. The main evidence for the normativity of the verb or predicate-final TCU structure is derived from instances of collaborative construction and completion of turns-in-progress as well as the positioning of overlaps.

4.3.1. *Turns ending with a predicate component*

It was suggested in Chapter 3 that a majority of turns in Japanese end with a predicate component, at least for the data set examined. This subsection examines participant orientations to this turn-shape. First, a search of the data does yield isolated instances of the standard S-O-V and O-S-V turn shapes where all three components are overtly expressed, but they are few and far between.[4] The following is an example of the former, S-O-V:

(50) [Tokyo 10 #2, p. 2] informal meeting; slightly simplified

The participants are discussing the suitability of Mr. Hirano to write an article for their journal.

G: → *Hi*: *Hirano san ga* *himoron* *kaita n* *jyanai*?
Mr Hirano NOM gigolo theory wrote VN not
[subject] **[object]** **[verb]**
'Wasn't it Mr Hirano who wrote about the gigolo theory?'

S: *Ah- so*: *datta n* (*desu ka*)
oh right COP VN COP QP
'Oh was it so?'

In the first line, the subject is *Hirano san*, marked postpositionally by the nominative particle (NOM) *ga*, the object is *himoron* 'gigolo theory' with an elliptical accusative particle (ACC) *o*, followed by the verb phrase *kaita n jyanai*? 'didn't ((subject)) write?'.

The alternative standard syntactical order, O-S-V, is described as a type of reordering of constituents preceding the verb, sometimes referred to as "scrambling" (Shibatani 1990: 259), involving the "fronting" of the direct object, the indirect object, or both, as exemplified by the following:

(51) [IMD: 252–3] telephone conversation; overlaps omitted

H is telling I about a doctor who played a major ceremonial role at a wedding that H attended.

1 H: *Kekkō sono taiyaku* *o*: **[object]**
rather AP major role ACC
2 (0.3)
3 nanka ano sensei e- **[subject]**
AP that doctor DF
4 yarihatte . . . **[verb]**
did and

Gloss: 'that doctor seemed to be playing a rather major role and . . .'

Line 1 is the object phrase which is marked by an accusative particle (ACC) *o*; the subject is *ano sensei* 'that doctor'; the verb is *yarihatte* 'did and'.

The existence of fragments such as the two presented above indicate in the first instance, that speakers sometimes do produce turns which conform to the S-O-V and O-S-V patterns.

Further inspection of conversational data, however, leads to the observation that the occurrence of both the subject and object components prior to a verb or predicate is not mandatory for participants to be able to project a potential verb or predicate component (see Hayashi and Mori 1998). As already noted in Chapter 1, various parts of speech such as subject, direct and indirect objects, as well as particles may be unexpressed. In fact, it is quite common for both the subject and/or object to be unexpressed due to ellipsis, so that a verb (predicate) may be projectable even after a speaker produces just a subject, object or even solely an adverb.

The normativity of such word order is further reinforced by instances of "anticipatory" or "collaborative completions" (Lerner 1987, 1991) indicating that the predicate-final structure may be at least one of the syntactic resources (in addition to contextual features) that coparticipants exploit in constructing a turn.

First, the following fragment shows a coparticipant implicitly furnishing a turn-final verb of an ongoing turn even when the direct object is unexpressed. After the current speaker produces a subject, the recipient enters the speaker's turn-space by incorporating the verb which was implied in the former's utterance.

(52) [Shakujii 1B (#3) p. 1] telephone conversation; slightly simplified

In this telephone conversation, T and H are discussing how to distribute some tickets for a community event.

1 T: *Ano:::- u::nto hhh chiketto moratta deshō=*
uhm uhm tickets received COP
'Uhm uhm ((you))'ve received the tickets haven't ((you))?'

2 H: =*'N: moratta*
yeah received
'Yeah, ((I))'ve received ((them))'

3 T:→ *Ano: ·hh Watanabe san ni wa anata ga*
uhm: Ms Watanabe DAT TOP you NOM
[indirect object] **[subject]**
'Uhm ·hh to Ms Watanabe, ((it))'s you ((who))'

4 ((baby's voice in the background))

5 H:→ *Uun atashi watashiteru:*
yeah I have handed over
[subject] **[verb]**
'Yeah, I have handed ((them)) over ((to her))'

6 T: *Sō yo ne*
right FP FP
'((You)) have, haven't ((you))'

In line 1, T is asking for confirmation as to whether H had received tickets she had previously sent H. To this, H responds in line 2 that she has received them. Within the context of talk about some tickets, the production by T in line 3 of an indirect object *Watanabe san* 'Ms Watanabe' and subject *anata* 'you' provide information for H to furnish the implicit verb *watashiteru* 'have handed over' in line 5, even though the direct object is unexpressed.[5]

Indeed, the object of T's utterance in line 3 (i.e. *chiketto* 'tickets') is recoverable from the context in lines 1–2 in combination with the specification of the indirect object. Therefore, at the end of line 3, T's turn-in-progress can be heard as referring to something that the addressee H has "done" to Ms Watanabe in connection with the tickets. The filled pause (baby's voice) in line 4 is employed by H (in line 5) as a chance to begin the next turn (see Lerner 1996; Hayashi 1997), in which she anticipates and affirms the possible upshot of T's turn-in-progress by starting out with *Uun* 'Yeah', then substitutes the subject *atashi* 'I' for the previously articulated subject *anata* 'you', and ends by supplying the action (i.e. the verb) which is projected by T's prior talk: *watashiteru*: 'have handed over'. Indeed, in response to T's incipient question: *Ano*: *·hh Watanabe san ni wa anata ga* 'Uhm ·hh to Ms Watanabe, (it))'s you ((who))', H produces the answer by filling in the missing verb: *Uun atashi watashiteru*: 'Yeah, I have handed ((them)) over ((to her))'. H's anticipatory response to T's question (as well as T's ensuing turn in line 6) suggests that the unexpressed object was heard by both participants as *chiketto* 'tickets'. In this connection, Hayashi and Mori (1998) argue that coparticipant completion of a current speaker's turn by supplying a final predicate is a powerful way in which participants attempt to achieve and display "congruent understanding". This example illustrates how the specification of a subject can be used to project an upcoming predicate even if the object is left unexpressed, in its interactive context, and also evidences the normativity of the S-V turn-structure.

The next case exemplifies a participant co-constructing a turn in which the object phrase has been articulated but the subject is left unexpressed:

(53) [Tokyo 10#2, p. 12] informal meeting, slightly simplified

The participants have been discussing how to organise a group event at their organisation.

1 H: *Nanka*: *are desho*? . . .
something that COP
'((You)) know what it is? ((It))'s something like this . . .'

2 *chūkaku ni natte kudasaru kata o* **[object phrase]**
nucleus P become person ACC
'the person who would be willing to act as the nucleus'

3 G: ***O*** *dare ni* ***suru*** *ka tte iu koto*
ACC whom DAT **select** QP QUOT say VN
[verb]
'To select whom for ((the person who would be willing to act as the nucleus))'

In the extract above, H begins in line 1 by indicating that he is going to suggest some aspect of the forthcoming group event. H's continuing talk in line 2 *chūkaku ni natte kudasaru kata o* 'the person who would be willing to act as the nucleus' is recognisable as the object phrase of the turn-in-progress by virtue of the post-positional attachment of the accusative particle *o* at the end of the line. At this point, G enters (line 3) by completing H's turn, first by repeating the particle *o*, followed by an indirect object phrase *dare ni* 'to whom', and then supplying the verb *suru* 'select'. This fragment illustrates that it is possible for coparticipants to project a verb (predicate) after a speaker produces an object, in its specific context (see Chapter 5).

In fact, within sequential exigencies, the production of an adverb may clearly project some predicate, even when there is no expressed subject:

(54) [Tokyo 10#3, p. 12] informal meeting

Prior to the extract shown, the participants have been talking about a range of problems associated with organising an event.

1 G: ((glottal)) *Na(g)ka(g)na(g)ka(g)*:: *g* [*mm*
'Quite' ['mm'
[adverb]
[
2 S: [*Muzukashii*
['Difficult'
[adjective]
[ ]
3 G: [*muzu(g)kashii(g)*
['difficult'
[adjective]

G begins (in line 1) with an adverb *nakanaka* 'quite', which in this specific context (i.e. discussing problems) is analysed by S (in line 2) as projecting a negatively phrased predicate *muzukashii* 'difficult', which is subsequently ratified by G (line 3).

As exemplified above, ellipsis is extremely pervasive, and the available data suggest that the appearance of all three components S, O, and V is more of an exception than the rule. To repeat, instances of the canonical S-O-V or O-S-V form were rare within the data corpora under consideration, with O-V or S-V patterns or simply V alone featuring far more frequently. Indeed, ordinary conversation massively relies on the simple production of a verb or predicate component, as illustrated below:

(55) [Shakujii 1A (#4), p. 15] telephone conversation; slightly simplified
K and Y have been talking about some strawberry jam that K had previously made for Y.

1 K: **>*tabeta*?<=**
ate
[verb]
'Did ((you)) eat ((it))?'

2 Y: **=>*tabeta*<**
ate
[verb]
'((I/we)) ate ((it))'

3 *oishikatta* <u>*yo*</u>=
was delicious FP
[adjective]
'((It)) was delicious'

4 K: =*Honto*
'Really?'

In this fragment, K's turn in line 1 is composed of just an expressed verb, with an unexpressed subject 'you' and unexpressed object 'it'. Likewise, Y's response in lines 2–3 consists of two TCUs: the first in line 2 with an unexpressed subject and object, the second in line 3 with an unexpressed subject and an expressed predicate *oishikatta* 'was delicious'.

The instances of collaborative constructions dealt with above—fragments (52)–(54)—exhibit participant expectations that the appearance of a subject, object and/or adverb may be followed by the situated production of some verb or predicate. Indeed, for each type of word order—including S-O-V, O-S-V, S-V, O-V, Adverb-Predicate—the feature that the verb (predicate) component might occur as the final expectable syntactic unit in the turn is shared. We can therefore tentatively conclude that the verb (predicate)-final order is at least one of the syntactic practices that participants normatively orient to. (see Chapter 5 for a discussion of the relationship between word order and the use of case and adverbial particles.)

4.3.2. *Post-predicate additions*

The foregoing discussion however, should not be taken to mean that all turns actually terminate with predicate components. Indeed, the verb-final (predicate-final) pattern is ostensibly "broken", from time to time, in natural conversation. Several studies have noted that the flexibility of word order in Japanese conversation is not limited to components prior to the predicate (as shown above), but that various components—such as subject, object, indirect object and/or adverbial expressions—may occur after the predicate component (Hinds 1982; Ono and Suzuki 1992; Simon 1989; Hayashi, Mori, and Takagi, to appear).

Various views have been put forward in previous research concerning the purpose and motivation for the employment of post-predicate additions (i.e. turns which have further components following the predicate). Shibatani (1990) describes the portion following the verb phrase as an "afterthought".

> Indeed the intonation pattern shows that the afterthought element is tacked onto the end of a sentence; the verb (and the final particle) is uttered with the falling intonation characteristic of a sentence-final element, and the afterthought element is uttered anew with a low, flat intonation pattern. (Shibatani 1990: 259)

Others have discussed the use of post-predicate additions for disambiguating an elliptical referent (Hinds 1982), for emphasis (Hinds 1982), to "defocus" semantically subordinate material (Clancy 1982), for "further specification, elaboration, clarification, repair" (Ono and Suzuki 1992), for emotive purposes (Ono and Suzuki 1992), and for the interactive achievement of collaborative talk (Hayashi, Mori, and Takagi, to appear). Moreover, Ono and Suzuki (1992: 436) go so far as to suggest that certain post-predicate forms produced within a single intonational contour such as *Nani sore* 'What's that?' are "in the process of becoming grammaticized".

It will be argued below that the analysis of the structure of post-predicate additions in relation to turn-taking further consolidates the case for the verb- (or predicate-) final orientation. The data indicate that the end of a predicate component is regularly treated as a possible transition-relevance place (TRP) regardless of whether speakers continue talking beyond the predicate. In conversation analytic terms, post-predicate additions turn out to be instances of "recompleters": i.e. when a further increment occurs after a final predicate component, the end of the predicate component is massively treated as a possible TRP, and the ensuing components are seen to be possible adjunctions to of the immediately prior TCU (see Chapter 3). The interactional (and specifically the turn-taking) consequences of this form are investigated below through the inspection of coparticipants' treatment of post-predicate additions (Section 4.3.2.1) and speakers' orientations to the phenomenon (Section 4.3.2.2).

4.3.2.1. *Coparticipants' treatment of post-predicate additions*

One method for identifying grammatical locations within utterances which are routinely treated as possible TRPs is to examine whether a regular pattern can be observed with respect to positions within a current speaker's turn where a second speaker begins to talk, thereby potentially displaying an orientation that the former's turn has reached completion. A review of cases of post-predicate additions in the present data set reveals a recurrence of instances where next speakers begin their turns after the predicate component can be heard without waiting for the post-predicate portion to be produced. Put another way, the post-predicate components are found to be a typical locus of overlapping talk between the current and next speaker. Coparticipants thereby treat post-predicate additions as recompleters by regularly beginning to speak towards the end of the predicate component. In the fragments in this section, the predicate components are highlighted in boldface.

We first consider below an example of the post-predicate addition of a subject phrase. B begins to produce a syntactically complete utterance *Mata jyūni ji goro kara itta ttsu no ne*: '((She)) says ((she)) went out again from about 12 o'clock', which ends with a predicate component *itta ttsu no ne*: (in boldface below). Note that at this point, the subject remains unexpressed. It is only after the predicate has been produced that B continues with the subject phrase *Yōko ga* (i.e., the name 'Yōko' followed by a postpositional nominative particle *ga* which marks *Yōko* as a subject). After B completes the predicate component, he is intersected by the next speaker F, overlapping B's production of the post-predicate subject phrase:

(56) [Shakujii 1A(#6), p. 3] telephone conversation; predicate component is in bold.

B is reporting to F about his wifeYōko who went to a beach the previous day.

B: → *Mata jyūni ji goro kara* ***itta ttsu no ne***:=
again 12 o'clock about from went say FP FP
'((She)) says ((she)) went out again from about 12 o'clock'
[*Yōko ga* (.) *'N*
[((name)) NOM yeah
['Yōko did, yeah'
post-predicate addition
=[
F: ['*N* ( )
['Yeah . . .'

In the following extract, the current speaker C begins with a predicate component *On'naji yo* '((It))'s the same' before adding a phrase *eri mo* 'the collar too', but is overlapped by the next speaker A as C continues to provide this phrase. By beginning after the predicate component and responding with a "change of state token" (Heritage 1984a), A displays an understanding of what it is that is being referred to as being 'the same' without waiting for the word 'collar' to be supplied (though this does not imply that the item implicitly furnished by A necessarily coincides with the phrase which C goes on to express). Note further that A comes in after C furnishes the predicate component even though there is no prosodic break or final intonational contour at the end of the predicate component.

(57) [OBS: p. 18] multi-party conversation; predicate in bold type.

One of the participants D has mentioned that her daughter is wearing one of her blouses which is exactly of the same style as that which is in vogue now. In the part shown below, C concurs that the style is the same, including the collar.

C: =***On'naji yo*** [*eri mo*
same FP [collar ADVP
'((It))'s the same [the collar too'
post-predicate addition
[
A: [*A! honto*::
[oh really
['Oh! really?'

Similarly, the next fragment shows a post-predicate addition of an adverbial phrase (produced within a continuous intonational contour) being overlapped by the next speaker embarking on her turn. H's turn is designed as the first part of an adjacency pair: a self-deprecation (see Pomerantz 1984a). I comes in after the predicate component *Uitotta n desu kedo*, by supplying a preferred second part of the pair (a disagreement which refutes the self-deprecation) even before the addition becomes hearable.

(58) [IMD: 149–150] telephone conversation; predicate in bold

H is talking about a wedding reception he went to, which was attended by many people of high social standing, where he felt totally out of place.

H: =*hijōni*:: (.) ***Uitotta n desu kedo***
extremely stood out N COP CONJ
'((I)) really stood out'

[*watashi tte. .hh e(H)e .hh*]
[I ADVP]
['as for me .hh e(H)e .hh']
post-predicate addition

[
I: [*Iya sonna koto nai n chau*?]
[no such thing not N different]
['No, that couldn't be, could it?']

The examples above illustrate that post-predicate additions are a regular locus of overlap by the next speaker. The observed recipient behaviour of beginning the next turn prior to the articulation of the subject or topic first of all suggests that the recipients have implicitly furnished it from the context, and that a subject or topic does not need to be expressed grammatically for an utterance to be treated as complete. Secondly, it reveals an orientation that the end of a predicate component is recognisable as a possible TRP in its sequential environment. Although only a few fragments have been dealt with above, the available data shows that expressions other than adverbial phrases also occur regularly in the post-predicate position and are likewise vulnerable to overlap by the next speaker, in their specific interactional contexts.

4.3.2.2. *Speakers' treatment of post-predicate additions*
Speakers also display an orientation that a post-predicate portion is liable to be heard as an adjunction to of the immediately prior TCU by regularly employing turn-holding strategies which are designed to over-ride a possible TRP occurring at the termination of a predicate component. For instance, the fragments above already illustrate how speakers typically attach post-predicate additions without any prosodic breaks. Further strategies include latching an additional increment contiguously to the preceding predicate component and/or using a sound stretch to deliver the last syllable of the predicate component before affixing the post-predicate portion. The regular deployment of such techniques for supplying additions after a predicate component is fitted to the possibility that a coparticipant might start up after the predicate, as demonstrated above. Presented below are fragments illustrating the two speaker strategies.

The following two excerpts exemplify the employment of the latching technique (denoted by an equal sign = below) precisely at the end of the predicate component, which connects the predicate component seamlessly to the ensuing post-predicate addition. Again, the predicate components are emphasised in boldface, and the post-predicate additions are labelled.

(59) [Shakujii 1A, #6, p. 6] telephone conversation

F and B are discussing the mistake they made the previous day by coming home early from the beach instead of staying until the temperature rose.

F: °*Shippai da yo*°
fiasco COP FP
'((It)) was a fiasco'

B: → °***Shippai da yo=*** *kinō wa hhh .hh*°=
fiasco COP FP yesterday TOP
'((It)) was a fiasco as for yesterday hhh .hh'
post-predicate addition

(60) [Shakujii 1A #4, p. 5] telephone conversation.

The two women in this extract are talking about K's baby who has a skin rash, which gets aggravated when he cries hard and becomes hot.

K: =*Dakara ūnto nai tari suru to sa=*
so a lot cry for instance do if FP
'So if ((he)) cries a lot or something'

Y: ='*N=*
'Yeah'

K:→ =*Kondo* ***ka:tto suru jyanai=*** *atama toka* [*mo*]
then hot do not head for instance [ADVP]
'Then ((it)) gets all hot, you know the head for instance [also']
post-predicate addition
[
Y: ['*N:*]
['Yeah']

Another speaker-conduct commonly found in the production of post-predicate additions is to stretch the last syllable of the predicate component to minimise any prosodic discontinuity, before appending a post-predicate component, as in the fragments below:

(61) [Shakujii 1A, #6, p. 5] telephone conversation
The speakers are talking about how cold it was the previous morning when they went to the beach.

B: → *Sorede mata* ↑***samukatta ne::*** *asagata::=*
and again was cold FP morning
'And it was again cold, wasn't it in the morning'
post-predicate addition

F: ='*N*=
'Yeah'

(62) [IMD 219–20] telephone conversation
I is asking H about a wedding that the latter attended.

I: [°*Etō:::*] *ntō ne:*°
[uhm] uhm FP
['Uhm uhm'

→ *.hh e dare ga* ***kiteta:::*** *kekkon shiki:.*
uhm who NOM came wedding
'.hh uhm who was there:::? at the wedding'
post-predicate addition

H: *Iya . . .*
'Well . . .'

At times, a speaker may combine the two techniques above, first by stretching the last syllable of the predicate component, and then latching on the post-predicate addition. The contiguous production or hurried start of the recompleter portion demonstrates speakers' orientation that a recipient may begin after the predicate component.

(63) [RKK 766–67] multi-party conversation
Prior to the part shown below, S has just mentioned that A's instructor had commented favourably on A's first research project.

A: → ***Ichiban saisho no darō::?=*** [*ano shi*]*gatsu no.=*
first one P COP [uhm April P
'The first ((one)) right? [uhm ((the one)) in April'
post-predicate addition
[
S: [*U::::n.*]
['Yeah']

The two techniques regularly exploited by speakers to display that more talk is to follow at the end of predicate components further demonstrate that these locations are typically oriented to as possible TRPs.

What emerges from the analysis in this section is the robustness of the predicate-final orientation in Japanese. In terms of the order of grammatical elements, components may appear in almost any order, together with the possibility that some components may not be expressed. The list of turn-shapes which were examined included (i) the standard S-O-V and O-S-V orderings, (ii) the elliptical forms S-V, O-V, and V, as well as (iii) post-predicate additions. In each case, participants regularly display a normative orientation that the end of the predicate component is a possible TRP. Indeed, for types (i) and (ii), collaborative completions massively involved recipients furnishing an anticipated predicate phrase; and even in case (iii) where the predicate phrase occurred before the production of other components, recipients regularly began to talk at the termination of the predicate phrase, demonstrating an orientation that the end of the predicate phrase is relevant for turn-transfer. Of course, speakers can choose to "violate" the predicate-final order—subject to possible overlap by the next speaker. However, speakers also enlist a variety of turn-holding strategies such as latching, contiguous talk, and avoidance of turn-final intonation to circumvent the relevance of turn-transfer at these points. Paradoxically, it is precisely these "deviant cases" consisting of "violations of the verb-final requirement" (see Shibatani 1990: 259) which provide the most vigorous evidence of participants' predicate-final orientation. Indeed, syntax is a normative system, and is not merely a description of how sentences are constructed. Syntactic organisation can serve as a resource for coparticipants to jointly construct a speaker's "sentence-in-progress" (Lerner 1991: 441), and more generally for turn-projection (Heritage and Roth 1995: 14).

Incidentally, some of the predicate components in the fragments above terminate with various grammatical elements such as verb nominalisers, copulas, and final particles, which serve to specify a preceding item as the final predicate of an ongoing turn. Although these elements are not the only kind of device available in Japanese for marking an adjective, verb or nominal expression as the final predicate, their utility for marking TRPs will be explored in greater depth in Section 4.5.

The picture is still quite incomplete, however, as we need to consider another important feature of turn-production and recognition in Japanese: the tentativeness and incremental transformability of the shapes of turns-in-progress. Indeed, the employment of postpositional particles to build an emerging turn-shape sometimes not only transforms an inchoate predicate expression into another type of grammatical category, but overwhelmingly results in reduced visibility of the trajectory of turns and delayed projectability of the ultimate turn-shape in Japanese (although it is also the case that interactional and contextual features can over-ride the impact of syntax).

4.4. Limited mid-turn projectability

Despite the evident orientation that the end of a predicate component is a possible TRP, the *onset* of for instance a verb phrase in itself is not necessarily treated as indicative that a turn-final verb component will be produced, nor for that matter that a turn is nearing completion (although exceptions are presented below in Section 4.5.4. This is because participants orient to the further possibility that what comes after a verb-stem can determine not only the mood of the verb but also may convert an incipient verb into another type of grammatical unit. For example, a verb expression may be transformed into a nominal phrase through the postpositional attachment of a verb nominaliser such as *wake* or *n*. This section explores the kinds of things that verb (or predicate)-suffixes can do for a turn: Section 4.4.1 pertaining to verb-following expressions which specify the mood of the verb, and Section 4.4.2 on further kinds of transformations which may occur thereafter.

4.4.1. *Expressions following the verb*

A predicate component which includes a verb stem can be followed by one or more suffixes. There are two major aspects of the structure of suffixes which contrasts with their equivalents in English.

First, suffixes can be prosodically and grammatically fused to a verb-stem to form a seamless unit—through a process referred to as *agglutinative morphology* (Shibatani 1990: 306; see Chapter 3, Section 3.2.3). This contrasts with the use of discrete words in English to accomplish similar ends. Many of the verb-suffixes in Japanese have no independent status as words nor can they normally be used separately from a stem to which they are attached. According to Shibatani (1990: 306–7), "Japanese shows a high degree of agglutination involving a fair number of suffixes (including auxiliary verbs) in a row", whose order is generally fixed, as in the following sequence:

Vstem–causative–passive–aspect–desiderative–negative–tense

Though expressions rarely employ every possibility for suffixes, some "commonly observed forms" are given by Shibatani (1990: 307):

a. *ika-se-rare-na-i*
GO-CAUS-POTEN-NEG-PRES
'cannot make X go'

b. *ika-se-rare-taku-na-i*
go-CAUS-PASS-DESI-NEG-PRES
'do not want to be made to go'

c. *aruka-se-tuzuke-ta-i*
walk-CAUS-CONT-DESI-PRES
'want to continue to make X walk'

The invented examples above sound somewhat unnatural, but nonetheless demonstrate the principle by which verb-following expressions may be affixed incrementally onto the verb stem in naturally occurring conversation.

Secondly, the suffixes in the Japanese version above do the interactive work performed by elements which in English normally precede the verb (e.g. compare the Japanese and English translations above), and therefore tend to occur relatively close to the beginning of an utterance in English. For instance, the negative marker *nai* or the thrust of an utterance such as 'want to make' someone do something can occur near the end of the Japanese verb phrase—items which massively get positioned closer to the beginning of an utterance in English (examples illustrating this contrast were given in Section 4.2). But there are additional reasons for coparticipants to wait until near the end of a turn to discover what is being done pragmatically in Japanese turns, to be discussed next.

4.4.2. *Transformability of the trajectory of a turn*

As suggested earlier, elements which might come after verb-following expressions can also have significant implications for what is performed in a turn both grammatically and interactionally. Even after a verb stem and verb-following expressions are produced, further postpositional suffixes may transform the foregoing expression into a different grammatical category such as a subject phrase, object phrase, or an embedded clause. It can therefore be difficult to anticipate whether an incipient verb expression will culminate as a turn-final predicate component of the turn-in-progress (and consequently herald a possible TRP), or if it might develop into something else which may project further talk. Moreover, important displays of the stance of the speaker and other types of actions are frequently reserved for the end of a turn (see Section 4.2).

This can partly be attributed to the postpositional structure of Japanese in contrast to languages such as English, which is predominantly a prepositional language (see Chapter 1). In comparison to English, for which it is claimed that a possible shape of a turn is regularly revealed early in the production of a turn (Schegloff 1987b: 71), the postpositional attachment of particles and other grammatical elements in

Japanese can result in the "incremental transformability" of an emerging utterance (see Chapter 5). Thus, a noun, adjective, or even a verb can become recognisable as a subject, object, indirect object, etc. by virtue of some particle which is attached at the end of the phrase containing the item, or an utterance potentially being constructed as a main clause can be transformed into a subordinate clause (e.g. through the appendage of a conjunctive particle) as a turn progresses.

It will be argued in Chapter 5 that the syntactic nature of a nominal element can remain somewhat equivocal until or unless a case or adverbial particle is expressed. Similarly, conjunctive particles can designate the syntactic form of a preceding clausal unit and project further talk (see Chapter 6). Briefly, conjunctive particles such as *dakedo* or *dakara* can be used to project a second component of a "compound turn-constructional unit" such as *although X–Y* or *if X–then Y*, as analysed for English by Lerner (1987, 1991, 1996). However, in contrast to English, the temporal emergence of such a compound turn-structure is regularly delayed until close to the end of the first component *X* rather than being revealed at the beginning of a turn (e.g. Lerner and Takagi, to appear; Chapter 6 this volume).

Due to the postpositional structure of Japanese, the type of a syntactic unit being constructed within the overarching structure of a turn may remain tentative and revisable as a turn unfolds in real time. Such possibilities have important consequences for how participants can anticipate the development of a turn or for the projection of a possible TRP. Thus, for instance, even after the production of a complete sentence, a particle following the sentence may transform it into a different kind of grammatical unit.

Despite the predicate-final orientation, then, it will first be shown that the simple production of a verb, adjective, or noun modifying a subject (i.e. items which can potentially develop into a predicate component) is not necessarily regarded as an incipient turn-ending, since it is not always possible to identify it as the final predicate without waiting to see what ensues. This is because what occurs after a verb expression can be critical for knowing what action the turn will ultimately be occupied with. Secondly, it will be argued that coparticipants display a normative orientation to the potential transformability of emerging grammatical units by regularly refraining from starting to speak even after a potential predicate of a turn is beginning to be produced.

First, a single fragment is used to demonstrate that what occurs after an initial verb expression (i.e. a potential final predicate) can influence the temporal evolution of a turn, through the possibility of mid-course adjustments of its trajectory.

(64) [Shakujii 1A, #4: 7] telephone conversation, slightly simplified

K is explaining to Y about her baby's ailment, in which the latter first developed a temperature, and then came out in rashes.

1 K: *Mō netsu ga mō- sagatta* to*
already temperature NOM already fell QUOT: that

2 *omot tara [ne:=*
thought CONJ:when [FP
[
3 Y: ['*N*
['Yeah'

4 K: =>*deta*<=
came out
'((the rashes)) came out'

5 Y: =↑*Ha::*
'Oh'

Gloss of lines 1–2: 'When ((I)) thought that already the temperature had already fallen, you know'

K's utterance from the beginning of line 1 to the asterisk constitutes a complete sentence in an analytic sense (with subject *netsu* and verb *sagatta*):

(a) K: *Mō netsu ga mō- sagatta** . . .
already temperature NOM already fell . . .
'already the temperature had already fallen . . .'

However, the recipient Y has not treated the verb *sagatta* 'fell' as a place to begin, waiting instead until near the end of K's turn in line 4 to start to talk. The incremental transformations of K's turn after the production of the verb *sagatta* 'fell' are charted below: .

To begin with, the postpositional quotative case particle *to* 'that' at the end of line 1 which follows *sagatta* 'fell' transforms the sentence-in-progress

(a) K: *Mō netsu ga mō- sagatta**
already temperature NOM already fell
'already the temperature had already fallen'

into a clause to be subsequently commented on (where the transforming elements are noted in bold):

(b) K: *Mō* *netsu* *ga* *mō-* *sagatta** **to**
already temperature NOM already fell **QUOT: that**
'**that** already the temperature had already fallen'

which then becomes an embedded clause within a new sentence with the new predicate, *omot-* 'thought' that follows:

(c) K: *Mō* *netsu* *ga* *mō-* *sagatta** *to* **omot**
already temperature NOM already fell QUOT: that ***thought***
'((**I**)) **thought** that already the temperature had already fallen'

This new emerging sentence is further transformed by the postpositional attachment of a conjunctive particle *tara* into the first part of a potential compound TCU of the form *when X–Y*:

(d) K: *Mō* *netsu* *ga* *mō-* *sagatta** *to* omot
already temperature NOM already fell QUOT: that thought

tara
CONJ: when
'**When** ((I)) thought that already the temperature had already fallen'

which now projects a clause *Y*. Indeed, the conjunctive particle *tara* 'when' syntactically projects the production of at least one more component, which is issued in line 4: *deta* '((the rashes)) came out'.

The fragment above exemplifies that a sentence-in-progress can be retroactively converted into an embedded clause, and that a compound turn-shape is often unprojectable until an actual conjunctive particle can be heard. Even from this single instance, it is possible to obtain a glimpse of how the postpositioning of particles can result in a step-by-step modification of the grammatical construction of an immediately prior segment of talk.

As a consequence, second, the occurrence of a verb-stem with verb-following expressions is typically treated as insufficient for participants to judge a turn-in-progress as nearing completion. In the fragments below, the verb constituents are highlighted in boldface, and the end of the verb constituents are marked by an asterisk *:

(65) [Shakujii 1A(#4), p. 5] telephone conversation

The two women in this extract are talking about K's baby who has a skin rash, and how scrubbing him in the bath aggravates the ailment:

K: . . . *kosuru* *to*
scrub if
'. . . if ((you)) scrub'

→ *mata* ***akaku naru**** *n da yo ne=*
again red become VN COP FP FP
'((it)) gets red again'

Y: =°*Ah: so kka:*°
oh so QP
'Oh ((I)) see'

The main sentential components (elliptical subject–elliptical object–verb) of K's turn have already been produced by the time she articulates the verb *akaku naru* 'gets red'. Even though the potential predicate already appears to have been produced, Y refrains from starting to talk. The addition of *n da* serves to present something as a state, the final particle *yo* emphasises or intensifies the action of the utterance, and *ne* elicits affiliation and an acknowledgement or speaker-change (Tanaka to appear-b, to appear-c). Considering that Y's response is accompanied by a "change-of-state" token (Heritage 1984a), it is interesting that Y "waits" until the ensuing elements *n da yo ne* are heard before she produces this token. This conduct raises the possibility that Y may have been open to an eventual "outcome" which diverges from what she may have been able to anticipate at the asterisk before the remaining elements were produced.

(66) [Tokyo 7: 6] multi-party conversation

H has been saying how much he can learn from his wife, especially about English ways of thinking. Below, he continues claiming this is because he is ignorant of such things.

H: *Ano:* ***shiranai-****
uhm don't know
'Uhm, ((I)) don't know ((it))'

→ *boku yappari* ***shiranai**** *desho?*
I after all don't know COP
'after all I don't know ((it)), ((you)) know?'

G: *Dakara sō naru to . . .*
then so become then
'Then that means that . . .'

Likewise, in the above fragment, although the verb constituents have already been produced at the two asterisks, it is only after the copula *desho* can be heard, that G begins to talk. Again, the significance of grammatical items such as copulas, verb-suffixes and final particles for announcing an imminent termination of a turn will be discussed in the next section.

Regular occurrences of examples such as the above offer reasons to believe that the production by Japanese conversationalists of the main syntactic constituents alone (and an incipient predicate in particular) is not necessarily sufficient for participants to consider an utterance-in-progress as somehow complete turns. As a general explanation for this behaviour, while a turn-in-progress may be syntactically complete taken out of context, it may not be complete intonationally and pragmatically (Ford and Thompson 1996). Furthermore, it appears that recipients refrain from starting up because they orient to the potential transformability of the already-produced thrust of an utterance through the possibility of the postpositioning of additional particles and other elements: one of the consequences of the postpositional structure of Japanese syntax. Indeed, as Heritage and Roth (1995) observe, withholding talk at certain points in talk can evidence a "situational normativity" of participants towards certain inappropriate grammatical and interactional positions within a current speaker's talk for the second speaker to begin to speak.

To summarise, the absence of recipient uptake at the junctures marked by asterisks in fragments (64)–(66) indicate that participants do not, as a matter of course, treat a verb-expression itself as heralding an imminent TRP (although as discussed below, the *iikiri* (truncated) form is an exception to this rule). The examples dealt with in this section show that Japanese participants regularly abstain from starting the next turn even after the main syntactical components (and in particular, a potential predicate) have been produced. Turns are built up incrementally through the possible addition of elements which can progressively modify the talk preceding it as well as the potential social action performed by the emergent turn. Furthermore, the additions crudely correspond to expressions which are usually produced in reverse order towards the beginning of a turn in English, that may be critical for projecting an upcoming turn-shape (e.g. expressions such as 'Since' or 'Doesn't this mean . . .'). In view of this limited visibility, how do participants in Japanese project possible TRPs?

4.5. Turn-final projectability: utterance-final elements and the *iikiri* (truncated) form

If turn-shapes are indeed transformable *ad infinitum* with no mechanism available to put a halt to the process, participants would presumably face major obstacles in managing a co-ordinated transfer of turns. In practice, however, Japanese conversationalists do not appear to experience special difficulties engaging in turn-taking activities, and in particular in producing and recognising TRPs.

It will be remembered from Chapter 3 that turn-endings in Japanese can be crudely classified into four types: utterance-final elements, the *iikiri* (truncated) format, recompleters and extensions. An examination of these turn-endings suggest that participants overwhelmingly rely on two major turn-exit devices (among others) to mark the potentially final transformation of the turn-trajectory and hence the arrival of a possible TRP: (i) utterance-final elements or (ii) pronounced prosodic features characteristic of the *iikiri* (truncated) format. The first of these devices is regularly employed at the end of some increment of talk to highlight it in one way or other as the turn-final verb or predicate component. Given the powerful verb-final orientation in Japanese (see Section 4.3), they can be highly effectual as markers of a possible TRP. The second device (pronounced prosodic contours) can also be occasioned at the end of predicate components as well as other junctures to signal finality. The relatively delayed projectability of turns in Japanese is to a large extent offset by the precision with which these devices can localise possible TRPs.

4.5.1. *Utterance-final elements*

One of the devices which may be employed to terminate the incremental transformation of a turn consists of a range of grammatical elements which have been referred to as *utterance-final elements*. In specific sequential contexts, these elements can be treated as marking a possible TRP by providing an ultimate sense of "closure" or "finality" to a turn. The pervasive use of utterance-final elements, which have no clear equivalents in English,[6] is perhaps one of the greatest contrasts between Japanese and Anglo-American conversational structures. In view of the normative orientation to the potentially indefinite step-by-step transformability of the grammatical unit under construction, utterance-final elements can play a pivotal role for indicating that no further transformations are in store.

To recapitulate (see Chapter 3), grammatical items which may be employed as utterance-final elements typically include one or more of those listed in Table 1. Speakers may invoke these grammatical items for instance to mark: one's social identity; social relations with coparticipants, referents and bystanders; as well as to formulate aspects of the interactional environment (e.g. Maynard 1993; Tanaka

Table 1. *Utterance-final elements (not exhaustive)*

- (a) (SFX) final verb suffixes such as *masu*, *mashita*, *mashō*
- (b) (COP) copulas such as *desu*, *deshō*, *da*, or *na*
- (c) (FP) final particles such as *ne*, *yo*, *sa*, *ka*, *no*, *wa*, *zo*
- (d) request or imperative: *kudasai*, *chōdai*, *nasai*
- (e) others, including nominalisers: *wake*, *mono*, *mon*, *n*

1996, to appear-b). But this is not the place to dwell on such "relational" implications. Instead, their consequences for turn-taking are discussed below. First, it will be shown that the situated use of utterance-final elements—either alone or in certain combinations—is treated as signifying a possible turn-ending. Secondly, I examine how the employment of a succession of utterance-final elements can "expand" the transition-relevance area where others may start up.

Utterance-finals can serve as integral resources for speakers to co-ordinate a precisely timed exchange of turns. In the following fragment, two coparticipants display concord in their judgements that the appearance of an utterance-final element is indeed an appropriate place to start the next turn. The utterance-final elements of interest in this section are marked in boldface.

(67) [Tokyo 7 p. 13] multi-party conversation

K is talking about how a particular relationship between two of the participants involves a repetition of the same pattern. Note that the utterance-final element *deshō* in line 2 below is just one word.

1 K: . . . *waku no sukima o dete nai to*
frame GEN corner ACC not go out QUOT
'. . . that ((it)) hasn't broken out of the pattern'

2 *kōiu koto* ***de*** *[****shō***
this sort thing COP
'is what it means, doesn't it?'
[
3 G:→ [*Daka* ↑*ra*
['Therefore'
[
4 W:→ [*Tsumari sa: ·hh . . .*
[in other words FP
['In other words ·hh . . .'

The current speaker K produces an open question/comment in lines 1–2, ending with the utterance-final copula *deshō* 'it is true, isn't it'. What is remarkable about this fragment is that immediately after K begins to enunciate the utterance-final element *deshō* in line 2, two self-selecting next speakers start up simultaneously, i.e. "turn-allocation rule (1b)" as analysed by Sacks, Schegloff, and Jefferson (1974). Both recipients have evidently treated this local invocation of *deshō* as an announcement of an imminent completion of the ongoing turn.

Likewise, the fragment below exemplifies two speakers finely tuning mutual entry into each others' turn spaces so that the overlaps occur precisely as the utterance-finals start to be produced, or shortly thereafter.

(68) [Tokyo 7: 26] multi-party conversation

W: '*N*: *sō* [***ne***
yeah so [FP
'Yeah isn't it?'
[
G: [*Sore wa aru* ***deshō*** [***: ne***
[that TOP exist COP [FP
['That's quite plausible, isn't it'
[
W: [*Sō* ***na*** ***n de***[***shō ne***
[so COP N C[OP FP
['That's probably right, isn't it?'
[
G: ['*N sore wa . . .*
[yeah that TOP
['Yeah that is . . .'

Here, the recognition of utterance-final elements results in an exquisite "chaining" of consecutive turns, overlapping the next turn only at utterance-final elements. These fragments demonstrate the potential utility of utterance-final elements for turn-taking by unequivocally signalling possible TRPs.

4.5.2. *Transition-relevance space*

Leaving until the next section a discussion of *how* the utterance-final elements might signify turn-completion, I take a moment to investigate the nature of the TRPs which are marked by these elements. An inspection of the data suggests that the next speaker does not always wait until the current speaker has finished producing all the utterance-final elements, but may start up at their *onset*. Presented below without commentary are several "straightforward" examples, fragments (69)–(72), in which the second speaker begins the next turn before the end of the current speaker's turn, either after the first of the elements can be heard or just as the last of the utterance-finals are issued (the utterance-final elements under consideration are highlighted in boldface):

(69) [Tokyo 7 p. 28] multi-party conversation

→ H: *Honto ni sō* ***na*** [***no***
really P SO COP [FP
'((It))'s really so'
[
G: [*Sō desu yo↑ne*
[SO COP FP FP
['((That))'s right, isn't ((it))?'

(70) [Shakujii 1B (#2), p. 6] telephone conversation

B: *Ofuro ireta no Yurika-chan*
bath put in QP ((name))
'Did ((you)) give Yurika a bath?'

Y: *Mada irenai yo*
not yet not put in FP
'((I)) haven't given ((her a bath)) yet'

→ *korekara gohan* ***da mo***[***n***
from now meal COP N
'((we))'re about to have dinner now'
[
B: [*Kyō dokka itta no*?
[today somewhere go FP
['Did ((you)) go somewhere today?'

(71) [Shakujii 1A (#9), p. 7] telephone conversation

→ H: *Mō nandemo utteru* ***wake yo*** [***ne***
INT anything sell VN FP [FP
'((They)) sell everything'
[
M: [*Na:ruhodo*
['((I)) see'

(72) [Shakujii 1B (#5) p. 5] telephone conversation

C: → *On- on'naji koto* ***na no*** [***ne***
same thing COP FP [FP
'((It))'s the same thing, ((you)) know'
[

H: [*Sō da wa* ↑*ne*
[SO COP FP FP
['((It)) is, isn't ((it))?'

The fragments above evidence a normative orientation that once utterance-final elements begin to be produced, there is a high likelihood that the current speaker is nearing the end of her/his turn: a grammatical position within the TCU referred to by Schegloff (1996a) as *pre-possible completion*. The duration of the transition-relevance *space* (see Jefferson 1986) appears to span the interval between the onset of the elements (i.e. pre-possible completion) until immediately after they have been produced. Thus, the typical use of several utterance-final elements in succession widens the window of opportunity for others to come in.

Furthermore, the expansion of the transition-relevance-space through multiple utterance-final elements may be regarded as an ingenious built-in mechanism which can compensate for the relative opacity of turn-trajectories. Recall that due to the postpositional structure of Japanese, there may be little prior information on the basis of which participants can project the possible onset of utterance-final elements. In particular, these elements—which can well be the first sign that a possible TRP is imminent—may occur rather suddenly, and often just before the end of a turn. The typical practice of producing a combination of utterance-final elements can, in effect, allow slightly more time for coparticipants to respond to the relevance of a turn-transfer, without giving occasion to regular occurrences of gaps after turn-completion.

Importantly, the fact that next speakers regularly begin their turn at the onset of utterance-finals without waiting until they have been produced in their entirety suggests that participants do not necessarily rely on the final intonational contours of a turn to determine that a turn has come to a completion, but that structural features—i.e. the situational deployment of utterance-final elements—may be oriented to as somewhat of an independent display of an imminent TRP. This view is further reinforced by the regular occurrences of possibly "inadvertent" overlaps when speakers talk past utterance-final elements even without a final intonation, as in fragments (56)–(57) examined in Section 4.3.2. Thus, although utterance-final elements frequently co-occur with a final intonational contour, it appears that they may contingently be treated as heralding a possible TRP even when they are not accompanied by a clear final intonation.

4.5.3. *Utterance-final elements and the predicate-final orientation*

This section seeks to explore features of utterance-final elements which underpin their situated utility as a turn-exit device. Broadly speaking, the mobilisation of utterance-final elements can be seen to be closely linked to the deep-rooted predicate-final orientation in Japanese. Specifically, utterance-final elements may signal turn-endings, for instance, by (a) marking what precedes it as a turn-final verb or predicate component, or (b) by incorporating next-speaker selection techniques, etc. The incremental progressivity of the turn-shape immediately before a possible TRP can reveal some characteristic ways in which the elements may engender the relevance of a turn-transfer. In the fragments below, the utterance-final elements have been highlighted in boldface.

A micro-analysis involving a step-by-step tracking of the penultimate trajectory of a turn in the fragment below ending with a series of four utterance-final elements illustrates some turn-taking implications of the postpositional attachment of these elements:

(73) [Shakujii 1A(#4), p. 5] telephone conversation
The two women in this extract are talking about K's son who has a skin rash, and that scrubbing him in the bath will aggravate the ailment:

K: →. . . *kosuru to mata akaku naru** ***n da yo ne=***
scrub if again red become **VN COP FP FP**
'. . . if ((you)) scrub, ((it)) gets red again'

Y: =°*Ah: so kka:*°
oh so QP
Oh ((I)) see

As noted previously with respect to fragment (65), K's turn is already grammatically complete in a "technical" or "analytical" sense at the asterisk (see Chapter 3):

(a) K: *kosuru to mata akaku naru**
scrub if again red become
'if ((you)) scrub, ((it)) gets red again'

However, instead of starting up after the production of the verb *akaku naru* 'to become red', Y waits to come in until the utterance-final elements have been produced. But what aspect of these elements are exploited by conversationalists to signal the end a turn?

The overall interactional activities which the subsequent utterance-final elements *n da yo ne* undertake can be glossed roughly as follows:

(b) K: ***n da yo ne=***
that it is the case indeed you know

It is necessary here to "unpack" the interactional significance of the sequential adjunction of the individual utterance-final elements. Each of these elements can be shown to be directed towards cumulatively terminating the turn and/or indicating the relevance of a turn-transfer.

To begin with, the verb nominaliser *n* (equivalent to something like 'that') which occurs after the verb *akaku naru* 'to become red' renders the turn-in-progress into a nominal unit:

(c) K: →*kosuru to mata akaku naru** ***n***
scrub if again red become **that**
'**that** if ((you)) scrub, ((it)) gets red again'

Then, the copula *da* converts this new nominal phrase, (c) above, into a predicate through a process of "predication" (Martin 1975: 40). Namely, the copula *da* which in this example may be glossed as 'it is the case' postpositionally marks the foregoing *akaku naru n* as the predicate of the emergent utterance:

(d) K: *kosuru to mata akaku naru** *n* ***da***
scrub if again red become that **it is the case**
'**it is the case** that if ((you)) scrub, ((it)) gets red again'

Given the powerful verb- (predicate-) final orientation in Japanese, the predicating effect of *da* provides robust grounds for judging that the current turn may be coming to a close.

Next, the final particle *yo* which is typically employed to emphasise an immediately preceding action, further reinforces the finality of the turn:

(e) K: *kosuru to mata akaku naru** *n da* ***yo***
scrub if again red become that it is the case **indeed**
'**indeed**, it is the case that if ((you)) scrub, ((it)) gets red again'

Finally, at the terminal boundary of the turn, the final particle *ne* serves as a kind of tag question similar to 'you know?', a method of allocating the next turn through a "current selects next" technique (see Sacks, Schegloff, and Jefferson 1974: 718):

(f) K: *kosuru to mata akaku naru** *n da yo* ***ne***
scrub if again red become that it is the case indeed **you know**
'indeed, it is the case that if ((you)) scrub, ((it)) gets red again, **you know'**

Thus, the adjunction of the combination of utterance-final elements *n da yo ne* here proposes in as many as three different ways that the current turn is being brought to a close. Coupled with their grammatical implications, the prosodic fusion of the series of four utterance-final elements *n da yo ne* through agglutination (Section 4.4.1 and Chapter 3, Section 3.2.3) and a turn-final intonation can result in an unequivocal signalling of turn-completion.

An exhaustive description of the grammatical and interactional significance of the entire assortment of utterance-final elements is not possible here. As exemplified above, the grammatical types of these elements are varied (Section 4.5.1), with each type (e.g. copulas, verb-suffixes, final particles, nominalisers, etc.) exhibiting somewhat distinctive ways for postpositionally marking or converting a foregoing spate of talk into a possible turn-final verb or predicate component. Moreover, even within one grammatical category such as final particles, there appear to be subtle differences in how individual particles may be invoked for bringing a turn to a close (see Tanaka to appear-c for a case study of the final particle *ne*). I have simply scratched the surface of this phenomenon, and indicated some representative ways in which utterance-final elements may be enlisted for marking turn-endings.

The fact that utterance-final elements can be used and recognised as undertaking the final possible transformation of the trajectory of a turn and for signalling a TRP has been discussed above. This, however, does not mean that utterance-final elements are always treated as turn-exit devices in their own right, regardless of the position or the specific context in which they appear. Indeed, like other grammatical elements, most utterance-final elements seem to have multiple uses in addition to signalling possible turn-endings. In short, utterance-final elements are contingently deployed for the performance of turn-ending activities.

It will be argued below that the employment of utterance-finals is ultimately fitted to (i) the particular sort of social action being performed and (ii) the grammatical and sequential positions in which they occur.[7] First, pragmatic projection is of prime importance in participants' judgement of turn-completion (see Chapter 3). In the interests of achieving an interactive task, participants may pre-empt a possible completion or indeed select not to speak at possible TRPs. In such cases, pragmatic considerations can outweigh the impact of syntax in projecting courses of action, as in the following instance, which demonstrates how some occurrences of utterance-final elements are treated as irrelevant for signalling turn-completion.

In the example below, the utterance-final element *kudasai* is not treated as relevant for marking a turn-ending, since it can be heard as a part of a quoted portion:

(74) [Shakujii 1A (#9), p. 13] telephone conversation; slightly simplified
M is conveying a message from his co-worker for H.

```
M: (Soitsu  wa)
   the chap TOP
   '(As for the chap)'

   setsumei shite kudasai [tte       ma: yu [tteta kara
   explain        please  [QUOT AP   say[ing  CONJ: because
   'because ((he)) was saying "would you please explain it ((to them))"'
                          [               [
H:                        ['N:            [Ah: yutteta ne:
                          [Mmm            [oh saying FP
                          ['Mmm'          ['Oh ((he)) was saying ((that)),
                                           was ((he))?'
```

Although the utterance-final element *kudasai* 'please' appears in the second line, the recipient H only acknowledges this, and does not actually begin her turn until after the turn-final verb *yutteta* 'was saying' begins to be produced. The appearance of *Soitsu wa* 'As for that chap' permits a parsing of the emerging talk as a possible quotation of something said by M's co-worker, and the utterance-final *kudasai* can be understood as belonging to the ending of the quoted speech rather than a possible termination of M's turn.

The following fragment illustrates the significance of the grammatical and sequential position in which an utterance-final element is occasioned for whether or not it is treated as a turn-ending device. Indeed, an utterance-final element occurring mid-turn (e.g. before the onset of a potential predicate) can be bypassed as a marker of turn-completion, as in the case of the following use of the final particles *sa* and *ne*:

(75) [Shakujii 1A (#4) p. 14] telephone conversation

1→ Y: *Tashō ame futte mo* ***sa***=
a bit rain fall even if FP
'Even if it rains a bit ((you)) know'

2 K: ['*N*
[uh huh
['Uh huh'
=[
3→ Y: [*icchatte kuruma de* ***ne***:=
[go and car by FP
['if ((you)) go by car and ((you)) know'

4 K: ['*N*
['Yeah'
=[
5 Y: [(*sa*)
FP

Here, the final particle *sa* (line 1) and *ne* (line 3) occur turn-internally, post-positionally attached to clauses which respectively project a further unit of talk. In detail, the particle *sa* occurs in line 1 after the clause 'Even if it rains a bit', the first part of a compound TCU of the format *if X* which foreshadows a *then Y* clause (Lerner 1987, 1991). Line 3 'if ((you)) go by car and ((you)) know' is also constructed as an *if X* portion of a compound TCU, an instance of a clause with a post-predicate addition, *kuruma de* 'by car'. The particle *ne* is attached at the end of this clause, which also projects a *then Y* clause to follow. In such instances, the employment of a final particle is treated as eliciting an acknowledgement rather than as a marker of turn-completion, as is evidenced by the coparticipant K's proffering of an acknowledgement in lines 2 and 4 respectively (see Tanaka to appear-c).

The situated uses of utterance-final elements for marking turn-completion have been examined. To summarise, some elements can serve as predicators of preceding expressions, and others can be deployed as next-speaker selection techniques when attached to a predicate component. In view of the predicate-final orientation in Japanese conversation, the effectiveness of these measures as turn-transfer devices should come as no surprise. Since utterance-final elements themselves can transform the grammatical or interactional sense of prior talk, these elements not only signal an imminent TRP but are treated as bringing about the final transformation of the turn-shape.

4.5.4. *The* iikiri *(truncated) form*

While turns in Japanese regularly do end with utterance-final elements, recall from Chapter 3 that there is also an entire class of turns characterised by a systematic absence of these elements, which was called the *iikiri* or truncated form.[8] Turns of this type end rather "abruptly" without a terminal attachment of any utterance-final element, and yet are treated as recognisably complete. The data indicate that these turns regularly, but not necessarily end at the occurrence of a verb or predicate component. But how do participants recognise and manage possible TRPs in the absence of utterance-final elements which are directed towards indicating that no further transformations of the ongoing turn are in progress? Though a fuller discussion must be left for future work (but see Tanaka 1998), an examination of this turn-shape indicates that (i) the signalling of turn-completion may be accomplished at least partly through the employment of a marked final prosodic delivery, such as stressing, pronounced falling or rising final intonation, sound-stretches or some other noticeable prosodic delivery, and (ii) sequential organisation is critical for the determination of a possible TRP.

First, I examine fragments which show that noticeable prosodic features may be used as an alternative method to signal turn-endings when utterance-final elements are not employed to end a turn. One type of prosodic marking is a sharp rise or fall in pitch, as in the following. Boldface is used to highlight the turn-endings in question.

(76) [Shakujii 1A (#1), p. 5] telephone conversation

Y's daughter Yurika had previously been suffering from an upset stomach. A asks Y if Yurika has recovered.

1 A: *Yurika-chan onaka no hō daijō*↑***bu***
((name)) tummy GEN as for all right
'Is Yurika's tummy alright?'

2 Y: '*N daibun mata naotte kita.* ((**falling intonation**))
yeah a lot again getting better
'Yeah ((it))'s getting a lot better again'

3 A: ↑***Ah*** ↓***sō***
oh right
'Oh, is ((that)) right'

In the above fragment, none of the turns end with utterance-final elements. A's turn in line 1 terminates with a predicate *daijō*↑*bu* without any utterance-final elements. The last syllable of this word is emphasised and uttered with a clearly rising final intonation. Likewise, Y's turn (line 2) finishes with a distinct falling intonation. The prosodic qualities are particularly pronounced in line 3, in which the rising tone of the first lexical item ↑*Ah* provides a sharp contrast to the falling second word ↓*sō*.

Another way in which the final prosodic contour may be marked is illustrated by the following instance in which the truncated turns (lines 1 and 2) are delivered in a pace more rapidly than surrounding talk:

(77) [Shakujii1A (#4), p. 15] telephone conversation; slightly simplified

In this telephone conversation, K and Y have been talking about some strawberry jam that K had previously made for Y.

1 K:→ ***>tabeta?<=***
ate
'Did ((you)) eat ((it))?'

2 Y:→ ***=>tabeta<***
ate
'((I/we)) ate ((it))'

3 *oishikatta yo=*
was delicious FP
'((It)) was delicious'

4 K: =Honto
'Really?'

Note that both lines 1 and 2 grammatically consist of just the past form of the verb *taberu* 'to eat', which rely on either a rising or falling final intonational delivery to characterise it as a question (line 1) or a declarative (line 2) instead of on utterance-final elements which could have been mobilised for this purpose (see fragment (64) line 4 for another example). Moreover, these two turns are produced in a quickened pace and clipped fashion. Their prosodic qualities stand in contrast to the relatively flat delivery of endings of turns with an utterance-final construction (e.g. fragments (67)–(70) and (72)–(73)).

The following fragment exemplifies instances of stressing and stretching. In lines 1 and 2, the entire turns are stressed. Alternatively, a sound stretch is employed in line 3 to fashion this turn as a question or complaint.

(78) [Shakujii 1A (#1), p. 2] telephone conversation

In this fragment, A inquires whether Y is coming back to see A.

1 A: ***Modoru***?
returning
'((Are you)) coming back?'

2 Y: ***Mada***
'Not yet'

3 A: ((laughing)) ***Ma: (h)da(h)*** *hm=*
not yet
'Not yet? hm'

Of note is the highly parsimonious construction of talk in the above example. In particular, the turns in lines 2 and 3 do not have expressed predicates. In the light of the predicate-final orientation discussed earlier, there would be an especially good reason to enlist another resource such as prosody to mark the relevance of a turn-ending. Importantly, participants do not rely solely on prosodic markings but also on the sequential context of talk to judge an utterance to be possibly complete. Thus, to the question *Modoru*? '((Are you)) coming back?', a turn which consists of simply an adverb *Mada* 'Not yet' in line 2 may well suffice for it to be treated as complete, even though it may not be syntactically complete when considered in isolation. Similarly, the same adverb *Ma*: (*h*)*da*(*h*) 'Not yet?' used to solicit confirmation in line 3 is recognisable as a complete turn. This fragment furthermore reminds us that grammar and prosody cannot be considered independently of their contingent relation to the accomplishment of social actions. In other words, a particular grammatical or prosodic realisation of talk is interrelated and interlocked within the sequential organisation of the courses of action that participants are engaged in. Thus, neither grammatical construction nor prosody alone plays a deterministic role in the localisation of possible completion points.

The instances above indicate that participants can arrest the expectation that further transformations of the turn-shape may be intended through the employment of a marked final prosodic contour towards the end of the turn. Moreover, the significance of the *iikiri* turn-shape should be regarded as an alternative to the typical use of utterance-finals which appears to be a statistically more prevalent turn-design signifying turn-completion (see Chapter 3). Given the overwhelming practice of attaching utterance-final elements to the end of a turn, a marked prosodic delivery serves a substantive purpose to inform coparticipants that a turn is arriving at an "early" completion (i.e. without utterance-final elements).

The foregoing discussion has addressed the dynamic role of utterance-final elements, prosody, and sequential organisation as resources for the localisation of possible TRPs. In spite of the limited projectability of turn-shapes in Japanese, then, Japanese participants have at their disposal at least two methods which allow them to judge when a turn is coming to a completion. The potency of these techniques as turn-exit devices can be explained in relation to the normativity of the incremental transformability of turn-shapes and the predicate-final orientation. In other words, recipients regularly withhold beginning a next turn while mid-turn transformations of the current turn are in progress, while at the same time parsing talk for *some sign* that a final transformation is being implemented. Both utterance-final elements and marked prosodic endings may be deployed to serve as such signs and contribute to forestalling further transformations of a turn. However, these devices are mobilised within their specific sequential contexts, in which a turn is recognisable as accomplishing a complete social action.[9]

4.6. Summary and discussion

The analysis of conversational syntax and its relation to turn-taking has unveiled major differences in turn-projection in Japanese and English. Previous research indicates that English syntax facilitates an early projection (relative to Japanese) of the type of turn being produced, since the social action performed by a turn is typically made available early in the progress of a turn. In other words, the substance of what is being talked about is commonly produced after the turn-shape has already been projected. Roughly the reverse can be said to hold in Japanese. Partly as a result of the predicate-final orientation and postpositional grammar, turns in Japanese are massively structured so that the substance of what is being talked about is articulated before the social action bearing upon that substance is made known. Put another way, turns in Japanese *do not necessarily project from their beginnings* what their ultimate shape and type will be. The features of projectability in languages such as English with a standard Subject-Verb-Object word ordering and prepositional syntactic structure may thus not necessarily be transferable *in toto* onto postpositional and predicate-final languages like Japanese. The following is a summary and discussion of key points raised in this chapter.

Major grammatical features which impact on turn-construction and projection in Japanese include the variability of word order and the pronounced verb- (or predicate-) final orientation. It was first noted that there is a degree of flexibility in the ordering of the major constituents of an utterance preceding the verb or predicate. Secondly, utterances were seen to be replete with ellipsis of various components such as the subject, object or both. Further, an examination of instances of post-predicate additions revealed that whilst the superficial structure of utterances can be varied, the production of a final predicate component is overwhelmingly treated as announcing an imminent possible TRP, wherever the predicate component may happen to be positioned within an utterance. Indeed, deviations from the canonical predicate-final order tend to be heard as already complete at the end of the predicate-component, with the subsequent production of additional components being treated as recompleters. It can therefore be said that the apparent versatility of the word order masks the normativity of the predicate-final orientation in Japanese.

Moreover, the postpositional grammatical organisation in Japanese allows for a high degree of revisability of a developing turn. Since a grammatical unit which has already been produced can be incrementally and retroactively converted into other grammatical objects as a turn progresses, the type of activity performed by a turn can likewise be subject to progressive transformations. For instance, a sentence-in-the-course-of-production may be reformed into a subordinate clause projecting more talk through the adjoining of a conjunctive particle delivered with a continuing intonation (see Chapter 6). Due to the revisability of the syntactic form of utterances, the type of syntactic unit being produced can remain relatively opaque until the end of a turn. As a consequence, participants would be motivated to listen towards the end of a turn to discover its eventual shape and the social action performed by the turn.

The inherent transformability of turns contributes to a relatively delayed projectability of the emerging turn-shape and the point at which a turn may be complete (in comparison to English). Thus, participants in Japanese massively resort to various syntactic, prosodic, and pragmatic cues that signal turn-completion. The data indicated the existence of two turn-exit devices which are recognised as marking a possible TRP. First, a variety of grammatical elements, referred to as utterance-final elements are regularly employed to mark turn-completion, typically consisting of some combination of turn-final suffixes, nominalisers, copulas, and final-particles. The situated employment of these elements is normatively recognised as announcing a possible TRP. The efficacy of these grammatical devices for flagging a possible TRP is furthermore explained by virtue of their role for marking an immediately prior increment of talk as the final verb (or predicate) component of the turn or as a tag question. As another option, participants may deploy a prosodically-marked turn-design (the *iikiri* truncated turn-shape) which is structured to end "abruptly" without utterance-final elements. However, the distinct delivery of the final item is heard as an alternative signal that a turn may be arriving at an early completion, which in effect over-rides the normative expectation that utterance-final elements are due. The sheer density of the resources available for explicitly marking TRPs may mean that Japanese conversationalists can determine with greater certitude when a turn is possibly complete, in contrast to English, where subordinate phrases and clauses are regularly used to extend an initial TRP with little advance notice.

In sum, since the production of the verb component including the accompanying auxiliary verbs, verb-suffixes, final suffixes, copulas, and final particles converges towards the end of a TCU, crucial information concerning the shape of turn being produced tends to be concentrated towards the end of a turn. These features can make it difficult for participants in Japanese to project a possible completion point or the type of activity which will be performed by a turn until slightly before the end of a turn. By the same token, the temporal organisation of Japanese syntax may be employed to delay until the end of a turn, any display of a stance on the topic of talk (e.g. wish, negativity, uncertainty, willingness) or the action to be accomplished by the turn (e.g. request, question, quotation, order, assessment).

The reasons cited above contribute to limitations of the projectability of turns until the proximity of the terminal boundary of a turn in Japanese. Hence, the particular importance in Japanese of waiting for the production of the thrust of an utterance towards the end of a turn. Recipients parse the speaker's talk for the first sign that either a predicate-component is recognisably being produced or that a turn is coming to an "early" termination. The predication of the final component (via utterance-finals) or distinct prosodic markings (in truncated forms) in a sense represents the ultimate transformation, which in "one fell swoop" can assemble the pieces of the jig-saw puzzle of the turn-in-progress. Thus, the organisation of turns in Japanese may be described as enabling a phenomenon which might be coined *retrojectability*.

The importance of studying turns *in situ* and in *real time* for gaining insight into the interdependence of conversational grammar and social interaction cannot be over-emphasised. Until fairly recently, much of the work on Japanese grammar has been based on idealised and invented examples as data, which do not take account of the sequential and pragmatic implications of turns as social actions. No doubt, there is a great deal that can be learned about linguistic structure from this voluminous literature. However, by examining fragments of naturally occurring conversational data and focusing on the temporal unfolding of turns, headway can be made in shedding light on issues which have long puzzled students of grammar. Consideration of how grammar is implicated in turn-taking has illuminated aspects of the normativity of the verb (predicate) -final word order, the pivotal role of utterance-final elements in turn-taking, the significance of prosodic features of *iikiri* forms, the treatment of post-predicate additions as recompleters, the possible interactional consequences of a postpositional as opposed to a prepositional language, as well as the inter-locking structure of alternative turn-ending designs constituting an overarching grammatical organisation. Importantly, conversational grammar is seen to be inextricably interlinked with turn-taking. The turn-taking system thus exhibits a capacity to change its outward contours to allow for its integration and interpenetration with the linguistic and socio-cultural orientations of a language community. Whereas Chapter 2 addressed the context-free structure of the turn-taking mechanism on the level of the basic rules, this chapter reveals its remarkable context-sensitivity in relation to Japanese.

Furthermore, the findings of this chapter suggest another angle for considering popular images of Japanese styles of communication as being illogical, unclear, indirect, and rambling (propounded by many *Nihonjinron* theorists). It may be useful to re-examine such characterisations in connection with a syntax which favours a delayed—and therefore, sometimes abandoned—production of the thrust of an utterance as well as facilitating modifications of the trajectory of an ongoing turn. Whilst it is difficult to imagine syntax having a determinate relation to social action, it is quite conceivable that the availability of divergent grammatical resources may present somewhat different possibilities for the styles in which social actions are performed.

Just to give one example, speakers in Japanese can apply grammatical resources to introduce a topic, engage in some discussion, and send out "feelers" to monitor coparticipant reactions prior to taking a final stand on a matter. In other words, speakers have relative freedom to modify the syntactical structure or the interactive work to be accomplished in an utterance while it is being constructed. Consider the following example (see Chapter 3 for a fuller extract):

(79) [Tokyo 7, p. 4, mid] multi-party conversation; simplified

W: ((complains about H))=

1 H: =*Sore wa sō ne*
that TOP SO FP
'That's right, isn't it'

2 (1.2)

3 H: *tto iu kara ikenai no*
QUOT say because wrong FP
'that ((I)) say things like that is what's wrong with ((me))'

4 (1.4)

5 ( ): *'N*
'Yeah'

This fragment illustrates how participants may retroactively modify the grammatical construction of a turn as it progresses. W has just complained about an aspect of her husband H's behaviour. To this, H initially provides an agreement incorporating a final particle *ne* as a tag item 'isn't it?' (line 1). But the way that H continues in line 3 indicates that H has interpreted the absence of any uptake (line 2) possibly as coparticipant disapproval that H had gone along with his wife so readily (in line 1). Indeed, in line 3, the quotative particle *tto* which is designed as a postpositional attachment to his prior talk transforms line 1 *Sore wa sō ne* 'That's right, isn't it?' into a clause 'X', embedded in the ensuing sentence: *X tto iu kara ikenai no* 'what's wrong with me is that I say things like X'. Thus, the pragmatic implications of the addition of line 3 can be seen as a realignment from an agreement (line 1) to a self-deprecation (line 3). Stylistically, however, the deployment of the quotative particle *tto* has enabled H to convert the grammatical trajectory of the prior TCU (line 1) by incorporating it as a part of a larger TCU (spanning lines 1 and 3) without engaging in overt repair of prior talk. In a discussion of TCU-endings in English, Schegloff raises a theme for reflection:

> How are non-uptakes of projected -possible-completions/designed-endings dealt with? By an increment to the same TCU? By addition of a new TCU? . . . If by an increment to the same TCU, *how does the prior talk shape the new increment*? (Schegloff 1996a: 83; italics added)

Interestingly, for Japanese, the reverse question can also be asked: "How does the new increment shape the prior talk?"

More generally, if the syntax of a language provides for an early production of the thrust—and therefore an early commitment to the kind of action performed in a turn (as in English), it may at the same time delimit the ensuing degree of manoeuvrability. On the other hand, a syntax which allows for a deferred positioning of the main thrust as well as the capacity for a retroactive revision of that thrust may permit greater inherent flexibility for modifying, qualifying, pre-empting or abandoning an action before it has run its course or even after an action has been performed. A possible agenda for future research could include an examination of how these resources may be interactionally invoked to produce potentially different types of turn-designs in the respective language environments. In this sense, the analysis of the interpenetration of cultural-linguistic resources and social interaction promises to have much to contribute to studies of cross-cultural similarities and differences.

The contrast made here between Japanese and English needs to be tempered by the possibility that the trajectory of utterances in English can also undergo revision. For instance, Goodwin (1979b) has demonstrated how the interactive consequences of utterances in American conversation can also be incrementally and progressively transformed as a result of the verbal and non-verbal interaction between speakers and hearers. Although speculative on my part, a crucial difference between English and Japanese suggested by Goodwin's case-study is that in English, this is typically accomplished through further additions and qualifications of what has already been produced. On the other hand, in Japanese, there is an extra potential for retroactively transforming the grammatical construction of a turn-in-progress, which can have important consequences for the social action performed by the turn as well as for the localisation of a possible TRP, as discussed in this chapter. Such potential contrasts require further investigation.

It is hoped that the focus on cross-linguistic differences in turn-projection reported here may go some way towards redressing an imbalance in conversation analytic work, which is presently heavily centred on the study of Anglo-American interaction. Even core notions such as "projectability" may merit a reconsideration in the light of the existence of a vastly divergent turn-organisation to that which has been described in the literature. The findings of this research may also have wider applicability to languages such as Korean which are reported to have grammatical features somewhat convergent with Japanese.

We have discussed in detail some of the major features participants orient to in recognising TRPs, particularly by examining two types of turn-endings in Japanese conversation. What then are the aspects of Japanese syntax which permit participants to monitor or mark the "progress" of an ongoing turn? A key to this question can be expected to lie in the role of certain particles, interspersed throughout talk, which act as signposts indicating what part of a turn has already been produced, and which parts are yet to be produced. The investigation of the role of particles in the construction of turns merits an in-depth discussion in its own right, and will be addressed in the remainder of this book.

Notes

1. The terms "shape" and "type" are both employed here in a non-technical sense to refer generally to various features of a turn, such as its grammatical structure, the activities occupying a turn, or the localisation of possible transition-relevance places (TRPs).
2. Kuno (1973: 4) reports that "(A)ccording to a large-scale statistical study of sentence structures conducted by the National Language Research Institute, Tokyo, Japan, the ratio of frequencies of occurrences between the SOV word order and the OSV word order in Japanese is 17 to 1".
3. In a seminal work on Japanese grammar, Martin summarises Oide's (1965: 107–8) portrayal of Japanese sentences, appealing to the analogy of the *furoshiki*,

that marvelous carryall kerchief which will expand or contract to just the size needed for the traveler to carry his belongings—and which can be tucked neatly away when not in use. It is of little concern that the contents may get rumpled in transit (or that the parts of the sentence may lose their overt signals of reference), since they can always be pressed out at the end of the journey (as the listener can infer the missing marks of reference). The English sentence, on the other hand, is like the unwieldy suitcase of the West—too big and too small at the same time, cruelly heavy, and cluttered with verbal coat-hangers piously designed to keep the contents unwrinkled to the very end of the journey. (Martin 1975: 35)

This analogy (which has some *Nihonjinron* type overtones) stresses the flexibility with which Japanese sentences may be constructed. Thus,

(so) long as you put the predicate . . . at the end, where it belongs in a well-planned sentence, you are free to present each of the built-up phrases early or late as you see fit. (Martin 1975: 35)

At the same time, there is an emphasis on the orderliness of the end of the sentence, as the proper place to position the predicate, and as a locus of novel or critical information (Martin 1975: 37). This view is echoed in Kuno's characterisation of Japanese as having a relatively free word order "(e)xcept for the very rigid constraint that verbs must appear in the sentence-final position" (1973: 3).

4. Though no empirical work has been done to date, it appears that the employment of a subject may be a marked activity, linked to specific interactional contingencies, e.g. specification of the topic when a topic change is involved.
5. In T's utterance in line 3, the nominal *Watanabe san* 'Ms Watanabe' is specified as an indirect object through the postpositioning of *ni wa* 'to'; and *anata* 'you' is identifiable as a subject by virtue of the nominative case particle *ga*.
6. However, conversational objects such as tag questions (e.g. 'you know?') and the turn-final attachment of the name of an addressee in English may accomplish activities convergent with some uses of utterance-final elements in Japanese.
7. These elements are predominantly employed in the Tokyo dialect. Other dialects share some of the same elements but also have others not included in this list.
8. See for instance, Tanaka (to appear-c), for a discussion of how the utterance-final particle *ne* can be used to engage in other interactive tasks such as for eliciting acknowledgments, as a turn-entry device, or a turn-final particle depending on the position in the talk where it occurs.
9. These turn-endings without utterance-final elements can be contingently employed to formulate a setting or relationship as "informal" or "intimate", and may be used for the direct accomplishment of an action (Tanaka 1996, to appear-b).
10. It should not be assumed, however, that utterance-final elements and turn-final prosodic features are employed solely for the purpose of marking TRPs. Although it is not possible to elaborate here, these endings seem to be employed for the achievement of finely differentiated social actions.

Chapter 5

Incremental projection: Case and adverbial particles

5.1. Introduction

Chapters 3 and 4 began to explore ways in which various resources available in Japanese and Anglo/American English are respectively enlisted in constructing a turn and projecting the completion of the current turn. In addition to interactional features, it was argued that members exploit prosodic features and their tacit understanding of syntactical organisation in the performance of such tasks. Continuing in the same vein, the next two chapters focus on how certain grammatical particles may relate to turn-taking contingencies in Japanese.

Particles are defined as "non-conjugative words which attach to words, phrases, or clauses, and indicate the relationship of the preceding word(s) to the following word or to the rest of the sentence" (McClain 1981: 93). Although particles lend themselves to alternative descriptions depending on the classificatory system used, they can be divided into several basic categories in accordance with the type of syntactic relationship they indicate. Shibatani's (1990: 334) categories, which will be employed here, include case, adverbial, conjunctive, and final particles.[1] A general property of particles is that they are normally postpositioned following some unit—actual or implied—and can retroactively specify the grammatical type, the action, or the sense in which the preceding unit is to be understood. This characteristic invests particles with a multitude of usages (depending on the type of particle) which augment the flexibility of turn-construction, provide a means to project the unfolding of a current turn, enable the construction and projection of extended turns, serve as turn-management devices, etc., as will be discussed in the remainder of this book. In diverse ways, particles provide resources for participants to project the progress of turns in Japanese, and it may not be an exaggeration to suggest that no account of Japanese turn-taking can be complete without a discussion of the myriad ways in which particles are implicated—both syntactically and pragmatically—in turn-taking operations.

At the same time, it is important to note that particles—especially those that mark a subject or object—are frequently unexpressed in conversation (see Chapter 1). Moreover, participants do not typically treat particle-ellipsis as an "omission", and the non-use of a case particle does not necessarily reduce the projectability properties of an utterance-in-progress. Nonetheless, it will be argued that the absence of a particle to mark prior talk may, in some instances, render its "intended" grammatical type somewhat equivocal. As a consequence, the determination of an unexpressed particle can, on occasion, become the object of negotiation between interlocuters (Section 5.6).

The discussion of particles in this book draws heavily on previous studies of grammar and interaction, and especially on those which have focused on the collaborative construction of emergent turns (e.g. Lerner 1987, 1991, 1996; Hayashi 1997; Hayashi and Mori 1998; Hayashi, Mori, and Takagi, to appear; Lerner and Takagi, to appear; Mori 1994, 1996a, 1996b; Fox, Hayashi, and Jasperson 1996). In the remainder of this book, two specific aspects of the relation between conversational syntax and turn-taking in Japanese will be examined: (i) case and adverbial particles for the incremental projection of a TCU in the present chapter, and (ii) conjunctive particles for the delayed projection of compound TCUs in Chapter 6. The analysis will be skewed towards Japanese, and it is left for others to develop the tentative observations made regarding turn-projection in English. The comparative analysis indicates that the availability of particles may permit a degree of flexibility in the construction of TCUs in Japanese which is not as apparent in English.

More specifically, this chapter compares and contrasts the diversity of resources available in the respective languages to project the unfolding of a turn, with a special emphasis on the role of case and adverbial particles in Japanese. It begins with a review of some major findings on the projection of the development of turns in Japanese and English conversation. Secondly, it is suggested that the shape of the beginning of a turn combined with the word order appears to be of paramount importance in English for projecting the course of a TCU. On the other hand, as discussed in Chapter 4, the incremental transformability of turn designs together with the concentration of projectability features in the vicinity of turn-endings in Japanese can result in delayed projectability (in contrast to relatively early projectability in English). This does not mean, however, that nothing at all can be projected about the shape of a turn being produced prior to its terminal boundary in Japanese. In the rest of this chapter, it is shown that case and adverbial particles provide one method (out of many other ways) of projecting the real time progress of a turn in Japanese, and enable coparticipants to anticipate at least one further increment of talk.

5.2. Previous research on the projection of the development of TCUs in English and Japanese

The growing literature on grammar and interaction indicates that there is a wide range of grammatical constructions, sequential features, non-verbal conduct, and productional features which can contribute to the projection of an emergent turn-shape or provide opportunities for coparticipants to jointly construct a TCU (refer to citations above). Much of this literature is based on the analysis of instances of coparticipant completion of the current turn. When parties collaborate in the joint construction of an emergent TCU, they not only mutually display their understanding of the social actions accomplished through interaction, but also display their orientations to conversational syntax. Thus, an examination of this type of activity provides an optimal glimpse into the possible salience of grammar for projectability.

It has been shown that some interactional features which are directed towards projecting the unfolding of a turn are shared in both English and Japanese, though their specific realisations may vary depending on the language. A number of common features (which are by no means comprehensive) employed for projectability include:

(a) "compound TCU" formats such as *If X–then Y*, *When X–then Y*, *Because X–Y*, and *Although X–Y* (original study for English by Lerner 1987, 1991; analysis for Japanese by Lerner and Takagi, to appear; Hayashi 1997). Hayashi, however, notes that these "strongly syntactic two-part formats appear to play a less prominent role in coparticipant completion in Japanese" (1997: 222);
(b) a recognisable two-part format involving quotations in conversation (study for English by Lerner 1991; for Japanese by Lerner and Takagi, to appear);
(c) recognition of an emergent "list structure" which adumbrates further items on the list (proposed for English by Lerner 1996; investigated for Japanese by Hayashi 1997);
(d) "parenthetical inserts" (Lerner and Takagi, to appear);
(e) "productional features" of the turn-in-progress such as "intra-turn silence", "sound stretches", "word searches", and "laugh tokens" which provide "unprojected opportunities" for coparticipant completion (originally proposed for English in Lerner 1996; Japanese study by Hayashi 1997).

Furthermore, analysis of Japanese conversation has revealed that the following syntactic features of Japanese can also strongly project further component(s) of talk:

(i) adverbials which typically precede a verb while intimating what kind of verb will be produced (Hayashi 1997; Hayashi, Mori, and Takagi, to appear; Hayashi and Mori 1998; Tanaka 1996);

(ii) grammatical construction of phrases which have already been produced by the current speaker, e.g. locative, accusative, or subject phrases (Hayashi and Mori 1998; Hayashi 1997; Chapter 4 in this volume);
(iii) the production of the first part of a recognisable compound verb format (Hayashi and Mori 1998);
(iv) the use of causal markers such as *datte*, *-kara*, and *dakara*, or "contrastive" markers such as *demo* and *-kedo* to construct and premonitor certain types of "opinion-negotiation sequences" (Mori 1996b; Hayashi and Mori 1998);
(v) contrast structures through the employment of the "contrastive *wa*" (Hayashi 1997);
(vi) recognition of incipient formulaic phrases or expressions which allow a recipient to produce the ending of the phrase (Hayashi 1997).

In his insightful discussion of coparticipant completion in Japanese, Hayashi (1997) remarks that it is not just the grammatical structure of an utterance-in progress which serves as a resource for coparticipant completion in Japanese, but that such opportunities are provided through a combination of grammatical construction, "locally emergent structures", as well as other interactional features of talk. The present exposition is also informed by this understanding.

This chapter attempts to add to the list above by specifically examining the role played by case and adverbial particles in the construction and recognition of the internal development of a TCU. But first, for purposes of comparison, I start out by making coarse conjectures about some possible ways participants monitor and project the development of a TCU in English.

5.3. The development of a turn in English

One of the first illuminating analyses of the connections between syntax and projectability in English and Japanese is found in a study by Fox, Hayashi, and Jasperson (1996). This section considers some implications of observations made in this work and Chapter 4 regarding the projectability of TCUs in English. While recognising that grammar is just one of the many features (including pragmatics and prosody) which contribute in complex ways to turn-taking operations, attention will be focused primarily on syntactical features which may be relevant for parsing the progress of a turn in English conversation. Though not all-inclusive, some significant aspects of conversational syntax in English are highlighted to provide potential contrasts with Japanese, through an inspection of the following fragment:

(80) [Rahman: C: 1: JS(15)]

1. Jenny: Hello: is that Sus'n,
2. Susan: Mm: ?
3. Jenny: ·h Oh is yih mum thea:h, (0.2)
4. Susan: Yes ah think soh (   )
                                        [
5. Jenny: Oh: .
6. Jenny: Well ahsk'err if she'd like tih come round f'r a coffee
7.   tell'er Ahntie Vera's coming up, h
8. Susan: A:lri :ght,
               [   ]
9. Jenny: So: w hen she's ready if she'd like t'come ferr a
10.   coff ee,
          [
11. Susan: Mm:?
12. Jenny: Okay?
13. Susan: Well ah'll find'er fuhr:st, ↑uhh!
                                          [
14. Jenny: Whadiyih doing eating yer
15.   breakfast ohr someth ing,
                               [
16.   Yes, . . .

As already noted in Chapter 4, the probable shape and type of a TCU is regularly revealed towards the beginning of a turn in English (Schegloff 1987b). In particular, whether a unit is projected as a lexical item, phrase, clause, sentence, or some multiple thereof is massively (though not always) exhibited early in the trajectory of a turn. In addition to pragmatic and intonational factors, the relatively rigid ordering of the main components of an utterance (e.g. SVO or Subject-Verb-Object for declarative sentences) is a resource that may be used to anticipate a possible form of an emergent TCU (see Fox, Hayashi, and Jasperson 1996):

1. A form of the verb *be* appearing before a subject can contribute to the projectability of an utterance as a question, e.g. *is* in lines 1 and 3.
2. Utterances beginning with a *wh*-word as in line 14 may also project a question.
3. The placement of a subject as the first main component of an utterance may project that a declarative form is being produced, e.g. lines 4 and 13.

4. An imperative form can be projected by the placement of a verb towards the beginning of a TCU, e.g. lines 6 and 7.
5. Beginnings such as *when* or *if* may announce a "compound TCU" (Lerner 1987, 1991), e.g. line 9.

The fact that the projection of the unfolding of an utterance depends to a great extent on word order is perhaps consonant with the absence of case markings for either the subject or object in English. Possible word ordering corresponding to the above types might include:

1. '*be*-verb'–Subject–X? (where X can be a nominal, adverb, verb, etc.)
2. wh-word–'*be*-verb'–Subject–Verb?
3. Subject–Verb–Object
4. Verb–Object
5. *when* + Subject–Verb–Object

The recognition of initial components (which can have a major bearing on what form of a TCU might be projected) together with a knowledge of normative orientations to word order may be cumulatively exploited by participants for projecting the ordering of the components for the ensuing part of the TCU. Thus, in 1. above, the production of a *be*-verb might indicate its possible shape as a question, and hence the syntactical components required for its completion. In the case of 3., since subject and verb ellipsis is relatively rare in English (in comparison to Japanese), the production of a subject such as 'I' may project a verb, which can then project a possible production of an object.[2] Likewise, a transitive verb at the beginning of an utterance as in 4. would make sequentially relevant the production of an object, after which the turn may be possibly complete. Moreover, since English is a prepositional language, there is little risk that an item initially produced as a subject would retroactively be converted into an object through the attachment of some particle following it, as is frequently the case in Japanese. Similarly, it is unlikely that a unit produced as a sentence may be converted into a clause through a further attachment. On the whole, the syntactical characteristics of a component seem to be exhibited either before or *as* it is being produced.

In sum, since turn-initial elements massively project the form of the utterance to be produced, once a turn has begun, those syntactical elements which would constitute the projected shape would become due, after which a possible transition-relevance place could occur. This would mean that the monitoring of the development of a turn massively involves confirming the production of the elements already projected. Nevertheless, these descriptions represent just general tendencies, and it can well happen that a turn may sometimes not have a beginning at all, as in collaborative completions (Schegloff 1996a), or that a turn may be extended beyond an initial TRP. As mentioned above, the observations made here concerning the role of turn-initial elements and word order in English are conjectural, and require further investigation in the future.

5.4. Projectability properties of case and adverbial particles in Japanese

Building on the previous literature on the collaborative construction of talk, the present chapter will be focused primarily on the use of case and adverbial particles to locally project the incremental unfolding of a turn in Japanese. While the works referred to in Section 5.2 touch upon issues of concern here (especially points (ii) and (v)), the systematic properties of these particles as tools for projecting upcoming units has not been fully explored. Combined with the sequential context of talk and other types of projectability features, it will be shown that these particles are treated as strong indicators that specific grammatical unit(s) *may* yet be produced. It is concluded that case and adverbial particles can serve as robust guides for participants in projecting a further increment of an emergent utterance.

The remainder of this chapter will be organised as follows. In Section 5.5, it will be proposed that the grammatical property of these particles to link a preceding element with some subsequent component can be enlisted by participants to project a further increment of talk. To substantiate this claim, it will first be shown that a degree of equivocality can emerge as to what action is being projected when a nominal phrase is not marked by a case or adverbial particle (Section 5.6). However, when these particles are physically present (i.e. expressed) in the stream of talk, they can serve as important resources for the projection of a further component. This point is demonstrated through their utility for forming questions (Section 5.7) and for coparticipant completion (Section 5.8). Further evidence of the projectability properties of case and adverbial particles is presented in Section 5.9, where it will be shown that participants may engage in a negotiation of the appropriate particle to employ for establishing a desired trajectory of talk. Further, Section 5.10 deals with instances of post-predicate additions, in which participants utilise the strong binomial linking made relevant by these particles to construct additions to a prior TCU. In spite of the utility of case and adverbial particles for local projection, however, it is also pointed out that the delayed projectability and incremental transformability of turn-shapes in Japanese (e.g. as a result of the variability of word order) set limitations on the accuracy with which coparticipants can judge the precise moment when a projected increment might actually be produced (Section 5.11). Finally, the cumulative effect of the use of these particles on possible interactional styles is investigated through an examination of a single case in Section 5.12.

5.5. Description of case and adverbial particles

Case particles (e.g. *ga*, *o*, *ni*, *de*, *no*, *to*, *e*, *yori*, *kara*) mark the "case" (e.g. as a subject, object, indirect object, etc.) of a noun phrase (NP) immediately preceding it, and are used to show a semantic or logical relationship between the NP and another nominal component, or between a NP and a predicate component (e.g. Shibatani 1990: 334). Adverbial particles (e.g. *wa*, *mo*, *koso*) are normally attached postpositionally to elements such as indeclinable parts of speech (that can serve as the subject) or adverbs, vesting them with an adverbial character and function, and modify ensuing predicates (*Kōjien* 1976: 1928). The literature refers to several varieties of adverbial particles with different properties, too complex to discuss within the scope of this chapter.

Through an examination of the sequential organisation of turns, it will be demonstrated that conversationalists do orient to the normativity of the descriptions noted above, and furthermore their knowledge of the syntactic relations created by these particles are mobilised for the purpose of projecting the progressivity of talk. In particular, case and adverbial particles have the general property of retroactively specifying the grammatical nature of the component immediately preceding the particle and simultaneously projecting some ensuing component (e.g. a predicate or nominal component depending on the particle), though not necessarily following on immediately after the particle.[3,4] It should be underscored that the postpositional properties of these particles implies that until (or unless) a case or adverbial particle is produced, the grammatical type (as a subject, object, indirect object, etc.) of a nominal can remain potentially indeterminate and therefore negotiable (although participants can and often do implicitly supply an "appropriate" unexpressed particle). Recipients seem to orient to this feature of particles by regularly waiting until a particle can be heard before co-constructing a projected component. By the same token, participants can display their understanding of the action as well as the emergent syntactic structure of a current speaker's utterance by furnishing a possibly projected item immediately or shortly after a particle is produced.

Put another way, these particles create a potential *binomial relationship*, as shown in the diagram below, where the arrow indicates how a nominal element marked by a case particle (the base of arrow) can project a further component (tip of arrow):

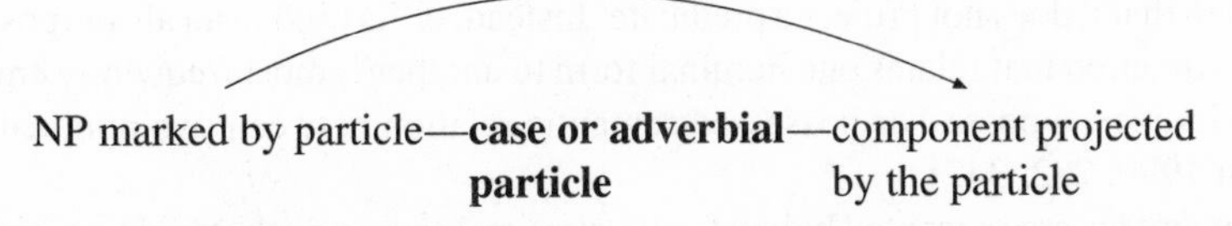

The following are some proposed projectability properties of the case particles *ga*, *ni*, *de*, *o*, and *no* and adverbial particle *wa* which are just several of the perhaps most abundantly observed particles in conversation.[5] (In the list below, "*ga*-marked NP" stands for "the noun phrase which immediately precedes *ga*".)

ga (nominative particle NOM):
- a *ga*-marked NP can be a subject;[6]
- can project a predicate component

ni (dative particle DAT; locative particle LOC; temporal particle)
- a *ni*-marked NP can be an indirect object or an oblique;
- can project a predicate component

de (locative particle LOC; instrumental particle INS)
- a *de*-marked NP can be an oblique;
- can project a predicate component

o (accusative particle ACC)
- an *o*-marked NP is a direct object;
- can project a predicate component

no (genitive particle GEN)
- equivalent to 'apostrophe-s' or 'of';
- can project a nominal component

wa (adverbial particle ADVP)
- a *wa*-marked NP is a topic;
- can typically but not always project a predicate component

All except the particle *no* listed above are generally used to link a nominal element with a predicate element: e.g. *ga* to mark the NP which directly precedes it as a subject and to connect it with an ensuing predicate; *ni* to mark the prior as an indirect object or an oblique, and to project a predicate; *de*, which can sometimes be glossed as 'by means of', 'at' or 'on', may mark the preceding expression as an oblique and projects a predicate; *o* to connect the prior direct object to the predicate which should follow. The adverbial particles *wa* and *mo* can have some projectability properties similar to case particles: by virtue of their use in connecting one nominal element or adverb with a predicate element, they also typically project a predicate element. Indeed, according to Shibatani, "the *wa*-marked topic nominal typically corresponds to the *ga*-marked nominative in grammatical function" (1990: 264). The genitive particle *no*, roughly equivalent to 'of' or 'apostrophe-s' is an exception in that it does not project a predicate. Instead, it "is used in an all-purpose attributive function that relates one nominal form to another", most frequently employed to indicate a possessor-possessed semantic relation between two nominals (Shibatani 1990: 282, 347).

Some examples are presented below for illustration (case and adverbial particles in boldface). Recall that the double parentheses indicate unexpressed elements.

For brevity, overlapped speech has been omitted from the examples.

(81) [Shakujii 1A #4: 22] nominative (case) particle *ga* marking subject

K: . . . *tomodachi* ***ga***: *ashita kekkonshiki na no ne=*
friend **NOM** tomorrow wedding COP FP FP
'. . . ((my)) friend is having ((her)) wedding tomorrow, you know'

(82) [Shakujii 1A #2: 1] topic (adverbial) particle *wa*

Y: *Sorede watashi* ***wa*** *niji chotto sugi ni koko dechau kara*
and I **TOP** 2pm a little past at here leave since-so
'And since I will be leaving here shortly after 2pm'

(83) [Shakujii 1A #9: 4] accusative (case) particle *o* marking an object

H: . . . *taikin* ***o*** *katte kureta kara sa=*
large amount of money **ACC** bought since-so FP
'. . . since ((she)) spent a large amount of money'

(84) [Shakujii 1A #3: 1] genitive (case) particle *no*, linking two nominals (self-identification in a telephone conversation)

K: *(Ah) Kawaguchi* ***no*** *Ōtsuka desu*
oh ((place name)) **GEN** ((name of person)) COP
'Oh, this is Ōtsuka of Kawaguchi'

The remainder of this chapter will be devoted to showing that the binomial relationships forged by these particles can serve as powerful resources for Japanese participants to project the incremental development of a TCU.

5.6. Equivocality of the turn-trajectory when particles are unexpressed

First, it is important to recognise that case and adverbial particles—like many other parts of speech in Japanese—are frequently unexpressed, especially in conversation. As mentioned previously, the situated non-use of particles does not normally appear to be an impediment to participants' understanding of syntax and the activities occupying a turn, since the elided elements are often recoverable from the context, or perhaps may even be treated as marginal for the participants' production and parsing of an utterance. An examination of the available data suggests that participants are often able to agree on roughly what is being projected without the benefit of particles. On the other hand, the non-deployment of particles can sometimes introduce a degree of equivocality about what type of nominal phrase has just been produced by the current speaker (Fox, Hayashi, and Jasperson 1996: 210), and consequently the type of action locally projected by a nominal phrase. Such instances can furthermore lead to some negotiation between participants as to what is being projected. What follows is a preliminary investigation into the possible ways in which projectability of the turn-shape might be affected when particles are unexpressed.

The two examples below initially exemplify how participants can sometimes implicitly furnish an unexpressed particle and display that understanding through a collaborative construction of an utterance. The fragment below follows immediately after fragment (102) (see p. 178) which will be dealt with later (to which the reader is asked to consult for a fuller background of this fragment). The excerpt is from an informal meeting, where the participants have been debating on the best person to ask to write an article based on a questionnaire survey. One of the participants G has mentioned that she is in favour of asking Professor Tamura to write an article. But H has shown some reservation about the latter, claiming that Professor Tamura is somewhat too serious, so could not be counted on to write an engaging article. Immediately prior to this fragment, however, H has just conceded that it would nevertheless be acceptable if Professor Tamura were asked to write an orthodox article. But H continues below to qualify this statement, beginning with *dakedo* 'but' which projects a contrastive statement to his prior stand (see point (iv) in Section 5.2).

(85) [Tokyo 10A: 15] informal meeting
The demonstrative *sore* 'that' in line 1 is referring to 'asking Professor Tamura to write an article'; the demonstrative *kono* 'this' in line 1 refers to the questionnaire survey:

1 H: =*Dakedo sore dake da to kono omoshiromi* Ø
but that only COP if this interesting aspect
'But if it's just that, then the interesting aspect of this'

2 H: [*detekonai su yo*
[wouldn't come out COP FP
['wouldn't come out'
[
3 G: [*gggDete(konai)*
[wouldn't come out
['Wouldn't come out'

In lines 1 and 2, H continues with the qualification that the points of interest in the questionnaire survey would be lost if Professor Tamura were to write the article. Through the overlapped production of *detekonai* 'wouldn't come out' in line 3, G displays a shared understanding of the trajectory of H's utterance (see Hayashi and Mori 1998). Moreover, the participants H and G display retroactive agreement that the nominal *kono omoshiromi* 'the interesting aspect of this' was a topic or subject phrase. In other words, their jointly produced utterance within its immediate context performs roughly the same action (i.e. pointing out a drawback of asking Professor Tamura to write an article) that would have been accomplished if the contrastive *wa* or the nominative *ga* had appeared in the position marked by Ø at the end of line 1: i.e. the negative assessment in lines 2 and 3 ratify that what they are doing is presenting a drawback *in contrast to* an advantage that H had just pointed out prior to the portion shown.

The following is another example illustrating that particles are not always necessary to project the progress of an utterance. The participants here have been discussing suitable people to ask to contribute an article, including Mr Katō. S begins to voice her uneasiness about Mr Katō below. The particle in question is the quotative (case) particle *tte* in line 2.

(86) [Tokyo 10A: 3] informal meeting

1 S: *Nanka Katō san intabyūā to shite wa dōka na*
somehow ((name)) interviewer as TOP whether FP
'Somehow, ((I)) wonder about Mr Katō as an interviewer'

2 → [***tte*** *iu kanji*
[QUOT say feeling
['that's the kind of feeling ((I have))'
[
3 G: [*iu kanji*
[say feeling
['((that's)) the kind of feeling ((you have))'

In line 2, S produces the quotative particle *tte*, which characterises line 1 as an expression to be commented on. However, G's completion of S's utterance *iu kanji* in line 3, which begins before S finishes uttering *tte* demonstrates that G was able to project the emerging shape of S's turn as a quotation format even before the quotative particle could be heard. Indeed, a quotation format is realisable either with a particle *tte* or *to* expressed (as in line 2) or unexpressed (as exemplified by line 3). Fragments (85) and (86) demonstrate that recipients are often able not only to project the course of an utterance without necessarily hearing an explicit case or adverbial particle, but can also implicitly furnish an unexpressed particle for all intents and purposes. The context and other grammatical features in such instances may provide enough information for a coparticipant to predict the emerging shape of an utterance.

However, as hinted above, a disagreement may emerge when coparticipants attempt to project the course of a current speaker's turn without waiting for the production of a case or adverbial particle. Not surprisingly, the nature of the disagreement relates to the possible grammatical sense of an unmarked nominal.

In the following conversation, four women are tasting a new dessert (which appears to be some form of crème brulée) and are attempting to guess what it is made of.

(87) [OBS: 1] multi-party conversation

1 B: *Chotto[mō chotto tabenai to ne:,]=*
bit [more bit not eat unless FP]
'Unless ((one)) eats a bit a bit more ((you)) know'

[ ]
2 D: [( ) shō.]=

3 C: → =*KASUTĀDO KURĪM [U **DE**] [(.)] [nanka] shite=*
custard cream INS(*with*) [something] do and
'Something done with custard cream and'

[ ] [ ]
4 B: → *[MU **NO**] [u::n]*
[GEN(of) ['yeah']

5 C: =*yaite[aru no yo*
bake[d FP FP
'baked, ((it)) is'

In the course of this tasting session, C suddenly exclaims that the dessert is something made with custard cream (line 3), beginning with the noun phrase *KASUTĀDO KURĪMU DE*, with the postpositional attachment of the instrumental (case) particle *DE* 'with' which projects a predicate. Before C finishes producing *KURĪMU DE*, however, B enters (line 4) in overlap by almost simultaneously producing the final syllable of the word *KURĪMU*, but with a different case particle *NO*, a possible occurrence of a genitive (case) particle meaning 'of', which at any event projects a nominal component rather than a predicate. At this point, it is possible that both C and B realise that there has been a different trajectory of talk respectively projected. C appears to display this through the microsecond hesitation (line 3) before continuing to characterise the dessert. On the other hand, B abandons the incipient collaborative construction of the utterance by dropping out and taking on a recipient role, as indicated by the acknowledgement which she proffers in response to C's turn-in progress (line 4). Interestingly, a disagreement on the case of the nominal 'custard cream' may have led to the termination of the incipient "collaborative" talk. This is not surprising, since the selection of *de* or *no* can respectively have quite divergent consequences for turn-projection: the former projects a predicate whether the latter projects a nominal.

Consider another example in which a coparticipant attempts to co-construct an emerging utterance without waiting for the production of a particle by the current speaker. In the following multi-party conversation, H is saying that his wife W frequently insinuates that he H must prefer a *sewanyōbō* 'a traditional motherly wife' over someone like herself (lines 1–3).

(88) [Tokyo 7: 4] multi-party conversation

1 H: *Kanojo wa boku ni ne mō*
she TOP me DAT FP INT

2 *sewanyōbō ga ii darō ii darō*
traditional motherly wife NOM good COP good COP

3 *tte iu n desu yo [ne.*
QUOT say VN COP FP [FP
[
4 (K:) ['*N*:::
['Mmm'

Gloss of lines 1–3: 'She keeps on saying to me, "Wouldn't a traditional motherly wife be good, wouldn't a traditional motherly wife be good", ((you)) know'

5→ H: *Dakedo boku* ***zenzen*** *sewa (heh) nyōbō-*(.) Ø
but I not at all traditional motherly wife

6→ T ***Iya***.=
don't like
'((Is something that you)) don't like'

7→ H: ***=o*** *hoshiku nai no yo.*
ACC don't want FP FP

Gloss of lines 5 and 7: 'But I don't want a traditional motherly wife at all'. (As mentioned before, it is not easy to provide a gloss of line 5 independently of line 7, since English does not normally permit for the possibility of an object coming before a verb.)

H continues in line 5, beginning with the connective *dakedo* 'but' and an adverb *zenzen* 'not at all' which indicate that H is about to disavow his wife's prior suggestion. What is of interest here is that after the nominal *sewanyōbō*, H does not immediately produce some particle which defines the case of *sewanyōbō* (in the position indicated by Ø). In other words, the syntactic role of *sewanyōbō* at this point has not been made explicit. A microsecond pause follows the nominal (end of line 5), providing an opportunity for another participant T to come in (line 6) with an "anticipatory completion" (Lerner 1996, point (e) in Section 5.2). Notice that T uses the adjective *iya* 'don't like', which ties into H's incomplete turn in line 5, and terminates it with the turn-ending: *sewanyōbō* ***iya*** (glossed roughly as 'a traditional motherly wife is something that ((you)) don't like'). The selection of this adjective *iya* 'don't like' shows that T has analysed *sewanyōbō* as either a 'topic' or subject of the completed utterance, thereby implicitly furnishing the contrastive particle *wa* or possibly the nominative particle *ga* to follow *sewanyōbō*. It happens, however, that H continues in line 7 where he left off in line 5, by starting out with the accusative particle *o* which retroactively revises T's characterisation of the nominal *sewanyōbō* (last item in line 5) into an object of the sentence being constructed. H's combined turn (lines 5 and 7) now becomes *sewanyōbō o hoshiku nai* '((I)) don't want a traditional motherly wife'. Thus, whereas T topicalises *sewanyōbō*, H subsequently renegotiates the case of the same word as an object.[7] Moreover, while T's formulation can be taken as a negative assessment of *sewanyōbō*, H has been able to refute his wife's assertion without directly criticising traditional motherly wives, by specifying *sewanyōbō* as an object.

The two examples above suggest that unexpressed (case or adverbial) particles can render the trajectory of talk negotiable, since a particle which may be implicitly supplied by a speaker or recipient—even if unarticulated—can be critical not only for what grammatical component is further projected, but also for the interactional consequences of an emergent turn.

5.7. Case and adverbial particles for formulating questions

In contrast to instances where case and adverbial particles are unexpressed, Sections 5.7–5.10 will attempt to show how the explicit use of these particles can be mobilised to project at least one further component of talk within its specific context. I begin by examining the employment of these particles for formulating questions, and continue in the next section to demonstrate their utility for the collaborative construction of a turn-in-progress.

An initial evidence of the projectability properties of these particles is their use in framing questions. In the fragments to be presented below, the current speaker designs a question employing the format:

Speaker: noun phrase + case or adverbial particle?

where a case or adverbial particle marking a noun phrase occurs turn-finally, delivered with a rising intonational contour. In each instance, the recipient provides a reply which attends to the properties of the case particle to project a predicate by either producing a predicate which can be binomially linked to the noun phrase via the particle or implying such a predicate.

The following fragment is from a telephone conversation between a husband H and his wife W. H has called home to say he will be coming home shortly, at about

2:30pm. In the part shown below, W asks *de- shokuji wa*? 'And how about lunch?', to which H replies not to bother.

(89) [Shakujii1A(#2): 1]

W: =*De- shokuji* ***wa***?
and meal TOP
'And how about lunch?'

H: >*Shokuji iranai*<
meal don't need
'((I)) don't need lunch'

W's turn is a question designed as a declarative form, but apparently utilises the feature of *wa* which projects a predicate. Indeed, H's reply, *Shokuji iranai* '((I)) don't need lunch' which is an elliptical version of *Shokuji* ***wa*** *iranai*, first repeats the topic *shokuji* 'meal' in W's turn, and then goes on to supply a candidate predicate *iranai* 'don't need', possibly projected by W's use of *wa*. H thus displays an understanding that a predicate was projected by supplying it in the "slot" made relevant through the use of *wa*. Notice, however that the unexpressed predicate in W's question opens up some room for interpretation as to *exactly* what predicate W may be projecting, as it is hearable as any of the following invented examples: *De- shokuji wa iru*? 'And do you need lunch?', or *De- shokuji wa iranai no*? 'And you don't need lunch?', or for that matter a combination of the two: *De- shokuji wa* iru *no iranai no*? 'And do you or don't you need lunch?'. H's answer, however, skilfully resolves any possible ambiguity by not leaving unexpressed the predicate *iranai* 'don't need'.

Let us look at another example in which a case particle—in this instance a locative particle *de* meaning 'at'—delivered with a rising intonation at the end of a turn is employed to ask a question. This fragment is from a telephone conversation between H and I, who have been talking about a grand wedding reception (of their mutual acquaintance) which was held at a magnificent banquet hall in an upmarket hotel. In the portion shown below, H goes on to ask if I (Imaoka-san) also intends to have her wedding there.

(90) [IMD: 12] slightly simplified

1 H: *Imaoka san mo izure shochira* ***de***?
((name)) ADVP in due course there LOC:at
'Are you also ((going to have your wedding)) there in due course?'

2 I: *.hhh IYA IYA*
NO NO
'.hhh NO WAY!'

3 H: HH HH [hehh!
[
4 I:→ [*zenze:::n sōyū: yotei wa nai n de:=*
[not at all such plan TOP not exist VN CONJ
['not at all, (I've got) no such plan'

H's question in line 1 leaves implicit the predicate of his utterance 'going to have your wedding'. However, in the context of a discussion about a friend's wedding at the banquet hall, the specification of Imaoka-san as the topic of the talk through the adverbial particle *mo* 'also', the use of the adverb *izure* 'in due course', as well as the phrase *sochira de* 'at there' (or more naturally 'over there') with the case marking *de* provide enough material for the recipient I to infer the unexpressed predicate, as indicated by her next turn in line 2 *.hhh IYA IYA* '.hhh NO WAY!'. This instance also demonstrates how I treats this case particle as directed towards formulating a question projecting an implicit predicate. As an incidental observation, this fragment contrasts with (89) above in that the unexpressed predicate is never made explicit: either in the question (line 1) or subsequently in the answer (line 4). I refers to the assumed predicate in line 4 by means of the deictic expression *sōyū: yotei* 'such plan', thereby rendering somewhat ambiguous whether she means that she has no plans of holding her wedding at the hotel *or* for that matter, whether she has any plans of getting married in the first place.

The two fragments presented here demonstrate how participants may utilise the projectability features of particles for formulating questions even without articulating the projected component.

5.8. Case and adverbial particles as resources for co-constructing a TCU

I next examine cases of collaborative talk which further demonstrate how case and adverbial particles can be employed as grammatical resources for projecting and co-constructing an emergent TCU in Japanese. As discussed in Chapter 4, speakers can construct their utterances incrementally by retroactively specifying the grammatical sense in which an immediately prior increment is to be understood. Needless to say, particles are not always used for this purpose, and there are various other features (including the sequential context, prosody, and other grammatical devices) which can also be mobilised for this end. Nevertheless, the examples below show that when a case or adverbial particle *is* occasioned, it can serve as a guide as to how an utterance is being constructed, and at least project one increment beyond it. Moreover, the type of increment projected depends to some extent on the type of particle produced (e.g. *wa*, *ga*, *ni*, *o*, *to*, etc. can project a predicate; the genitive particle *no* projects another nominal element), allowing participants to exclude those which cannot be grammatically linked with a given particle. The enlisting of a case or adverbial particle permits coparticipants to avoid projecting mutually divergent trajectories of talk, as in fragment (88) above where a particle was unexpressed. In the examples presented below, a second speaker joins in the co-construction of the TCU-in-progress of the current speaker either *immediately* or *shortly after* a case or adverbial particle can be heard.

The following case of anticipatory completion illustrates participants' orientation that a predicate should follow the production of *ga*. The sequential context is also consequential for the recipient H to project the specific predicate which would be appropriate in a particular situation:

(91) [Shakujii 1B(#3): 1] telephone conversation; slightly simplified

The two women in this extract are talking about some tickets that H received which are to be distributed to other members of their group.

1→ T: *Ano*: *·hh Watanabe san ni wa anata* ***ga***
uhm Ms Watanabe DAT TOP you NOM
'Uhm, ·hh to Ms Watanabe, ((it))'s you ((who))'

2 ((baby's voice in the background))

3→ H: *Uun atashi watashiteru*:
yeah I have handed over
'Yeah, I've handed ((them)) over ((to her))'

4 T: *Sō yo ne*
right FP FP
'((You)) have, haven't ((you))'

In line 1, T's utterance stops at *ga*, which marks *anata* 'you' as a subject. After a brief "filled pause" (a baby's voice), H responds with a sentence *Unn atashi watashiteru*: 'Yeah, I've handed ((them)) over ((to her))', in which H replaces the subject *anata* 'you' with *atashi* 'I', and supplies the projected predicate *watashiteru* 'have handed over'. H thereby displays the understanding that T might be inquiring whether H had already handed over the tickets to Ms Watanabe, an understanding which is subsequently ratified by T (line 4). At the same time, both participants exhibit an orientation that a predicate was projected or implied by T's syntactically incomplete utterance in line 1. Hayashi (1997) notes that certain productional features such as a pause, a hitch, or in this case a filled pause frequently provide an opportunity for a coparticipant to finish another's utterance, as observed for English by Lerner (1996) (point (e) in Section 5.2).

We next show below how the production of an accusative particle (which marks the preceding item as a direct object) can also provide a resource for a coparticipant to project a predicate component. The participants have been discussing how to organise a group event at their organisation. One of the events involves an informal forum to which anyone can attend to talk about whatever they are interested in.

(92) [Tokyo 10#2, p. 12] informal meeting, slightly simplified

1 H: *Nanka: are desho*? . . .
something that COP
'((You)) know what it is? ((It))'s something like this . . .'

2 → *chūkaku ni natte kudasaru kata* ***o***
nucleus P become person ACC
'the person who would be willing to act as the nucleus'

3 G: →***o*** *dare ni* ***suruka*** *tte iu koto*
ACC whom DAT **select** QUOT say VN
'to select whom for ((the person who would be willing to act as the nucleus))'

H first indicates he is going to make a suggestion (line 1), and then continues in line 2 by specifying an object phrase *chūkaku ni natte kudasaru kata o* 'the person who would be willing to act as the nucleus'. In the context of talk about how to set up a group event, the articulation of the phrase in line 2, which is recognisable as an object phrase through the terminal attachment of the accusative particle *o*, enables G to come in (line 3) with a verb and indirect object which might complete H's prior incomplete turn: 'to select whom for ((the person who would be willing to act as the nucleus))'. Furthermore, by repeating the particle *o* at the beginning of her contribution, G strongly displays that her talk is a continuation of H's turn (Makoto Hayashi, personal communication).

Similarly, the particle *ni* in line 3 in the fragment below marks the preceding phrase as an adverbial phrase, and is treated as projecting a predicate. Prior to this fragment, M has been explaining that experts would be able to tell just by looking at the price of a gold jewellery whether it is 'value for money' since they would know the current market price of gold. In the portion transcribed below, M is referring to some gold jewellery which is sold by his company, saying that the price tag already reflects a discount, so that a knowledgeable person (X) would simply have to look at the price tag to see that it is good value.

(93) [Shakujii 1A (#9): 11] telephone conversation, slightly simplified

1 M: . . . *mitara* (.) *Ah*: >*kore dattara*:< *yasui to*:=
see-if Ah: this if-then cheap QUOT
'. . . if ((X)) sees ((this)), "Oh if it's this, then it's value for money"'

2 H: ='*N*=
'Yeah'

3 M: =*iu fū* ***ni*** [( ) *hito wa* ***wakaru*** *yōna mono o ne*=
in this way [person TOP can see kind of thing ACC FP
'in this way [a ( ) person would see this kind of thing'
[
4 H: → [( ) ***wakaru*** *wake* ↑*ne*
[can see reason FP
[( ) ((X)) can see, right?

Shortly after the particle *ni* 'in' is produced in line 3, H supplies the projected predicate *wakaru* 'can see'. In contrast to the two cases examined previously (91) and (92), the original speaker continues with his utterance (in line 3), ratifying the predicate anticipated by H by repeating the same predicate *wakaru* 'can see' with a slight time gap.

The next instance involves a coparticipant supplying a predicate after the production of the topic (adverbial) particle *wa* by the first speaker K. In this multi-party conversation, K and S have been talking about men (their husbands in particular) who come home after work to enjoy a few hours of concentrated "quality time" with their children and claim that they are contributing to childcare, whereas the wives (K and S) must deal with the day-to-day routine of taking care of the children. After claiming that these different ways of relating to children are not equivalent, K continues below, beginning to say that according to the logic that men use, they would not be able to appreciate the tediousness of the daily care that is required to bring up children.

(94) [Tokyo 6: 2–3] multi-party conversation

1 K: *Otoko no sōiu ronri tte no wa* (.9)
men GEN that kind of logic QUOT N TOP
'As for that kind of logic that men use'

2 *mainichi zu:tto sono kakawatteru sono*: (.)
everyday continuously AP relating AP

3 → *wazurawashisa toka iyarashisa tte no* ***wa*** (.) *.hhh*
tediousness for instance onerousness QUOT N TOP

Gloss of lines 2–3: 'concerning for instance the tediousness or onerousness of relating ((to the children)) continuously, everyday'

4 S: →*Wakara* [*nai.*
cannot appreciate
'((They)) cannot appreciate'

[
5 K: [wakaranai to ne?
[cannot appreciate QUOT FP
['that ((they)) cannot appreciate, ((you)) know?'

The context of the prior talk and the use of the contrastive *wa* (in line 3) to project a contrasting predicate to follow, combined with productional features (a microsecond gap and in-breath following the particle) set the scene for S to anticipate how K is developing her utterance (see Hayashi 1997; point (v) and (e) in Section (5.2). And in line 5, K continues with an endorsement of S's choice of the predicate *wakaranai* 'cannot appreciate'.

Each of the instances presented above involves another speaker completing a current speaker's turn by supplying a final predicate. In this connection, Hayashi (1997) suggests that "(t)he majority of coparticipant completion take the form of 'terminal item completion'", in which "a second speaker supplies a verb or an adjective that completes an emerging TCU". Hayashi attributes this pattern in part to the predicate-final orientation in Japanese, as also discussed in Chapter 4. I believe that this observation can also be explained by virtue of the fact that case and adverbial particles play an important role in projecting further talk in Japanese, and since most case and adverbial particles are employed to strongly project an eventual production of a predicate component. Indeed, a large proportion of terminal item completions examined in the data corpora for this study also occurred immediately or shortly after one of these particles was occasioned.

From time to time, however, coparticipants complete an emerging utterance by supplying a nominal rather than a predicate component. The examples below indicate that the type of grammatical unit selected to complete a current speaker's turn can be specifically fitted to (1) the kind of particle used by the current speaker which triggers the completion in the first place, and (2) the context and the social action performed by the talk.

Recall that the particle *no* is frequently used as a genitive particle (GEN) to indicate a relation of possessor-possessed, roughly equivalent to an 'apostrophe-s' or 'of' in English, e.g. *Furansu* ***no*** *hitobito* 'people **of** France'. A function of *no*, therefore is to connect one nominal component with another. A knowledge of this grammatical property can be mobilised as a resource by coparticipants to project a further nominal element. Consider the following case of collaborative talk, which demonstrates participants' orientation that a nominal should follow a genitive particle in its local context. In this face-to-face conversation among four women in their forties, the participants have been discussing the current fashion trend which they take to be a reversion to the styles of the time when they were younger. In this context, D has just pointed out (a few turns before the excerpt shown below) that she found some old 'things' which presumably fitted that description. D continues in line 1 below that Miho (her daughter) is now wearing it. There is some ambiguity as to what D is referring to by 'things' (discussed in detail in Hayashi, Mori, and Takagi, to appear), and some exchanges ensue to identify this referent, in the form of questions by B (in lines 2 and 4) directed towards D.

(95) [OBS: 17] multi-party conversation

```
1 D:      Miho ga   [kiten     no.
          Miho NOM  [wearing FP
          'Miho is wearing ((them))'
                    [
2 B:                [Mukashi no   shashin?
                    [past    GEN  photos
                    ['((You mean)) the old photos?'

3 C:      A!=
          'Oh!'

4 B:→ =E!  [jibun          no    [mono o?
      oh   [oneself        GEN   [things ACC
      'Oh! [((your)) own         [things?'
           [                     [
5 C:       [Ho:nto::.
           ['Really'
                                 [
6 D: →                             [Un.  burausu.
                                   [yeah blouses
                                   ['Yeah blouses'
```

Notice that in line 4, B asks D, *E! jibun no mono o*? 'Oh! ((your)) own things?', ending with the accusative particle *o*. According to the analysis that has been undertaken in this section, the production of the object marker *o* can be expected to project a predicate component to follow. However, the way in which D continues co-constructing B's emergent turn in line 6 is composed of an acknowledgement *Un* 'Yeah' plus a nominal component *burausu* 'blouses' instead of a predicate. A clue as to why D furnishes a nominal element here can be gleaned by examining more closely at exactly what point in B's turn D enters. Indeed, D has not waited until the accusative particle *o* has been produced at the end of line 4, but has in fact started to speak immediately after the genitive particle *no* is hearable. In other words, all that D could have heard at this point is B's incipient question/exclamation: *jibun no* 'your own'. Thus, it is plausible that D first agrees with this characterisation by B through an acknowledgement *Un* 'Yeah', and then goes on to link onto B's utterance-so-far to jointly produce the expression: *jibun no burausu* '((my)) own blouses'. On this level of detail, therefore, it becomes apparent that D is attending to the projectability property of the genitive particle *no* that projects another nominal element to which the first nominal will be linked. Thus, in contrast to the other particles examined above, the production of a *no*-marked nominal (i.e. *jibun*) is treated by a coparticipant as projecting another *nominal* (i.e. *burausu*) instead of a predicate element. However, like other particles examined above, this particle shares the property that it projects a further increment of talk.

The next instance demonstrates the importance of the context and interactional implications of talk for a determination of what kind of item is projected. In the fragment which follows, the current speaker produces a *wa*-marked nominal phrase, which provides an opportunity for the current and next speaker to collaboratively supply another nominal component (instead of a predicate component) in the specific interactional context. In this excerpt from an informal meeting at an organisation, there has been an extended discussion of having three of its part-time members write a joint article regarding the results of a questionnaire survey. One participant suggests that a fourth member S should also be asked to join the three in contributing to the article. A debate follows during which another member (who is one of the "three") says that S shouldn't have to participate, as she is of a different standing, and not to be lumped together with the three rank-and-file members. To this, the chairperson G replies:

(96) [Tokyo 10 #4: 11] informal meeting

1 G: *'N (.) ma- sore wa: tomokaku konkai* **wa**
yeah well that TOP set aside this time TOP
'Yeah (.) well, setting that to the side for now, on this occasion'

2 S: *Konkai* **wa** [*san'nin de*
this time TOP [three people INS
'On this occasion [the three people to
[
3 G: [*wa san'nin de*
[TOP three people INS
['the three people to'

G first begins to dismiss the prior comment through a turn full of hesitations and hitches *'N (.) ma- sore wa: tomokaku konkai* **wa** 'Yeah, (.) well, setting that to the side for now, on this occasion,' using the contrastive topic particle *wa* at the end of line 1. At this point, S enters (line 2) by first repeating the last topic phrase

Konkai ***wa*** 'On this occasion', after which S and G almost simultaneously produce continuations, both containing the nominal phrase *san'nin de* 'the three people to' without producing any predicate here at all. Observe that the instrumental (case) particle *de* at the end of this phrase implies that the three people are the ones who should write the article. In this manner, both S and G display a common understanding that the bone of contention here is the number of people (i.e. three or four) who should be involved in the writing of the article, and not the actual task of writing itself. They display their shared understanding: first, via S's repetition of the topic phrase *Konkai wa* 'On this occasion' in line 2; secondly, through G's repetition of the topic particle *wa* in line 3; and third, by the joint production (by S and G) of the nominal phrase 'the three people to' rather than a candidate predicate.

The fragment above demonstrates that participants do not simply attend to the grammatical linking properties of particles by automatically projecting a predicate as the next appropriate component, but that contextual and interactional features are of paramount importance in the co-construction, and therefore projection, of further talk (see Hayashi 1997). This brings us to the next crucial feature of case and adverbial particles: their role in the projection of a course of action.

5.9. Case/adverbial particles and action projection

Case and adverbial particles are not only directed towards projecting certain grammatical components to be produced, but also for foreshadowing and implementing the kind of action which will occupy an emergent turn. It will be argued here that the choice of particle can have a significant impact on setting the trajectory of talk. Three examples are presented below in which participants revise the choice of particle in the interests of modifying the course of talk in some way. The first case involves a repair of a particle by the current speaker, "self-repair", followed by two instances of repair by another speaker, "other-repair" (see Schegloff, Jefferson, and Sacks 1977).

Consider the following example of a self-repair of a particle.[8] In this telephone conversation, H is ringing I about a pre-arranged meeting with I the next day to attend a mutual friend's wedding. After a greeting sequence, H immediately launches into the reason for the call, saying that on the following day, he wants to stop by somewhere before joining I, and that meeting each other inside the station (as previously arranged) would entail his re-entering the station. (This would normally necessitate the purchase of another ticket just to go through the wicket.) H continues, saying:

(97) [IMD: 21–24] telephone conversation

1 H: → >*Dakara dokka*< *eki no soto::* ***de***::,=
therefore somewhere station GEN outside LOC: at
'Therefore, **at** somewhere outside the station'

2 I: =*U::n.*
'Yeah'

3 H:→ ***ni*** *machiawase: no basho o kaetai nā*
LOC: to[9] meeting place P place ACC want to change FP
'**to** ((somewhere outside the station)), ((I)) wish to change the meeting place'

4 *to*[: *omou n yakedo.*]
QUOT think VN although
'that's what ((I))'m wondering, but'
[ ]
5 I: [*A! .h hai ha:i.*]
['Oh! .h yeah yeah']

H originally designs his turn by using the locative particle *de* 'at' at the end of line 1, which is hearable as projecting a form of a verb such as *au* 'to meet'. But after a slight hesitation (the sound stretch and the space for I to proffer an acknowledgement), H repairs the original particle *de* 'at' to a different locative particle *ni* 'to' which also changes the set of verbs which may be usable with the new particle. Although the obvious verb which would follow *de* is *au* 'meet' as noted above, some verbs that would typically be associated with *ni* include *suru* 'make' or *kaeru* 'to change' as we see in line 3 (where *kaetai* is a desiderative form of *kaeru*). Had H continued with the original particle *de*, the main thrust of his turn may have resulted in a request to *meet* outside the station. However, by repairing the particle, he now makes it possible to fashion a slightly different outcome: to a request to *change* the meeting place to outside the station. An interactive consequence of repairing the case particle has been to render the request less imposing: i.e. from one that might have been designed as a direct request to *meet* outside the station to one that emphasises a wish to *change* the meeting place.

The next instance involves an "embedded" other-repair of a particle produced by the current speaker (see Jefferson 1987). In the following telephone conversation, I and H are talking about a recent wedding reception of their mutual friend Yōko, which was heavily attended by medical doctors who are friends and colleagues of the bride and groom.

(98) [IMD: 254–257] telephone conversation

1 I: . . . *ano* *Yōko* (.) *tte* *naika* *deshō:?*
uhm ((name)) QUOT internal medicine COP
'. . . uhm Yōko is ((a specialist in)) in internal medicine, isn't ((she))?'

2 H: *U::n*
'Yeah'

3 I: → *Danna san* ***wa:***?=
husband TOP (as for)
'How about ((her)) husband?'

4 H:→ ***=mmo*** *naika* *tte* *yutteta* *yo.*
ADVP: is also internal medicine QUOT were saying FP
'**is also** ((a specialist in)) internal medicine, ((they)) were saying'

In line 1, I requests confirmation about whether Yōko specialises in internal medicine. H affirms this in line 2. Then, I asks about Yōko's husband in line 3 by deploying the topic particle *wa* in turn-final position, delivered with a rising intonation (as discussed in Section 5.7). The juxtaposing of her question *danna san* **wa**:? 'How about ((her)) husband?' in relation to her earlier query in line 1 displays I's assumption that she knows the husband is also a doctor, but does not know what his speciality is. This employment of *wa* (a possible use of the contrastive *wa*) further displays I's assumption that the husband must be a specialist in some branch of medicine other than internal (see point (v) in Section 5.2). It happens, however that H replies that the husband is also in internal medicine (line 4). But in order to pave the way for this embedded repair, H has been forced to replace the earlier topic particle *wa* in I's question (implicit of a contrast) by another adverbial particle *mo* 'is also' which is used to project "sameness". In the sequential context of the preceding confirmation of Yōko's speciality, this replacement is necessitated by the fact that the employment of *wa* in this position (in line 4) would project a type of speciality which contrasts with that of Yōko's. In a covert way, then, H has not only repaired the particle appropriate in this position, but has also "corrected" the assumption implicit in I's choice of topic particle *wa* that Yōko's husband may have a different speciality to that of Yōko.

We inspect another instance where a coparticipant replaces a particle in a current speaker's turn to subvert the course of talk. In the following example, W is complaining about her husband H by recounting a past episode, in which H allegedly told her that 'it is no fun playing tennis with you'. But this is the second time W brings up this topic in the course of the conversation.

(99 [Tokyo 7: 7] multi-party conversation

1 W: *Dakara kimi to ·hh [tenisu shitat te omo [shiroi koto*
so you with [tennis do even if fun N
[[
2 K: ['*N* ['*N*
['Yeah' ['Yeah'

3 W: *nai n da yo [to iu koto* **de** *sa, ·hh*=
not N COP FP [QUOT say N and FP
[
4 K: ['*N*
['Yeah'

5 K: =***ni***: *kakawatte kuru wake ne*?=
to related become reason FP
'to ((that)), ((it))'s related, is it?'

6 W: ='*N*::
'Mmm'

7 K: *A*: *A*: *Naruhodo.*
oh oh ((I)) see
'Oh oh ((I)) see'

Gloss of lines 1 and 3: 'That "it's no fun to play tennis with you" and, you know'

W begins repeating the said episode in lines 1 and 2. Towards the end of line 3, W projects a further component through the particle *de* (which is used similarly to a conjunctive particle) and the employment of the final particle *sa* (used in a turn-internal position) which can request others to "keep paying attention to the following" (R. Suzuki 1990: 317). The continuing intonation and the in-breath at the end of line 3 also suggest that W intends to continue. At this point, however, K latches onto the end of line 3, and displays recognition of the story: 'to that, it's related, is it?' It is the way K designs her turn which is of interest here. First, K "replaces" the particle *de* 'and' with a case particle *ni* 'to'. Whereas a conjunctive particle can be used to project a further clause or sentence (see Chapter 6), a case particle marks a nominal element and can project a predicate component. Thus, this occurrence of *ni* marks W's utterance up to . . . *koto* in line 3, since *koto* nominalises what precedes it. K's "sequential deletion" of W's conjunctive particle seems to be designed to forestall further talk, in view of the possibility that the previously told story might be repeated. What appears to be happening here is a specific targeting of the conjunctive particle for replacement by a case particle, after which the newly projected course of talk is swiftly brought to a completion simply with a further predicate component (line 5). We see in line 6 that W cooperates through an agreement and a display of recipient orientation.

The three examples examined here illustrate that the specific particle which is used not only marks the part of speech of a foregoing unit and projects a certain type of grammatical component, but also has significant implications for the kind of action which is projectable through the use of the particle in question. This feature of case particles may then be exploited for redirecting the trajectory of talk.

5.10. Nominal phrases produced after a predicate

It has been demonstrated above that case and adverbial particles not only strongly project a further predicate or nominal element, but are critical for the performance of some action. The linkage between case or adverbial particles and particular actions is further demonstrated by their use in constructing post-predicate additions: i.e. turn-designs in which the speaker furnishes a subject, object, indirect object phrase, etc. marked by one of these particles, *after* the final predicate is produced (see Chapters 3 and 4). In such cases, the projectability properties of the particles (together with contextual features) work in the reverse direction: by permitting participants to recognise a particle-marked nominal phrase as an addition to the just produced TCU, instead of projecting a new TCU. This claim is warranted by the presence in the data set of instances where next speakers display an understanding that a particle-marked phrase is fitted to a previously produced predicate by starting to talk immediately after the production of a case or adverbial particle instead of waiting for some further predicate which might be projected by the particle. For the sake of argument, this point is illustrated through an examination of occurrences of case particles *ga* and *ni* at turn-final positions.

(100) [Shakujii 1A (#6), p. 3]

1 B: →. . . >*wakan* *nei n* *da* *sore* ***ga***<=
understand not VN COP that NOM
'. . . ((I)) don't understand, that'

2 F: =(*Hore* *naoru* *mo* *omae to* *dake datta n* *da(g) yo(g)*)
Look(EXC) get better ADVP you with only COP VN COP FP
'(Look! It was only with you that one gets better)'

Drawing on the analysis of turn structure in Chapter 4, we see in line 1 that *wakan nei n da* 'don't understand' is a predicate phrase ending with utterance-final elements *n* (verb nominaliser) and *da* (copula), and moreover, modifies the nominal phrase *sore ga* 'that' which is recognisable as a subject through the postpositioning of *ga*. Line 1 can therefore be seen as an "inversion" of the hypothetical sentence:

B: . . . sore **ga** wakan nei n da
that NOM understand not VN COP
'. . . that's what ((I)) don't understand'

in which the *ga*-marked nominal *sore* 'that' is modified by *wakan nei n da* 'don't understand'. Returning to fragment (100), the fact that F starts up immediately after B utters *sore* ***ga*** 'that', suggests that F must have attended to the prior production of the description. In such a case, the binomial relation does not project forward, but links the nominal that it marks backward with a previously-produced predicate (in boldface) as in the diagram below:

1 B: . . . ***>wakan nei*** *n da* ***sore*** *ga<=*
understand not VN COP that NOM
'. . . ((I)) don't understand, that'

As in the case of *ga*, it can happen that a next speaker starts up immediately after the first speaker's production of the particle *ni*. But this occurs massively when the predicate phrase linked with a *ni*-marked nominal has already been produced or can be furnished from the context, as in the following instance:

(101) [Shakujii 1A (#7) p. 1] telephone conversation

1 H: . . . *Naoki san irasshai °masu deshō* [*ka°*
name is there SFX COP [QP
'. . . Is Naoki san there?'
[
2 Y: [*A- ima de=*
[oh now DF
['Oh right now'

3 →Y: =*sochira* ***ni*** *mukatteru to omou n desu kedo*:=
over there LOC heading towards QUOT think VN COP CONJ
'((I)) think ((he)) is heading over there'

4 H: =*E- sochira tte*:
what over there speaking of
'What? What do ((you)) mean by "over there"?'

5 (.8)

6 →Y: *Ano:- ie* ***ni*** [*Hagiwa kun no*
uhm house LOC [((name))-suffix GEN
'Uhm to the house [Hagiwa's ((meaning 'yours'))'
[
7 →H: [*Uchi desu ka*?=
[((my)) house COP QP
['((You)) mean ((my)) house?'

8 Y: =*E*:
'Yes'

In the fragment above, when H asks for Y's husband, *Naoki san* (line 1), Y replies in lines 2–3 that he is heading towards H's house *A- ima de sochira* ***ni*** *mukatteru to omou n desu kedo*: 'Oh right now, ((I)) think ((he)) is heading over there'. When the particle *ni* appears in line 3, Y has not yet produced the predicate of her utterance: *mukatte iru to omou n desu kedo* '((I)) think ((he)) is heading over there'. Thus, this first occurrence of *ni* can be heard as projecting a predicate, as discussed in previous sections. Then, H displays difficulty in understanding what is meant by 'over there', and requests clarification in line 4: *E- sochira tte*: 'What? What do ((you)) mean by "over there"?'. To this repair initiator, Y begins to answer in line 6 using a *ni*-marked nominal *Ano:- ie* ***ni*** 'Uhm **to** the house'. Immediately after the production of *ni*, however, H intersects Y's continuing talk with another repair initiator, requesting confirmation: *Uchi desu ka*? 'My house?' in line 7. One explanation for why H enters here instead of waiting for Y to finish speaking is that the second occurrence of *ni* is recognisably establishing a backward binomial relation with the same predicate component which followed the initial use of *ni* in line 3: *mukatte iru to omou n desu kedo* '((I)) think he is heading over there'. And in this sense, the beginning of Y's utterance in line 6 *Ano:- ie* ***ni*** 'Uhm **to** the house' can be heard as a post-predicate addition.[10] This example illustrates that the strength of the binomial relation between this particle and an action can be utilised by participants to link in the reverse direction to a predicate which has previously been articulated. Thus, whether or not a particular occurrence of a particle is treated as projecting a further predicate or linked to a prior predicate depends on its positioning *vis-à-vis* a final predicate and on contextual features.

5.11. Limitations to the projectability properties of case and adverbial particles

In the sections above, the efficacy of case and adverbial particles to project and establish a linkage with specific grammatical components and actions has been explored from a number of different angles. Even though case and adverbial particles can be shown to project the type of a forthcoming increment of talk within a local sequential context, it is nevertheless important to observe that *these particles do not necessarily project the temporal sequence in which a turn may develop, nor the eventual shape of an emergent turn*. This point is evidenced by instances where coparticipants do not always agree on the appropriate moment when a projected item should be produced, demonstrating the variability of word order in Japanese. Moreover, due to the transformability of turn-shapes discussed in Chapter 4, incongruities regularly emerge as to what that projected component will ultimately develop into. These observations suggest that case and adverbial particles typically help to project only one further component which will be produced at "some point" during the current TCU, consonant with the discussion of the limited projectability of turn-shapes in Japanese (Chapter 4). Two fragments which illustrate some of these patterns are dealt with below.

Before the part reproduced in the following fragment, the participants had been considering whom to ask to contribute articles to an annual gazette. One of the projects they had been discussing is to have someone write a piece based on a questionnaire survey. In this context, G proposes asking Professor Tamura to write an article. To this, H first voices a reservation, that because he is somewhat too serious, whatever he writes is destined to be rather uninteresting. However, when G suggests that he would still be a good person to ask since he has expertise in "case-work theory", H begins to make a concession as follows:

(102) [Tokyo 10A: 14] informal meeting

1 H: *Sorejya ne* (.) *a::no sensei* ***ni*** *ne*: *.hh*
then FP that professor **DAT** FP
'Then you know, to have that professor'

2 G: → *Ma-* [<u>*mazu*</u> *yonde ita-*
ini [initially have read
'Ini- [initially to have ((him)) read it'
[
3 H: → [( ) *o- ōsodokkusu no* ↑*ne*
[orthodox P FP

4 G: *Hai*
Yes

5 H: → *mono to shite* **kaite kudasaru** (.) *koto* wa (.)
thing as write N TOP

6 → ***itadaku*** *koto wa*
have ((him write)) N TOP

7 *ii to omou no=*
good QUOT think FP

8 G: = *Hai hai hai*
'Yes yes yes'

Rough gloss of lines 3, 5–7: 'that ((he would)) write (.) to have ((him)) write it as an orthodox piece would be a good thing, ((I)) think'

H indicates that he might be ready to settle for Professor Tamura after all, by beginning with the discourse marker *Sorejya ne* 'then' in line 1. Then he continues, *a::no sensei ni ne* 'to have that professor', thereby marking 'that professor' as an indirect object. At this point, G enters by beginning to continue H's turn by furnishing a predicate expression: *Ma- mazu yonde ita-* 'Ini- initially, to have ((him)) read it' projected by the particle *ni*, i.e. that Professor Tamura can initially be asked to read the questionnaire. It happens, however, that H starts to overlay G's talk by first inserting an adverbial phrase *( ) o- ōsodokkusu no* ↑*ne . . . mono to shite* 'as an orthodox piece' in lines 3 and 5 before going on to produce a predicate phrase in lines 5 to 6 projected by the *ni*-marked phrase in line 1. Incidentally, H begins to produce the predicate expression *kaite kudasaru* 'write' in line 5, but repairs this to . . . *itadaku* 'have ((him write))' in line 6, possibly realising that the former compound verb *kaite kudasaru* 'write' does not link grammatically with the indirect object phrase he produced in line 1.[11] After H's continuation starts to be produced, G cuts short her attempt to co-construct the utterance-in-progress, and takes on a recipient role, as indicated by her proffering of an acknowledgement in line 4.

Among other things, the fragment above exemplifies the variability of the word order of components in Japanese conversation, especially prior to the production of the final predicate (as discussed in Chapter 4). Furthermore, the projected incipient predicate expression *kaite itadaku* 'have him write' in lines 5–6 is subsequently reshaped into a nominal expression through the postpositional attachment of the verb nominaliser *koto*, again illustrating the incremental transformability of the trajectory of TCUs in Japanese conversation (see Chapter 4).

We reconsider a similar fragment which was examined earlier (fragment (93)):

(103) [Shakujii 1A (#9): 11] telephone conversation, slightly simplified

1 M: . . . *mitara* (.) Ah: >kore dattara:< yasui to:=
see-if Ah: this if-then cheap QUOT
'. . . if ((X)) sees ((this)), "Oh if it's this, then it's value for money" '

2 H: ='*N*=
'Yeah'

3 M: =*iu fū* ***ni*** [( ) *hito* *wa* ***wakaru*** *yōna* *mono o* *ne*=
in this way [person TOP can see kind of thing ACC FP
'in this way, [a ( ) person would see this kind of thing'
[
4 H: → [( ) ***wakaru*** *wake* ↑*ne*
[can see reason FP
['( ) ((X)) can see, right?'

The appearance of the *ni*-marked phrase in line 3 permits H to anticipate a forthcoming predicate *wakaru* 'can see' that M then ratifies, but as noted earlier, there is a "time gap" in the moment when M utters the predicate. This is due to the insertion by M of a topic phrase ( ) *hito wa* 'as for people like ( )' prior to the production of the predicate *wakaru*, again exemplifying the permutability of the word order in Japanese. Notice also that the possible final predicate *wakaru* in line 3 is thereafter transformed into a nominal object phrase *wakaru yōna mono o* through the postpositional attachment of suffixes and the case particle *o*.

Therefore, although the particle *ni* can help to project the production of a predicate *at some point* within a TCU in progress, such a predicate may not necessarily occur immediately after the *ni*-marked phrase (as seen in the examples above). The very fact that such misalignments in "timing" occur provides further evidence of word order variability prior to the production of the final predicate in Japanese. Fox, Hayashi, and Jasperson (1996: 208) may be alluding to this feature in characterising syntactic units in Japanese conversation as being structurally "loosely associated" with one another.

The observations made above are congruent with Hayashi's (1997) finding that "(t)he majority of coparticipant completion (in his data) take the form of 'terminal item completion' " (parentheses added). Re-inspecting the instances of coparticipant completion above (e.g. fragments (91)–(94) and (96)), it appears that coparticipants often refrain from taking the first possible opportunity for co-construction which is afforded by case or adverbial particle(s) occasioned fairly early in a current speaker's turn, and hold off until some of the possibly many particle-marked components have been produced before participating in the collaborative activity. Just one instance (fragment (94)) is re-examined below:

(104) [Tokyo 6: 2–3] (same as (94) above)

1 K: → *Otoko no sōiu ronri tte no* **wa** (.9)
men GEN that kind of logic QUOT N TOP
'As for that kind of logic that men use'

2 *mainichi zu:tto sono kakawatteru sono*: (.)
everyday continuously AP relating AP

3 → *wazurawashisa toka iyarashisa tte no* **wa** (.) *.hhh*
tediousness for instance onerousness QUOT N TOP

Gloss of lines 2–3: 'concerning for instance the tediousness or onerousness of relating ((to the children)) continuously, everyday'

4 S: → *Wakara* [*nai.*
cannot appreciate
'((They)) cannot appreciate'
[
5 K: [*wakaranai to ne*?
[cannot appreciate QUOT FP
['that ((they)) cannot appreciate, ((you)) know?'

The coparticipant S does not begin her co-constructing activity at the first occurrence of a topic particle *wa* near the beginning of K's turn (end of line 1), but refrains until she has heard two full topic phrases, both of which provide a cumulative basis for determining what probable type of predicate might be projected. In retrospect, both the topic phrase in line 1 and the one in lines 2–3 can be seen to be binomially linked to the projected predicate *wakaranai* co-produced by S and K in lines 4 and 5. The reader can also re-inspect fragments (91)–(93) and (96) for further examples.

One possible explanation for the generally observed delay in joining in the collaborative talk is that there may be relatively little grammatical resources or contextual information towards the beginning of a turn to formulate a sense of how the current speaker's utterance is evolving (cf. "delayed projectability" in Chapter 4). But as the turn progresses, even if a final predicate has not yet been produced, the "cascade effect" or accumulation of incremental bits of syntactic binomial projections together with other projectability features of the locally emergent talk can reach a kind of "threshold level", thereby improving the visibility of the possible trajectory of the turn-in-progress (but please refer to Section 5.12 for a contrastive example). Another explanation may be that the likelihood of the current speaker inserting additional phrases before the final predicate (as in (102) or (103)) is likely to be relatively reduced, the longer one waits to come in. Indeed, if S had attempted to supply a possible predicate component after the first topic particle *wa* produced in line 1 in fragment (104) above, she may have come into conflict with K's insertion of the second topic component (in lines 2–3). This explanation is somewhat speculative, and requires further investigation. However, these possible orientations may partially explain Ono and Yoshida's observation that "co-construction of syntactic units is not very common in Japanese" in comparison to English (Ono and Yoshida 1996: 115–16).

This section has pointed to some limitations of the projectability properties of case and adverbial particles. In spite of their utility to project a particular component which will eventually be produced, it was suggested that the variability of word order and the incremental transformability of utterance-structure (Chapter 4) can "conspire" to restrict the ease with which participants can predict the exact moment when such a component might be produced or the ultimate trajectory of the course of a current speaker's turn. Coparticipants seem to display their orientation to this constraint by delaying the point at which they begin to engage in a collaborative construction of a turn-in-progress, until they have a "reasonable" sense of how the utterance may be developing.

5.12. Interactional styles

The discussion above has highlighted both the utility and limitations of case and adverbial particles in the projection of the unfolding of a turn. On the one hand, many of the fragments examined above suggest that these particles may be deployed in orderly ways to make explicit the logical relationship between a component of talk produced and a forthcoming increment of talk, serving as resources for coparticipant completion. At the same time, it should also be noted that these same resources can be employed in complex ways which may render opaque the possible trajectory of talk. I next look at the potential implications that a successive linking of nominal and predicate elements through such particles may have for the production of certain interactional styles in Japanese conversation. (The arrow indicates the relationship forged by a case particle: nominal element → the predicate or nominal phrase projected by the particle.)

(105) [Shakujii 1B #2, p. 4]

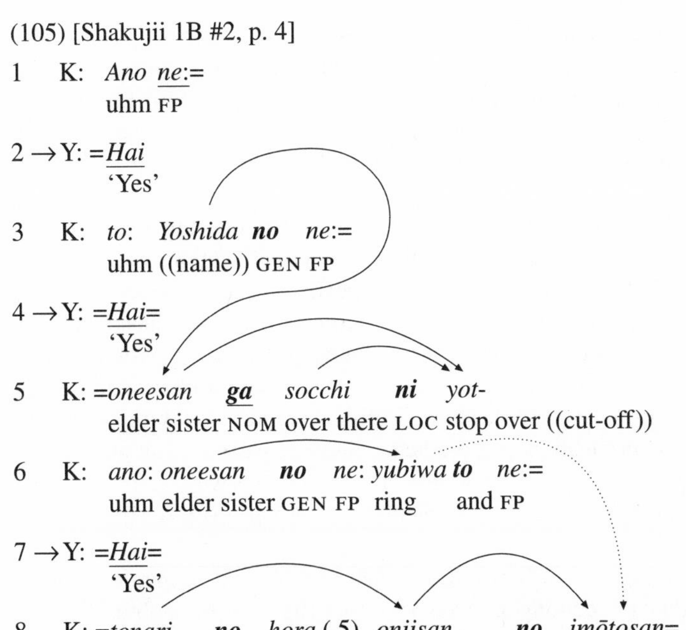

1 K: *Ano ne:=*
uhm FP

2 →Y: *=Hai*
'Yes'

3 K: *to: Yoshida* ***no*** *ne:=*
uhm ((name)) GEN FP

4 →Y: *=Hai=*
'Yes'

5 K: *=oneesan* ***ga*** *socchi* ***ni*** *yot-*
elder sister NOM over there LOC stop over ((cut-off))

6 K: *ano: oneesan* ***no*** *ne: yubiwa* **to** *ne:=*
uhm elder sister GEN FP ring and FP

7 →Y: *=Hai=*
'Yes'

8 K: *=tonari* ***no*** *hora* (.5) *oniisan* ***no*** *imōtosan=*
next door GEN you know elder brother GEN younger sister

9 *=iru de* ↑*sho*
exist COP

Rough gloss of K's talk: 'Uhm: ((my)) elder sister Yoshida is stopping over ((cut-off)) there, uhm there is ((her)) ring and uhm ((you)) know the younger sister of ((my)) older brother next door?'[12]

In line 3, the genitive particle *no* in *Yoshida* ***no*** 'Yoshida's' projects the production of another nominal element, which follows in line 5: *oneesan* 'elder sister'. The latter nominal *oneesan* 'elder sister' is marked by the nominative particle *ga*, possibly linking with the predicate: *yot-* 'stop over', though this phrase is cut off before it is fully articulated. Nested within this last loop is the *ni*-marked locative phrase *socchi ni* 'over there' which also links to the aforementioned cut-off predicate *yot-* 'stop over'.

After the cut-off, K makes a restart with *ano*: 'uhm' in line 6. Then, on the same line, *oneesan* ***no*** 'elder sister's', a nominal form with a genitive particle *no* again projects an ensuing nominal: *yubiwa* 'ring'. The nominal *yubiwa* in turn, is marked by the case particle *to* 'and', which projects a further nominal element. However, since the projected element does not actually seem to have been produced, the location where it might have occurred is indicated by a dotted line.

Within this larger loop in line 8, there are two nested case relationships indicating a possessor–possessed relationship: *tonari* ***no*** 'of next door' which links with *oniisan* 'elder brother'; *oniisan* ***no*** 'of elder brother' projecting the nominal *imōtosan* 'younger sister'. The current turn is brought to a close in line 9 with the production of a verb *iru* 'exist', followed by a copula *desho* marking the end of the turn (see Chapter 4).

The fragment above illustrates that the projection and monitoring of the development of a turn may proceed as a concatenation of binomial relations, relying partly on the prospective-linking (and sometimes retrospective-linking) and nesting operations enabled through case and adverbial particles. A consequence of this organisation is the possibility of the creation of a lengthy chain of nested nominal and predicate elements linked by such particles within one turn before the arrival of a possible TRP, as in the example above. Before an initial TRP is imminent, and certainly before the production of a predicate element, particles can also be employed to limit projectability to progressive local increments which offer little clue as to where it is going, not only to recipients, but perhaps even for the speakers themselves.

This instance suggests that it is not so much the inherent properties of these particles, but rather the contingent ways in which they can be mobilised which may be responsible for the image of Japanese interactional styles as illogical, rambling, and unclear. While case and adverbial particles may be deployed for elucidating the syntactic, logical, and interactional trajectory of talk, these very resources may likewise be utilised to incrementally and gradually build up a point, while leaving the ultimate shape of an emerging utterance inconclusive until close to the end of the turn. The speaker can, for instance "float" various ideas before taking a stand (by delaying the production of a predicate). What is more, syntactic binomial relations which are projected towards the beginning of an turn may be truncated or abandoned before a turn reaches completion, and new relations projected within the course of a turn, as in the example above. Some further cultural implications of the use of particles on turn-taking are considered in the concluding chapter.

5.13. Concluding remarks

In summary, differences in the production and monitoring of the progress of turns were examined for Japanese and Anglo-American English. In English, the early projectability of turn-shapes and subsequent word ordering can provide a robust guide to the possible unfolding of a turn. In Japanese, due to the transformability of the shape of an ongoing turn, post-positional structure, and resultant delayed projectability, word order is not always informative concerning the progress of a turn. However, it was argued that one means for producing and recognising the progressivity of ongoing talk is through case and adverbial particles, which allow for incremental projections over the course of a turn.

Since case and adverbial particles are post-positioned, they refer backward to the words/phrase/clause immediately preceding it, marking the prior component as the subject, object, indirect object, topic, etc. depending on the particle. At the same time, they are also prospective-linking or anticipatory, connecting the component preceding the particle with what should projectably follow. For instance, if *ga* (subject-marker), *o* (object marker), *ni* (indirect object or oblique marker), or *wa* (topic marker) occurs, there will be a strong expectation that a predicate component is due, unless the latter is recoverable from the context. Likewise, the production of a *no*-marked nominal projects a nominal element. However, no further talk may be projected if the associated component has already occurred prior to the case or adverbial particle in question.

The features of case and adverbial particles noted above are relevant to turn-construction and projection. Although context and other features of talk (as discussed in Section 5.2 often provide a good basis for coparticipants to project the local trajectory of talk even when particles are unarticulated, it was shown that an early attempt at collaborative completion (i.e. without waiting for the production of a particle) can be "risky", as there is no way of knowing for certain what type of nominal phrase has just been produced (until sometimes later in the utterance), and consequently no assurance of what action is being projected in the turn-in-progress. As evidence for this, I examined occurrences of misalignments between current speakers and coparticipants who attempt to co-construct an emergent TCU before the advent of a case or adverbial particle. In such cases, it was shown that the parties may implicitly or explicitly furnish different particles which can then project divergent trajectories of talk. On the other hand, the physical presence of a case or adverbial particle can provide information as to what syntactic component has just been produced and furthermore what grammatical component should expectably follow at some point in the utterance. For instance, the occurrence of *ga* informs participants that what preceded *ga* is the subject, and that now a predicate phrase is due. The said turn would not be projectably complete until the predicate has been produced. Thus, even though the ultimate shape of a turn may not be fully revealed, case and adverbial particles at the minimum provide a strong foundation for the local projection of certain components. Furthermore, the utility of these particles for the projection of social action was illustrated through instances where participants negotiate the selection of particles for setting the trajectory of talk.

Nevertheless, it was shown that even after the production of a case or adverbial particle, it is possible that the speaker would insert other non-projected phrases before the projected component is produced, partly as a reflection of the variability of word order in Japanese. Moreover, particles alone may not provide adequate contextual grounds on which to anticipate the specific ways in which a turn is being projected. Participants display an orientation to these constraints by frequently passing up opportunities for co-construction, waiting for a later point at which to join in the collaborative activity.

Pictorially, the parsing of talk when particles are employed could be represented as follows:

nominal phrase + case or adverbial particle

↓

permits participants to project a possible predicate or
nominal component *and* a set of components
potentially usable with a specific particle.

the context of the talk and other grammatical features
can further narrow down the range of possible elements
(e.g. particular verbs, adjectives or nouns) which are
projected

productional features can provide further "unprojected
opportunities" (Lerner 1996) for co-completion

↓

incremental projection
and
coparticipant completion

In other words, a case or adverbial particle seems to act as a kind of "trigger" setting in motion the dialectic process of ascertaining where the talk is progressing against other grammatical features and the sequential context of talk. Additionally, productional features of the speaker's utterance may provide an opportunity for a coparticipant to display that understanding through a collaborative construction of talk.

In this manner, case and adverbial particles not only serve to foreshadow the progress of a turn in-the-course-of-production, but also as local floor-holding devices (e.g. fragment (105)). Moreover, a succession of such particles can be used to serially link together an entire string of nominal and predicate elements without passing through a TRP, as each occurrence of a particle could be used to incrementally project further elements.

Notes

1. Shibatani's classificatory system includes two other types of particles, which will not be discussed here. Nevertheless, they are the *kantō-joshi* (interjectional particles) "that occur freely within a clause and whose presence or absence does not affect sentence formation" and the *kakari-joshi* (a variant of an adverbial particle) which "comprises those particles that affect the entire predication, and figure prominently in the classical language of the Heian Period" (1990: 334).
2. Other relevant syntactical features may include the following: a subject and object are the only cases which have no case marking, and are indicated solely by word order (i.e. subject precedes object); all other cases are indicated by prepositions such as *to*, *of*, *for*, etc. (Umegaki 1988: 199–200).
3. In cases of post-predicate additions, however, a case particle links the marked nominal with a preceding component (see Chapter 4; also Section 5.10).
4. Of course, it sometimes happens that the projected components are not produced.
5. Particles often serve more than one purpose, and those shown here represent only one or more possibilities out of a variety of roles and projectability properties that each particle can have depending on the context and position in which it is used.
6. Oide (1965: 147) presents examples to show that the use of *ga* is actually much more varied than just marking a subject. It can in rare cases mark a direct object.
7. I am grateful to Makoto Hayashi for pointing out to me that T employs the equivocality of the grammatical role of *sewanyōbō* as a resource to retroactively contextualise it as "nominative" or "topical" in this example.
8. The idea of looking at self-repair to examine action projection was suggested through a reading of Fox, Hayashi, and Jasperson (1996).
9. Note that *ni* can also be labelled as DAT: dative particle.
10. H's repair initiation (line 7), which requests confirmation of the location rather than the action also suggests that H had already established a connection between the *ni*-marked phrase and the prior predicate *mukatte iru* 'is heading'.
11. The first version *kaite kudasaru* 'write' would be grammatically incorrect, as it would require *Professor Tamura* to be the subject, whereas the second version which repairs just the second part of the compound verb *kaite kudasaru* into *kaite itadaku* 'have him write' is a grammatical continuation of H's turn-beginning in line 1.
12. To provide some background information on kinship terms for avoiding confusion, K is not referring to her own sister (by birth) by the expression 'the younger sister of my older brother'. Instead, the 'younger sister' is a younger sister of the man (referred to here as 'older brother') who is the husband of K's older sister-in-law.

Chapter 6

Delayed projectability: The 'compound turn-constructional unit'

6.1. Introduction

The intimate relation between syntax and turn-taking is also exemplified in the achievement of extended talk through the "compound TCU" format (see Lerner 1987, 1991). As mentioned in earlier chapters, the compound TCU has been reported as a technique available in both languages to extend a TCU by one further unit. While this description is broadly accurate, the divergent "grammatical realisations" of this format in English and Japanese (as pointed out by Lerner and Takagi, to appear, among others) have an important bearing upon turn-taking operations. This chapter is devoted to an analysis of the differential implications of this format for the projection of extended units of talk in the respective languages, which draws on previous research in English and Japanese (Lerner 1987, 1991, 1996; Hayashi 1997; Hayashi and Mori 1998; Lerner and Takagi, to appear; Mori 1996b; Ford and Mori 1994).

In a study of collaborative completions in Japanese, Hayashi makes an observation which touches upon the possible limited projectability of this format in Japanese (in comparison to English).

> In contrast to this claimed prevalence of syntactically-defined two-part formats that provide major resources for co-participant completion in English, a preliminary inspection of the database for the present study suggests that such strongly syntactic two-part formats appear to play a less prominent role in co-participant completion in Japanese. That is not to say that syntax plays no role in Japanese co-participant completion . . . , but it does not appear that Japanese conversational participants have available as robust syntactic resources as compound TCUs in English which strongly project a place and a form for co-participant completion. (Hayashi 1997: 222)

It will be argued here that the relative degrees of robustness of this resource to project further talk can be associated with three differences in the mobilisation of compound TCUs in English and Japanese.

First, while compound TCUs in English are "pre-positional" devices normally requiring pre-planning at the beginning of a clause, compound TCUs in Japanese are typically constructed through the attachment of selected postpositional conjunctive particles at the end of a component, and can therefore be used in somewhat of an *ad hoc* manner. As a result, the point at which a compound TCU is recognisable in Japanese may be delayed (Lerner and Takagi, to appear). Secondly, compound TCUs in English syntactically project two-part TCUs consisting of the preliminary and final components (Lerner 1991). On the other hand, conjunctive particles are employed *either* to project a further component or as a turn-ending device (see Mori 1996b; Hayashi 1997). Therefore, when a conjunctive particle is produced, participants must determine which type is involved. One of the objectives of this chapter is to suggest some ways in which participants arrive at a judgement as to whether a conjunctive particle is employed turn-internally or turn-finally. Third, the "prospective" projection of an upcoming compound TCU in English limits the "compounding" to at most two units (with a potential expansion of the preliminary component), after which a possible TRP may occur (Lerner 1991). In contrast, it will be shown for Japanese that the placement of conjunctive particles at the end of a component engenders the practical possibility of connecting more than two clauses, so that speakers may locally and serially project an indefinite number of clauses before the occurrence of a possible TRP. These three features of compound TCUs in Japanese respectively result in: a delay in the temporal emergence of the compound TCU format, an ambiguity in the type of turn being constructed, and an indeterminacy of the point at which the turn-in-progress might reach completion. It is concluded that the complexities accompanying the employment of the compound TCU format in Japanese may therefore restrict its robustness as a resource for participants to engage in coparticipant completion. These features of conjunctive particles may have additional implications for possible styles of interaction in Japanese.

Conjunctive particles (*setsuzoku-joshi*) are commonly employed to conjoin two clausal or sentential units into a compound TCU, and can indicate a "logical" relation between two juxtaposed clauses or sentences. Examples of conjunctive particles and rough glosses include *te* (and then), *shi* (and, besides, moreover, and what with), *ka* (or) *ga* (but, however, and yet, still), *keredomo* or *kedo* (but, although, notwithstanding), *dakara* (accordingly, because, consequently), *dakedo* (despite, yet, nevertheless). The interactional implications of the employment of specific conjunctive particles have been investigated by others (e.g. Ford and Mori 1994; Mori 1994, 1996b). However, this chapter will be focused primarily on the specific uses of this class of particles for turn-taking, rather than on their salience for social interaction.

6.2. The compound TCU format in English

In English, the production of *if* at the beginning of a first component X can project the occurrence of the second component Y. Lerner observes that "participants orient to and use *if X* and *then Y* (and related forms such as *when X–then Y*; *because X–Y*) as sequential components of a single turn-constructional format", which "delays, by at least one turn-constructional component, the occurrence of the next possible turn-transition place" (Lerner 1991: 442–3). This format can therefore be used to connect components without passing through a TRP, as in Vic's turn below:

(106) [US] (from Lerner, 1991: 443)

→ Vic: **If** yer intuh one I'll take one too.=
Mike: =Yeh.

Lerner furthermore demonstrates how the recognition of a first component of a compound TCU "makes it sequentially possible to produce a next utterance that can be affiliated to the turn-constructional unit-in-progress as a fitted completion of that unit" (1991: 445), as in the following instance of coparticipant completion:

(107) [US] (from Lerner, 1991: 445]

Rich: if you bring it intuh them
Carol: ih don't cost yuh nothing

Moreover, a more flourished version may include an "expanded preliminary component" such as a succession of *when X*, *unless X*, a parenthetical insert, *if X*, (in boldface below), before the onset of the final component:

(108) [Gerald] (from Lerner 1991: 444)

J: .hh **when** you go to France **unless** you cn speak perfect French er: ·h mosta the French-speaking countries in Europe anyway like in Belgium 'n stuff ·h **if** you can't speak French 'n speak it fluently 'n the way they speak it **they don't wan anything t'do with you**.
R: They don' ( )

A possible TRP is postponed so long as the final component is unfinished. But since "the preliminary component projects in its course the form its final component will take", "at the onset of a recognizable final component, recipients can then examine the utterance for its upcoming transition-relevant completion and . . . begin speaking just at that completion". (Lerner 1991: 444)

The summary of Lerner's analysis above highlights aspects of the grammatical realisation of the compound TCU structure in English which prove to be germane for considering possible differences in the projectability properties of this format in the two languages. First, this format serves as a *pre-emptive strategy* to project two components, which is dependent on the placement of the word *if* (or other words such as *although* or *when* for related formats) at the beginning of the first component. In this regard, pre-planning is required for this format to be implemented. This feature of the compound TCU format provides a prime example of the early projectability of turn-shapes in English (see Chapter 4). Secondly, once a recognisable second component has begun, a possible TRP may occur at its completion. Thus, the compound TCU in English is essentially a two-part format permitting not only the projection of one further component, but also of the likely point at which a TRP may occur.

6.3. Delayed temporal emergence of the compound TCU in Japanese

Previous work on compound TCUs in Japanese have identified some differences and similarities with respect to the grammatical realisation of this format in the two languages. These findings are reviewed in this section, before embarking on a detailed analysis of potential cross-linguistic differences in the ensuing sections. In the first instance, examples can be found which suggest that the use of conjunctive particles do permit participants to syntactically project a further component in Japanese, albeit with a temporal delay in the point at which a compound TCU structure may be revealed. However, it will subsequently be argued that much more than syntax is involved in the complex productional and parsing process implicated in the construction and recognition of the compound TCU format in Japanese.

In the fragment below, the first component [A] begins with *moshi* 'if', and after an expansion of the first component [B], the speaker produces the final component [C]:

(109) [Tokyo 7: 16] multi-party conversation, simplified

W: (　　) ***moshi*** (　　) *watashi ga　uwaki o　·hhh shi tara* [A]
　　if　　I　NOM affair ACC　do if-then
　'If I had an affair'

　[*de　dareka　to* (.) *icchat　tara* [B]
　[and someone with ran away if-then
　['and if ((I)) ran away with someone'
　[
( ): [(　　)

W: *dō shita*? [C]
what did
'what would ((you)) have done?'

The fragment above has a structure broadly congruent with fragments (106)–(108), with the word *moshi* 'if' appearing at the beginning of the first component. As in the case of English, this structure serves as a resource for the collaborative completion of the TCU-in-progress. The recognisable beginning of an *if X–then Y* structure allows coparticipants to complete the second component of the two-part compound TCU, as illustrated below:

(110) [Shakujii 1A 9: 13]

1 M: ***Moshi***: *gg* >*zenzen teika de kacchat te*
if not at all list price at bought and

2 *yasuku nakatta n da*:<
was not cheap VN COP

3 *to omowareta n* ***nara*** [*ne*
QUOT thought VN **if-then** [FP
[
4 H: ['*N* '*N*::=
['Yeah yeah'

Gloss of lines 1–3: 'If what she thought was that ((she)) had bought it at the list price and that it was not at all value for money, then'

5 M: =*Eg*:*g*: [*g*: ( ) *zan'nen da*]*kara*=
DF [unfortunate because-so
'((that)) would be unfortunate, so'
[ ]
6 H: → [*Sō suru to tsuman'nai kara ne*]
[then a shame because FP]
['Then ((that)) would be a shame']

However, it is also the case that an *if X–then Y* format is realisable even without lexical items such as *moshi* 'if' appearing turn-initially in Japanese, as in the following example consisting of two components connected by a conjunctive particle *kara*.[1] Lerner and Takagi's (to appear) schematic representation for denoting the "temporal emergence" of connective expressions is useful here. The arrow in *because → therefore* is used to indicate the property that the conjunctive particle *kara* meaning 'because' simultaneously embodies the meaning 'therefore'. As a result, the occurrence of *kara* in a component-final position "transforms" the TCU-in-progress into the first component of a compound TCU while at the same time projecting a further *therefore* component.

(111) [Tokyo 7: 7] multiparty conversation

G: *Datte sōiu chikara o motte irassharu* ***kara*** **[X]**
after all that sort power ACC have because → therefore
'After all, because ((she)) has that sort of power, therefore'

shigeki ni nariuru wake deshō?= **[Y]**
stimulation P can become reason COP
'((it)) provides a source of stimulation, doesn't ((it))?'

K: '*N*: *dakedo* . . .
yeah but
'Yeah but . . .'

G's turn above has the form

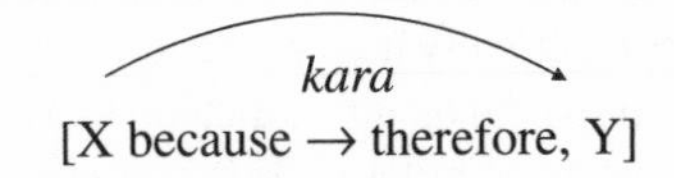

where the conjunctive particle *kara* marks X as a "subordinate" clause of Y. The capacity of conjunctive particles to create a binomial link between a clause that it marks with a prospective clause can be mobilised to project a second component. Although the shape of this turn is not revealed until the production of *kara*, this single particle accomplishes the task undertaken by the two items *because* and *therefore* in a *because X–therefore Y* format in English (Lerner and Takagi, to appear).

The localisation of Japanese turn-endings—discussed in Chapter 4—is relevant here. Recall that in Japanese, there is a strong expectation that a predicate or verb component should come last in an utterance, and is massively marked by utterance-final elements which are treated as a prominent announcement of a TRP. In two-part compound TCUs, a conjunctive particle appears where otherwise a series of utterance-final elements may have been occasioned to bring the first component to completion. In this manner, a possible transition-relevance-place may be by-passed, and instead, a new component is projected. By postpositioning a conjunctive particle as the terminal item of a component, a speaker can project an *if X–then Y* format, and propose that there is at least one more component to follow beyond the current component.

Some differences in the construction of compound TCUs in the two languages have been noted above. First, a turn-initial item such as *moshi* 'if' is not required for Japanese participants to construct a two-part format. Secondly, a conjunctive particle is employed at the end of the first component to project such a format, in comparison to English, where the projection occurs at the beginning of the first component. This feature results in a relative temporal delay of the point within a turn that the compound TCU can be anticipated in Japanese.

However, the remainder of this chapter explores other features of the use of conjunctive particles which may have consequences for the point at which a possible TRP may occur. Irrespective of what has been suggested above, I first proceed to show that the use of a conjunctive particle in a component-final position does not necessarily project a second component, but may alternatively be treated as a complete turn at the occurrence of the conjunctive particle.

6.4. Conjunctive particles used turn-finally or turn-internally?

Recall from Chapter 3 the existence of an entire class of turn-endings terminating with "extensions" consisting of grammatical elements which syntactically project further talk (including conjunctive particles, among others). Turns ending with extensions form a class of syntactically incomplete turns which are nevertheless pragmatically complete. The statistical results indicated that turns of this type were regularly treated by participants as complete actions, as evidenced by others massively starting to talk at their termination. Thus, even though these elements "syntactically" project further talk, they can be employed turn-finally (within their immediate sequential context) when delivered with a final intonation or other means such as non-verbal conduct which display finality.

In particular, this means that conjunctive particles can be directed either towards terminating a TCU or to indicate that the speaker intends to continue speaking beyond a conjunctive particle, thereby projecting a further component. Because of this dual possibility, there is an inherent "equivocality" with respect to the finality of conjunctive particles. As Hayashi (1997) notes,

> (n)ow, if clauses marked with *kara*, *kedo*, etc. are sometimes followed by main clauses, and sometimes not, it is possible that recipients of such clauses face the problem of ambiguity at the clause juncture regarding whether the speaker moves on to produce the main clause or not. (Hayashi 1997)

Building on previous work on these particles (e.g. Lerner and Takagi, to appear; Hayashi 1997; Ford and Mori 1994; Mori 1996b), examined below are features which are relevant for displaying and recognising the finality or non-finality of conjunctive particles depending on the sequential context and other aspects of the talk. As in the previous chapters, an investigation of collaborative completions is an optimal way to discover coparticipant orientations to this phenomenon. Parts of the following discussion relating to certain particles such as *dakara*, *kara*, and *kedo* have already been dealt with by Mori (1996b).[2] However, none of the research cited above has dealt systematically with the overall projectability properties associated with conjunctive particles.

6.4.1. *Turn-final position*

There appear to be at least two ways conjunctive particles are occasioned in a component-final position to signal the end of a turn. First, these particles can be employed at the end of a "subordinate" clause which is linked to some prior talk either produced by the speaker her/himself or by another participant (Mori 1996b). It is important to note, however, that the prior talk need not necessarily have occurred immediately before the production of the subordinate clause. In addition to such contextual linkages, speakers indicate that a conjunctive particle is being employed in a turn-final position by delivering it with a final intonational contour.

The following example illustrates a current speaker first producing a main sentence before attaching a subordinate clause. In this conversation with tragicomic overtones, a married couple W (wife) and H (husband) are talking about their marriage. W has been implying that she has only herself to blame for not having ended the marriage long ago. In the excerpt below, she continues in a bantering tone, that she even tried to recommend someone to her husband as a prospective wife to take her place. After extended laughter from coparticipants, H responds in lines 5 and 8 in a similarly playful manner:

(112) [Tokyo 7: 2] multiparty conversation, slightly simplified

1 W: *Datte ano toki dattara kare datte::*
after all that time if he even
'After all, if it was back then, even in his case'

2 *Atashi- ·hhh suisen made shita koto aru n dakedo na::,*
I recommend even made VN exist N although → FP
'although I even made a recommendation'

3 *ano kata to dattara ii n [jyanai ka to.* ((laughter))
that person with if good N [not P QUOT
'that if it was with that person, it would have been good ((for H to marry))'

[
4 (others) [((laughter for 2.9 seconds))

5 H:→ *Sonna no mō: jitsu ni motte ·hhh katte da to [boku omou.*
that P INT truly wilful COP QUOT [I think
'I think that is really truly wilful ((of her))'

```
6 ( ):                                                [
                                                      [('N:    )
                                                      [('Mm    ')

7 ( ):       heh heh heh heh ·hh heh heh

8 H: → dare datta ka mō      wasurechat [ta kedo. [Ahh hah [hah hah hah hah
       who COP  P  already forgot           although →
       'although I've already forgotten who it was'
                                          [
9 ( ):                                    [heh heh [heh heh
                                                   [
10 (many others):                                  [(laughter )]
```

In line 5, H initially constructs a main sentence, expressing his outrage towards his wife's actions. But after an intervening burst of laughter by a coparticipant in line 7, H continues by making light of this matter in line 8, claiming that he has already forgotten whom she had recommended as a replacement wife. Note that line 8, which is marked with the conjunctive particle *kedo* can be heard as a subordinate clause of the main sentence appearing in line 5 within the context of talk about his wife's "efforts" to try to find him another partner. Furthermore, the conjunctive particle is delivered with a falling intonation.

The fragment above illustrates a case of a post-predicate addition or "re-completer", whereby a subordinate clause Y ending with the conjunctive particle *kedo* 'although' occurs after the production of a complete turn X in line 5. In other words, Y extends the turn X by a clausal increment after the initial possible TRP at the end of line 5.

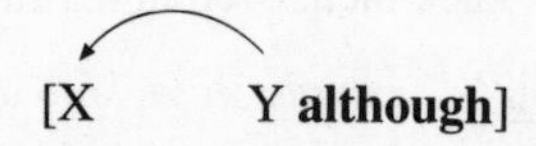

In this case, the conjunctive particle establishes a binomial retrospective link between the *although*-marked clause Y and a main sentence X produced earlier by the same speaker. To repeat, the final intonational delivery of the conjunctive particle (or other means to display finality) may be critical for participants to recognise Y as a recompleter of X.

Consider another instance, this time where a subordinate clause ending with a conjunctive particle links retrospectively to a prior speaker's talk:

(113) [Shakujii 1A (#1): 4] telephone conversation

A has rang Y to say that she has arrived at Y's house while Y was away. In the following portion, Y asks A if she intends to go home.

1 Y: → *Mata kaecchau* *no*
again going home FP
'Are ((you)) going home again?'

(1.4)

2 A: → *'N:: chotto yōji ga aru* ***kara*****::**.
yeah a little work NOM exist **CONJ** (because → therefore)
'Yeah, because ((I've)) got some work to do'

3 (.7)

4 Y: ↑'*N* (.) *Jya: denwa suru yo*
yeah then telephone do FP
'Yeah? then ((I))'ll call you ((sometime))'

To the question 'Are ((you)) going home again?', A answers with a subordinate clause ending with a conjunctive particle delivered with a final intonation: *'N:: chotto yōji ga aru* ***kara*****::**. 'Yeah, because ((I've)) got some work to do' in line 2. Furthermore, since this answer clearly links to the prior question by Y, it is treated by Y as complete and not requiring a second component, as evidenced by Y's next turn (line 4) which displays an understanding of A's utterance as a complete action. In the two examples shown above, not only are the subordinate clauses in question hearable as linked to a prior main sentence (either of the speaker or hearer), but the speaker also employs a falling intonation to indicate finality.

Secondly, conjunctive particles may also signal finality without any main sentence being expressed either before or after the subordinate clause ending with the particle (see Chapter 3; Mori 1996b; Hayashi 1997). In the following, the participants have been talking about an eventuality, with respect to which H comments that it is not something that one can do anything about. To this, W responds: 'if you had told me sooner'. The background of this fragment is provided in Chapter 3, Section 3.4.2.

(114) [Tokyo 7: 19] multiparty conversation, simplified

H: *Sore wa mō shōganai desu yo.*
that TOP any more nothing can be done COP FP
'There's nothing that can be done about it any more'

W: → *gg Motto hayaku itte ku[re re* ***ba***. **[X]**
more soon say CONJ: if → then
'If ((you)) had told ((me)) sooner'
[
others: [((laughter))

( ): (*Osoi ka*)
late QP
'Too late, is ((it))?' ((rhetorical question))

Notice that the "main clause" is not expressed at all in this instance but is left implicit. W does not continue after the conjunctive particle *ba*, and another participant begins to talk, displaying an understanding that W's turn is complete. The binomial linking in this case might be visualised as follows:

[X **if → then** ((Y)).]

where ((Y)) is the implicit "main" clause.

Consider another instance, where a speaker constructs a subordinate clause ending with a conjunctive particle, in which the next speaker begins speaking immediately. The participants have been talking about the possibility that K will go to visit a mutual acquaintance. In the following portion, Y expresses a hope to meet K there.

(115) [Shakujii 1A (#4): 13] telephone conversation

1 Y: (*De*) *mata*-=
and again
'(And) again'

2 K: ='*N*=
'Yeah'

3 Y: → =*ne*: *itta toki* [*ni aeru to ii n* ***dakedo*** *ne*.=
FP went when [P meet if good N **CONJ**: although→ FP
'Although it would be good if ((we)) could meet when ((you)) go there'
[
4 K: [*Sō*
['Right'

5 K: =*Sō da ne*:.=
right COP FP
'((It)) would be wouldn't ((it))'

In this example, Y ends line 3 with a conjunctive particle *dakedo* + final particle *ne* delivered with a final intonational contour. Again, even though no main clause is expressed, K displays an understanding that Y's turn is complete, by agreeing in line 5 with Y's statement in line 3.

The fragments above suggest that a combination of contextual factors and a turn-final intonational delivery of a conjunctive particle (or alternatively, some indicator of finality such as a conjunctive particle followed by a turn-final use of a final particle) appears to inform participants that a turn is possibly complete, even though the utterance-in-progress may be syntactically incomplete. Recall from Chapter 3, Section 3.4.2 that participants may also resort to non-vocal displays of finality such as closing one's mouth. The possibility that a first component can in some instances be treated as a complete action, therefore, implies that the feature of a conjunctive particle to potentially project further talk is not automatically implemented simply by virtue of its grammatical construction.

6.4.2. *Turn-internal positions*

The discussion above highlights a need to re-examine the situated employment of conjunctive particles, to gain an understanding of the implications of alternative possibilities with regard to participants' judgements of whether or not a conjunctive particle projects another unit. What aspects of the current speaker's utterance permit participants to differentially produce and recognise these two usages? Hayashi reports that productional features such as hitches and silences following a conjunctive particle are regularly taken as opportunities by coparticipants to engage in co-construction using this format (Hayashi 1997). It is likewise important to note that speakers seem to project a second component by delivering a conjunctive particle with a continuing intonation, or through other means that indicates that the speaker is not finished speaking.

To begin with, the following fragment (same as (110) above, but with revised notation for conjunctive particle) is re-inspected in order to identify some features which reveal that a second part is being projected.

(116) [Shakujii 1A 9: 13]

1 M: *Moshi*: *gg* >*zenzen teika de kacchat te*
if not at all list price at bought and

2 *yasuku nakatta n da:<*
was not cheap VN COP

3 → *to omowareta n* ***nara*** [*ne*
QUOT thought VN **if→then** [FP
[
4 H: ['*N* '*N*:=
['Yeah yeah'

Gloss of lines 1–3: 'If what she thought was that ((she)) had bought it at the list price and that it was not at all value for money, then'

5 M: =*Eg:g:* [*g:* ( ) *zan'nen da*]*kara*=
DF [unfortunate because→so
'((that)) would be unfortunate, so'
[ ]
6 H: → [*Sō suru to tsuman'nai kara ne*]
[then a shame because FP]
['Then ((that)) would be a shame'

In contrast to the cases examined in Section 6.4.1, the conjunctive particle *nara* 'if→then' in M's utterance (line 3) does not end with a turn-final intonation. Moreover, M indicates that he is going to continue by employing the final particle *ne* to elicit an acknowledgement from H in line 3 (see Tanaka to appear-c), as well as through the disfluency at the beginning of line 5. These productional features not only serve as an "unprojected opportunity" (Lerner 1996; Hayashi 1997) for H to co-complete the grammatically projected *then Y* component, but also indicates that M intends to continue speaking.

Consider another case involving a coparticipant completion of a clause which ends with a conjunctive particle. In the following fragment, the participants have been planning a forum to which they are hoping to ask various people to come to talk frankly about their experiences. G has just asked K (and another coparticipant) whether they know of anyone with whom they are on intimate terms, who can open their hearts and relate to one another. After a long silence of 12 seconds, K answers in a very tentative manner, employing many conditional clauses as shown below.

(117) [Tokyo 10A: 6] informal meeting

1 (12.0)

2 K: *Soko made wa osshatte kudasatte mo*
there until TOP say CONJ (even if→)

3 *sono ato ni nat te*
afterwards P become CONJ (and→)

4 *on'naji kotoba ga* ((gradually getting fainter))
same words NOM

5 (*dekiru*) *to wa kagirimasen desu shi*
can make P TOP not limited COP CONJ (although→and)

Gloss of lines 2–5: 'Even if they might reveal ((themselves)) to that extent, later on, ((it)) does not necessarily mean that ((they)) will continue to say the same words, and'

6 (3.5)

((faintly))
7 → *on'naji kurikaeshi jyanakute mo ii* ***keredo***,
same repetition not even if alright CONJ (although→)
'although it does not necessarily have to be a repetition of what ((they)) said'

8 (2.0)

9 G: → (*Futsū*) *on'naji jyanaku tatte*
normally same not even if
'(Normally), even if ((it))'s not the same'

10 *sore ni chikai hyōgen* [*de*(*aru*) *wake desho*?
that P close expression [COP reason COP
'((it)'ll be an expression which is close to that, wouldn't it'
[
11 K: [*Eh*::::::: *eh*:::
['Yes yes'

K displays much hesitation and tentativeness in presenting her solicited opinion, as indicated by the tone of her voice which gradually becomes fainter and fainter. Her tentativeness is further displayed in line 7 where K reverses what she had been saying up to that point. The conjunctive particle appearing at the end of line 7, however, is marked with a continuing intonation, which projects a further component to follow after *keredo* 'although'. There ensues a 2-second silence, which is taken as a chance by G to collaborate in constructing the TCU which has been left in limbo (cf. analysis of a similar case by Hayashi 1997). G does this (lines 9–10) by first rephrasing part of K's utterance in line 7, and continuing in line 10 with a projected second part to follow *keredo*.

Participants' treatment of a conjunctive particle as signalling finality or continuing talk, therefore appears to depend on the sequential context, the intonational contour (final or continuing), as well as on other features such as non-verbal behaviour. Now, a determination of whether a conjunctive particle is delivered with a final or non-final intonation is not fully ascertainable until the particle can actually be heard in its entirety. Although a more detailed study is required to verify the importance of prosody, the fact that coparticipants frequently wait for some time after a conjunctive particle can be heard before starting to speak (e.g. fragments (113), (116), and (117)) and the regular occurrences of short intervals of silence following the production of conjunctive particles (fragments (113) and (117)) are strong indicators that coparticipants are monitoring the delivery of the conjunctive particle for some characteristic which will help determine whether it is used turn-finally or to project further talk. This point is adumbrated by Lerner and Takagi (to appear):

> We are not suggesting that the non-finalness (or finalness) of a clause is always projectable. It may be that recipients (and speakers?) must sometimes wait until the clause-final particles have begun to be produced before it is possible for them (or professional analysts) can determine whether the imminent possible component completion is a TCU possible completion.

Recall also Hayashi's (1997) observation that the compound TCU syntactic structure does not seem to provide as robust an opportunity for coparticipant completion as is found to be the case in English. The ambiguity regarding the finality/non-finality of conjunctive particles may thus be relevant to the relatively reduced degree of effectiveness of this format for projecting compound TCUs in Japanese. The examples investigated here also provide further evidence that the grammatical structure of this format in itself is typically not treated as sufficient for participants to co-construct a further component (but see Section 6.6 for exceptions). The importance of prosodic contours in relation to the parsing of conjunctive particles should come as no surprise when syntax does not always serve as a reliable guide for determining whether a further component may be projected.

This brings us to the final crucial difference between the projectability of compound TCUs in the two languages. Whereas in English, participants can look towards the termination of the second component as a possible TRP, this is not necessarily the case in Japanese, where the second component may not end at a TRP, but another component projected before the second component comes to a completion. The next section considers the structure of these multi-unit TCUs and some possible implications for interactional styles in Japanese.

6.5. Conjunctive particles for an indefinite expansion of a TCU

The discussion thus far suggests that participants do attend to the role of conjunctive particles to binomially link two clauses when they are delivered with a continuing intonation. Certain conjunctive particles therefore share with compound TCUs in English at least the capacity to project a further component and to connect the first component with a second. When focusing on one conjunctive particle at a time as in the examples above, it may be possible to analyse the relation between components, and to map out the "subordinate-main" relationship between the corresponding clauses.

However, since a conjunctive particle occurs as the terminal item of one clause and before the second, i.e. between the first and second component, speakers can construct compound TCUs composed of a chain of components without passing through a possible TRP, through serial application:

X CONJ Y CONJ Z CONJ W . . .

This might allow an expansion as in the invented schema below:

X if→then Y because→therefore Z and W . . .
(*-tara*) (*dakedo*) (*-shi*)

The use of conjunctive particles therefore permits "iteration", i.e. potentially, an indefinite number of components can be linked in this way through a serial binomial linking of juxtaposed components, possibly resulting in an ambiguation of categories such as dependent-head. This operation is examined in some detail below, through a consideration of the construction of an extended compound TCU via a combination of turn-internal and turn-final deployments of conjunctive particles.

In the following fragment (also presented in Chapter 3, Section 3.4.2), the participants have been talking about W's marriage which W has been describing as problematic. K asks W if the latter feels that the institution of marriage or co-living itself is unjust. To this, starting in line 6, W constructs an elaborate disagreement, a dispreferred turn-shape involving many hesitations, pauses, restarts, as well as various accounts for why she disagrees. Nevertheless, W constructs her turn (lines 6–27) as one TCU through incremental additions. W's turn from lines 6 to 27 forms a single compound TCU, with conjunctive particles appearing at the end of lines 12, 14, 16, and 26 to serially project further components, and ends with a conjunctive particle signalling finality in line 27. Note that on the right hand side of this transcript, the letters [X], [X′], [X″], and [X‴] are used to stand for clauses analysable as subordinate clauses in the first instance, and [Y], [Y′], [Y″], and [Y‴] for the corresponding main clauses to which each of the subordinate clauses are respectively connected through a binomial relation. As will be discussed below, the equivalence [Y] = [X′] describes a situation where clause [Y] which might serve as the main clause for [X] can simultaneously be seen as a subordinate clause [X′] for a further main clause [Y′].

(118) [Tokyo 7 p. 1] simplified

1 K: *Nantonaku rifujin na kanji ga shi masu?* (.)
somehow unjust feeling NOM do SFX
'Does ((it)) somehow seem unjust?'

2 *sono* (.)
'the (.)'

3 *kekkon seido sono mono tte iu ka,=*
institution of marriage itself QUOT say or
'should ((I)) say, the institution of marriage itself or'

4 =*ma*:: *nan te iu ka,*
AP what QUOT say or
'uhm what shall ((I)) say'

5 [( ) *dōkyo sono mono ga.*
[living together itself NOM
['( ) living together itself'
[
6 W: [*Ss seido,* **[A]**
[institution
['the institution'

7 (1.0) **[A]**

8 ((slowly)) *ssseido sonomono* ***to iu***::, ·*hhh* (1.3) **[A]**
institution itself QUOT say
'((rather than?)) the institution itself ·hhh'

9 *datte ma*: ·*hhh*
because after all well
'because after all, well ·hhh'

10 *ssssss*: (.)

11 *seido no mondai yori* (.) **[X]**
institution GEN problem more than
'more than ((it being)) a problem of the institution (.)'

12 *min'na ga kojin kojin no mondai* ***dakara*** [↑*ne? ·hhhh* **[X]**
everyone NOM individual GEN problem because→so [FP
'because ((it))'s an individual problem for everyone, so you know ·hhhh'
[
13 K: [*Nnnnnnnn.*
['Mmmmmmm'

14 W: *kō ga yoi toka kō ga warui toka yuenai* ***kara,*** **[Y]=[X′]**
this NOM good e.g. this NOM bad e.g. can't say because→so
'because((one)) can't say if this way is good or that way is bad, so'

15 *atashi wa seido sono mono no mondai ·hhh* **[Y′]=[X″]**
I TOP institution itself GEN problem
'as for me, as for the problem of the institution of marriage itself ·hhh'

16 *mukashi wa* (.) <u>*atta*</u> ***kedomo*** [↑*ne?* (.7) **[Y′]=[X″]**
past TOP existed although→but [FP
'although ((I)) did have that problem in the past, but ((you)) know'
[
17 K: [((nodding))

18 W: *ima wa*, (3.0) **(lines 18–26)=[Y″]=[X‴]**
now TOP
'as for now'

19 *seido sonomono-* (.)
institution itself
'((as for)) the institution itself (.)'

20 (*ra*) *atakushi jishin to shite wa ima wa, ·hhh*
I myself QUOT do TOP now TOP
'as for me, at this point in time ·hhh'

21 *sss*: (.) *seido sono mono yorimo,*
institution itself more than
'more than the institution itself'

22 (1.0)

23 K: *Nnnn*
AP

24 (2.8)

25 W: ((looking at K)) *ma::: yappari ·hhhh* (.)
AP after all
'well after all ·hhhh (.)'

26 *oso sugita* **to** **iu ka**, *·hhh*
too late QUOT say or
'that it was too late, should ((I)) say, or that ·hhh'

27 → *jiki o* [*shisshita* **to** **iu ka.** ((closes mouth)) **[Y‴]**
timing ACC [missed QUOT say or
'the chance was [missed, should ((I)) say, or'
[
28 K: [((nodding)) '*N*:: '*N*:: .
'Mm Mm'

29 K: *Osoku umareta hiai mitaina desu* ↑*ka*?
late born woe like COP QP
'Is it something like the woe of having been born late?'

The marked beginning of W's reply in lines 6 to 8 (with restarts *ss seido* . . .) not only foreshadows a possible disagreement, but itself constitutes a part of the disagreement (see Ford and Mori 1994). Indeed, line 8 employs the format NP (nominal phrase) + case (quotative) particle *to* + *iu* 'say', which may be the beginning of something like 'rather than the institution of marriage . . . ', but the elements corresponding to *rather than* are left unexpressed: an implicit production of a dispreferred response. W restarts in line 9 with disagreement markers: *datte ma*: *·hhh* 'because after all well ·hhh' (see Ford and Mori 1994) and continues to produces a complex clause *ssssss*: (.) *seido no mondai yori* (.) *minna ga kojin kojin no mondai dakara* ↑*ne*? *.hhhh*' 'more than ((it being)) a problem of the institution, because it's an individual problem for everyone, so you know ·hhhh' in lines 10–12.[3] But at the end of this component, W does not bring the TCU to a possible completion with some utterance-final element such as in:

min'na ga kojin kojin no mondai ***desho***?
everyone NOM individual GEN issue COP
'((it))'s an individual problem for everyone, isn't ((it))?'

Instead, just where the copula *desho* in the invented ending above might have occurred, W produces a conjunctive particle *dakara* followed by a final particle ↑*ne*, which characterises lines 10–12 as a subordinate clause [X].

The first heuristic question we might ask is: where is the main clause or sentence for which [X] is a subordinate clause? One possibility is the truncated beginning of the disagreement in lines 6–8 (denoted by [A] in the transcript) which may implicate a turn-final use of this conjunctive particle *dakara*. However, through a continuing intonation and use of the final particle ↑*ne* to claim the floor at the end of line 12, W displays her intention to continue. The coparticipant K reciprocates by aligning as a recipient through the proffering of an acknowledgement (line 13). Thus, through the syntactic properties of this particle, W projects a second component Y of the shape [X because→so, Y] (English equivalent *because X–so Y*). Thus the 'main' clause could just as well be heard as [Y] in line 14.

The projected second component [Y] of the above binomial relation is then produced in line 14: 'because ((one)) can't say if this way is good or that way is bad, so'. However, since line 14 ends with a further conjunctive particle *kara* 'because →so' delivered with a continuing intonation, this line (i.e. [Y]) not only serves as the second component of [X], but is simultaneously designed as the preliminary component [X′] of a new compound structure [X′ because→so, Y′]. Hence, the notation [Y] = [X′]. Thus, at the end of line 14, another component [Y′] has been projected.

Continuing with the analysis of this fragment, the syntactically projected second component [Y′] seems to be produced in lines 15–16: 'as for me, as for the problem of the institution of marriage itself ·hhh, although ((I)) did have that problem in the past, but ((you)) know'. While fashioned as the second component [Y′] of [X′], however, the spate of talk in lines 15–16 concurrently serves as the preliminary component [X″] of a further compound structure [X″ although→but, Y″] through the appendage of a conjunctive particle *kedomo* 'although→but' towards the end of line 16, projecting yet another second component [Y″]. Indeed, the acknowledgement-soliciting use of ↑*ne* can again be heard as W's intention to continue speaking.

What appears to be the second component [Y″] is then produced in lines 18–26, which itself has a highly complex structure, as described below. Lines 18–21 is a slightly elaborated recapitulation of lines 6–11: 'as for now, ((as for)) the institution itself (.), as for me, at this point in time ·hhh, more than the institution itself'. Syntactically, each of these increments projects further nominals and predicate elements through the use of the topic particle *wa* in line 18, a cut-off in line 19, and again, the topic particle *wa* used twice in line 20 (see Chapter 5). After making these pre-starts, W produces a repetition of her original formulation *sss*: (.) *seido sono mono yorimo* 'more than the institution itself' in line 21. W's talk has returned full circle to 'the problem of the institution of marriage itself'. There is an intra-turn pause in line 22 (analysable as W's silence because W stops after projecting more talk), followed by an appositional in line 23, a further lengthy intra-turn pause of 2.8 seconds in line 24, and finally the "thrust" of the second component [Y″] begins to be produced in lines 25–26: 'well after all ·hhhh that it was too late, should

((I)) say, or that ·hhh'. But note that even as W is producing this component, she has projected a further unit [Y‴] through the postpositional attachment of the conjunctive particle *ka* 'or' at the end of line 26. Finally, the component projected by *ka* at the end of line 26 is produced in line 27: 'the chance was missed, should ((I)) say, or'. Again this line ends with the same conjunctive particle *ka*. On this occasion, however, the particle is delivered with a falling final intonation, followed by a gesture (closing mouth) through which W suggests she has stopped talking (see Chapter 3, Section 3.4.2). Thus, the highly elaborate compound TCU is now possibly complete in spite of the fact that the particle *ka* syntactically projects more talk.[4] The next speaker treats this as the end of W's turn, and starts to speak (line 29).

Summarising the analysis above, W's turn crudely consists of the chaining of four compound structures: [X because→so, Y], [X′ because→so, Y′], [X″ although→but, Y″], and [X‴ or Y‴] where [Y]=[X′], [Y′]=[X″], and [Y″]=[X‴]. Thus, as the turn progresses, the second component [Y] of the first compound TCU structure is transformed into the preliminary component [X′] of the second compound TCU structure, and likewise, the second component [Y′] simultaneously serves as the first component [X″] of the next compound TCU structure and so on, allowing the speaker to cumulatively link further components without passing through a possible TRP. It is only at the end of line 27 that it emerges that there will be no further components produced beyond [Y‴].

As a consequence of the identification: [Y]=[X′], [Y′]=[X″], and [Y″]=[X‴], what may have been designed as the main clause [Y] for the form [X because→so, Y] concurrently serves as the supposed subordinate clause [X′] for the form [X′ because→so, Y′]; similarly, the main clause [Y′] of the relation [X′ because→so, Y′] also acts as the supposed subordinate clause [X″] of the relation [X″ although→but, Y″], etc., resulting in an elaborate chaining of binomial relationships. Despite the complexity of the corresponding "logical relationships" that have been set up by these particles, the speaker W constructs the entire turn as an integral "package" addressing the initial question/comment made by K in lines 1–5 as to whether W considers the institution of marriage to be unjust. Likewise, even when faced with the elaborate string of clauses linked by conjunctive particles, the coparticipant K does not appear to treat the sequence as interactionally problematic.

When multiple components are attached in the above manner to form highly compounded TCUs, it is quite possible that participants may not necessarily be orienting to the analytical distinction "subordinate-main" for understanding the progressivity of the talk. Rather, from the point of view of the primacy of interactional concerns, participants may be parsing talk at each successive occurrence of conjunctive particle, and also in terms of whether the turn-so-far is designed to be final or non-final. This conjecture is further supported by Mori's observation:

> . . . the clauses marked by the connective particles may be produced as a unit, or even as a turn, or transfer of the speakership. That is, these clauses, which have been described as a "dependent" or "subordinate" clause, could be produced not as a unit preplanned with the corresponding "main" clause but as a unit planned rather "independently" as speakers make each contribution reflecting their moment-by-moment analysis of the interactional context. To this end, the classification such as "dependent" versus "independent", or "subordinate" versus "main" may require reevaluation in the analysis of conversational data. (Mori 1996b: 42–3)

Thus, the projectability properties of conjunctive particles can be utilised as a resource by speakers to incrementally add onto an ongoing TCU, syntactically linking each successive component with the next, more or less independently of a consideration of the strict logical link between the components. The potential equivocality of the finality (or non-finality) of conjunctive particles can also be exploited to continue or terminate a TCU-in-progress seemingly at will.

Finally, the next fragment (119) from an informal meeting at a voluntary organisation further illustrates some stylistic implications of the serial deployment of numerous conjunctive particles for forming a single TCU. The issues raised above (particularly the blurring of subordinate-main relations) become even more pertinent where a large number of components are involved. Recall that in the previous fragment, W employs conjunctive particles to build her turn, which as a whole, can be seen to be fitted as an answer to a question by a coparticipant. In contrast, the following fragment demonstrates how a current speaker may sometimes employ primarily the turn-holding feature of conjunctive particles with little apparent regard for their overall "logical" linking property. A speaker can make full use of these particles particularly when coparticipant speakership rights may be restricted, as seen in the systematic absence of acknowledgement tokens such as *'N* in the extract. The speaker G who happens to be the chairperson for this meeting, uses conjunctive particles liberally to extend her turn as she goes along.

In this meeting, the participants have been holding an editorial briefing to discuss plans for articles to be included in a forthcoming journal published by the organisation. The talk has revolved around the pros and cons of holding a forum based on which someone would be requested to produce an article and/or asking someone to write an article based on interviews. In the part shown below, the chairperson begins by engaging in a kind of summing-up of the session.

(119) [Tokyo 10A p. 9] Conjunctive particles indicated in boldface

1 G: °*Ma mo*::: ·*tz*::::° *do*: *tomokaku*::: **[A]**
((pre-starts)) anyway
'Anyway'

2 *gutaika shite ika na kya nara nai:: wake* **dakara** *·hhh* **[A]**
go on to concretise must reason **because→therefore**
'**because** ((we)) must go on to concretise ((this)), **therefore** ·hhh'

3 *soshite:: (.) sono hon o tsukuri* ***naga↑ra=*** **[B]**
and that book ACC make **while→**
'and **while** making that book'

4 *=yappari otagai ni benkyō dekiru to omou n* ***de*** *·hh* **[C]**
after all mutually P study can do P think VN **since→so**
'after all, **since** ((I)) think((we can)) learn from each other, **so**'

5 *ano::g (1.0) ma kyō mo sō desu* ***kedomo=*** **[D]**
uhm well today ADVP such COP **although→**
'**although** well, ((that)) can also be said of today'

6 *=sōiu koto ni yotte ironna koto ga* (.) **[E]**
that kind thing P through various things NOM

7 *kō hatsugen mo at tari* **[E]**
in this way expression ADVP exist and/or

8 *wakatte iku wake* ***dakara***: ·hhh (2.0) **[E]**
come to understand reason **since→therefore**

Gloss for lines 6–8: '**since** through such things, various things ((come about)) such as the expression of opinions and/or ((deepening our)) understanding, **therefore**'

9 *hashira to shite wa* (.) **[F]**
pillar P be as TOP
'as a pillar (.)'

10 *kore mo ankeeto mo hitotsu dasu desho*? **[F]**
this ADVP questionnaire ADVP one submit COP
'((we)) would for one also be submitting this questionnaire, won't ((we))?'

The fragment above is constructed as a single TCU which is a concatenation of binary relations created through serial linking of six components [A] to [F] through conjunctive particles. The formal "logic" traced by the use of these conjunctive particles can be roughly described as follows:

[A] because→therefore, [B] while→, [C] since→so, [D] although→,
[E] since→therefore, [F]

The chairperson G uses these particles to link up the components to expand a single TCU locally and consecutively, without having to claim a new TCU.

After stating that the group needs to firm up the plans in [A], G extends her turn by employing the conjunctive particle *dakara* 'because→therefore' without a final intonation, but followed by an in-breath to display that more talk is to follow. On the basis of the analyses in the foregoing sections, this conjunctive particle shapes lines 1–2 or [A] as a subordinate clause, and simultaneously projects a 'therefore' component (at the end of [A]). But it appears that the projected component is not produced at this point. Instead, G simply exploits the turn-extending property of the particle to maintain her speakership rights, and goes on to insert a somewhat unrelated expression *and while making that book*, beginning with *shoshite*:: 'and' which formulates [B] as something other than the projected second component.

This last clause [B] projects another clause through the adjunction of the conjunctive particle *naga↑ra* 'while→' which is again produced with a continuing intonation. Indeed, G raises the pitch at the end of *naga↑ra*—thereby avoiding a turn-final intonation – and continues to latch on the next component [C] without any break. In this instance, however, the clause [C] projected by *naga↑ra* does ensue immediately: 'after all, since ((I)) think that ((we can)) learn from each other, so'. In sum, after G projects a component at the end of clause [A], she defers its production, and changes course by inserting in its place another format [B] while→[C]: 'and while making that book, after all, since ((I)) think ((we)) can learn from each other, so'.

But again, [C] is extended with a conjunctive particle <u>de</u> 'since→so' which is used to project a further component through a non-final intonation followed by an in-breath *·hh*. As analysed for fragment (118), the next clause [D], 'although well, ((that)) can also be said of today', which ends with the conjunctive particle *kedomo* 'although→' can be seen simultaneously as the main clause projected by <u>de</u> at the end of [C], but also perhaps as a plausible subordinate clause of an ensuing main clause [E]: 'since through such things, various things ((come about)) such as the expression of opinions and/or ((deepening our)) understanding, therefore'. Further, the clause [E] also ends with a non-final use of a conjunctive particle *daka<u>ra</u>*: 'therefore' and an in-breath, which is followed by a candidate "main" sentence [F]: 'as a pillar (.) ((we)) would for one also be submitting this questionnaire, won't ((we))?'.

Now, it is possible to analyse this last sentence [F] either as the component projected by [E] as just suggested, or possibly as the "deferred" component projected by the first clause [A] in G's turn. In the latter case, it is plausible that G is proposing the questionnaire as one way to concretise the plan for the journal. Such alternative possibilities for parsing can make it hazardous for the analyst and perhaps also for participants to "tease out" the intended "logical" linkage between and among the various components which are progressively foreshadowed by the multiple use of conjunctive particles. Needless to say, a more extensive and detailed examination of other cases where coparticipants' understandings are displayed in interaction is required to better appreciate how participants process the logical implications of complex turns composed through many conjunctive particles.

Apart from such potential difficulties, this fragment clearly demonstrates the utility of conjunctive particles to incrementally expand the size of a turn under construction. At each invocation of a conjunctive particle, G employs a variety of techniques to specify that it is intended as a turn-internal occurrence. First, none of the conjunctive particles in this fragment is delivered with a turn-final intonation. Secondly, an in-breath repeatedly follows a conjunctive particle, as in [A], [C], and [E]. Third, the component syntactically projected by a conjunctive particle is sometimes latched onto the particle, as in [B] and [D], thereby discouraging others from beginning to speak. Finally, a clear rising intonation may be employed to signal that the conjunctive particle is not employed turn-finally, as exemplified in [B].

In the above manner, a speaker can exploit the turn-holding feature and the prospective and retrospective linking properties of these particles to connect an unspecified number of clauses to gradually and freely build up the talk within one TCU. Moreover, the combined use of conjunctive particles with case and adverbial particles (see Chapter 5)—as in this fragment—allows a speaker to construct highly intricate turns, which give rise to the dual possibility of an articulation of complex logical relationships and/or an ambiguation of the logical relationships which are created within a turn.

The examples in this section point to an important difference between the mobilisation of the compound TCU format in the respective languages to construct turns and to project a possible TRP. As mentioned previously, in English, the completion of the first component can signal that a second component may be produced next. Moreover, participants parse talk for the arrival of the end of the second component as a potential completion point of the two-part format in English. On the other hand, Japanese participants must first of all determine whether or not the end of the first component projects a second component by examining the contextual features and prosodic delivery of the conjunctive particle marking the end of the first component (or other indicators of "finality"). Even in the event the current speaker starts to produce a second component, a TRP may still not be imminent, as there is an additional possibility that the attachment of another conjunctive particle at the end of the second component may be used to further extend the current TCU. Thus, the projectability properties even in cases of speaker-continuation may be limited to the local projection of one more component, which may not necessarily be the final component of the compound TCU-in-progress.

Summarising the points made so far, the postpositional use of conjunctive particles in Japanese means that: (a) no pre-planning is necessary at the beginning of a component to implement this type of expansion. This grammatical property of conjunctive particles permits participants to construct multi-part formats such that (b) any number of components (within practical limits) can be locally and serially projected by these particles without passing through a possible TRP. Furthermore, it has been suggested that (c) the distinction between preliminary component and final component can be blurred when many components are connected. Thus, while compound TCUs in English typically enable participants to project one further component and a possible TRP on its completion, conjunctive particles can be employed to consecutively connect juxtaposed components into one compound TCU, as a cumulative "logical" linking of two or more components, while "indefinitely" suspending the occurrence of a TRP. Therefore, while the capacity of conjunctive particles to project a possible TRP may be more limited than in English, they are nevertheless a major strategy that Japanese participants can employ for claiming extended units of talk.

6.6. Conjunctive particles for social action

In spite of the aforementioned equivocality inhering in the mobilisation of conjunctive particles, it is also the case that participants may choose to disregard potential ambiguities in the interests of setting or influencing the course of talk. In the following fragment from an informal meeting, the members have been talking about suitable people who can be requested to write an article for their organisation. G has just been saying that unless one is cautious in selecting whom to ask, things could get out of hand. Immediately before the portion shown below, S starts to talk about some trouble she had when she asked some clients of the organisation to engage in such an exercise.

(120) [Tokyo 10A: 5] informal meeting, slightly simplified

1 S: *Sorede chotto kaite itadaita kata mo atta n* ***dakedo***=
and a little had write person ADVP existed VN although→
'And although ((I)) had some people write a little ((piece))'

2 G: =*Demo kai- kaku no wa*
but wri- write P TOP
'But as for writing'

3 → ↑*dō*[*mo*: *umaku nai wa* [*ne*:::
rath[er not adept FP [FP
'((they)) don't seem to be very adept'
[[

4 S: → [*Kaku no wa dame mitai* [((*nod to G*))
[write P TOP no good seems
[‘((They)) seem to be no good at writing’

S begins to say ‘And although ((I)) had some people write a little ((piece))’ in line 1, with the conjunctive particle *dakedo* in the component-final position. This occurrence of *dakedo* seems to provide an optimal opportunity for G to begin speaking (line 2), to reinforce her earlier view concerning the difficulty of selecting a candidate to write an article. Notice that G enters (by latching her turn to the end of S’s utterance) before she has a chance to fully ascertain the prosodic contour of the conjunctive particle *dakedo* ‘although→’.

Likewise, in the following fragment, the onset of the conjunctive particle *tara* ‘if→then’ provides an occasion for a coparticipant to complete the current speaker’s turn. Here, the parties are discussing whom to ask to lead an informal forum. In particular, they are debating on the merits of asking Mr Ueda. Prior to the following excerpt, some of the participants have been raising a drawback: that Mr Ueda sometimes gets carried away, as though he has a tremendous amount of pent-up energy. However, H mentions that the saving grace is that Mr Ueda at least knows where to stop. Then H continues below ‘if that ((the state of being carried away)) continues a long time’ employing *tara* ‘if→then’. Given the context of the prior talk, the onset of the particle *tara* serves as an opportunity for S to join in by collaborating in producing a second component: ‘((it)) would be serious, quite serious, wouldn’t it?’:

(121) [Tokyo 10 3: 12] informal meeting
H: . . . *are ga nagaku tsuzui* ***ta**[**ra*** *taihen nan dakedo*
that NOM long continue **if→then** serious N although→but
‘. . . if that continues a long time, then ((it)) would be serious, but’
[
S: [*Taihen taihen* ↑*ne*::
[serious serious FP
[‘((It)) would be serious, quite serious,
wouldn’t it?’

Again, not only does H come in before the final prosodic contour of the conjunctive particle *tara* (‘if→then’) can be heard, but even before the particle is produced in its entirety. These two examples demonstrate that participants are ultimately free to choose whether or not to attend to the possible equivocality and indeterminacy of a particular employment of a conjunctive particle.

6.7. Closing comments

The compound TCU format provides a prime example of the early projectability of turn-shapes in English. It indicates at the outset of a turn, the probable shape of the turn, and roughly how it may unfold before the turn reaches a possible TRP. This format is therefore a robust way of syntactically projecting a further unit in English. In contrast, it was shown that conjunctive particles are a retroactive and *ad hoc* device occasioned at the end of a component to possibly (but not necessarily) project a further component. When a conjunctive particle is heard, coparticipants must resolve the initial ambiguity by examining several features to determine how it is likely to develop within the immediate sequential context. First, it is necessary to ascertain whether the conjunctive particle is produced in a way which displays that the turn is coming to an end, or alternatively, if the speaker intends to continue speaking, thereby projecting a possible second component which is fitted to the first component. Since participants cannot rely on syntax alone for the determination of finality, contextual, prosodic, and other productional features may be crucial for projecting the trajectory of the talk. Moreover, even when a second component begins to be produced, its probable completion does not always provide a place to project a TRP, since speakers regularly replicate the above procedure by employing a further conjunctive particle at the end of the second component. Therefore, although the occurrence of a conjunctive particle can sometimes locally project at least one more component, there is no guarantee that such a component will culminate as the final component which will be produced within the space of a current TCU. It appears that coparticipants parse each occurrence of a conjunctive particle within a stream of talk independently and incrementally as it is produced, for an indication of whether or not more talk is projected. Furthermore, the consecutive employment of these particles can retroactively and serially convert successive emerging "main" clauses into subsequent "subordinate" clauses. It is also possible that a multiple compound-TCU terminates with a conjunctive particle (as in fragment (118)), so that grammatically, every clause which is produced is subsequently recast as a subordinate clause without any expressed main clause.

The fragments examined in this chapter cumulatively lead to a similar conclusion about interactional styles in Japanese as in the preceding chapter. In one sense, the compound TCU is a format that participants can exploit for projecting and influencing the course of talk through a "logical" linking of components. However, its inherent equivocality and flexibility may also be directed towards producing elusive interactional styles which may reveal little about the probable trajectory of a turn-in-progress.

Notes

1. Therefore, even though the turn-initial *Moshi* 'if' may not be redundant interactionally, it is redundant from the point of view of syntax.
2. Some conjunctive particles such as *dakara* and *demo* regularly occur as connectives at the beginning of a turn (Mori 1996b), but will not be discussed here.
3. After restarting *ssssss*: *seido* 'the institution of marriage' in lines 10–11, the next spate of talk 'more than it being a problem of the institution' ends with a case particle *yori* 'more than' which not only projects a further component, but forshadows a component of a specific type: [A]-more than, [B] (English equivalent: *more than* [A]–[B]). The projected component B occurs in line 12: 'because it's an individual problem for everyone . . .'.
4. By ending with a conjunctive particle *ka*, W has in effect circumvented a direct disagreement with K's suggestion. If instead, W had used utterance-final elements at the terminal boundary of her turn, W may have had to overtly "take a stand", as in the imagined:

   line 25 *jiki* *o* [*shisshita to* *iu* ***koto desu***
   timing ACC [missed QUOT say VN COP
   'the chance was [missed, that is to say.'

   However, W manages her "disagreement" with K without making her stand explicit, by incorporating an "uncertainty-marked" turn-design: 'that it was too late, should I say, or that the chance was missed, should I say, or'. The disagreement has been downgraded by avoiding finishing with utterance-final elements, and instead terminating with the conjunctive particle *ka*.

Chapter 7

Concluding remarks

The complex interpenetration of grammar, prosody and social interaction has been investigated through a comparison of turn-taking in Japanese and Anglo-American English. Social action is realised in talk through an interplay of communicative resources and, conversely, the vicissitudes of such realisations have further implications on action. This chapter summarises the main results and possible implications of the findings, and indicates some areas for future research.

7.1. The applicability of Sacks, Schegloff, and Jefferson's Model of Turn-Taking to Japanese

The model of turn-taking for English proposed by Sacks, Schegloff, and Jefferson (1974) (SSJ) served as the starting-point for exploring potentially generalisable and culturally specific features of turn-taking with reference to Japanese talk-in-interaction. In contrast to other major models of turn-taking mentioned in this study, SSJ's model is characterised as a context-free and context-sensitive system, through a distillation of the essential generic structures without "reference to one or another aspect of situatedness, identities, particularities of content or context" (p. 699). Chapter 2 has suggested that the rudimentary components (turn-construction and turn-allocation) and rules of SSJ's turn-taking system are manifest in broadly similar ways in Japanese, adding to the list of languages which are compatible with the model. In either socio-linguistic context, there are common interactional problems to be resolved, such as the projection of TRPs and the management of transitions from the current to the next speaker. The turn-taking mechanism exhibits a capacity to orchestrate the diversity of locally available resources for the performance of such interactional objectives. Thus, for Japanese, projectability of TRPs is possible; turn-allocation techniques also operate on a local, turn-by-turn basis, and are organised along a similar order of priority as identified in SSJ. Turn-taking in Japanese is likewise seen to be an "interactionally managed system" fitted to the performance of social action as its primary goal. On this basic level, then, the turn-taking organisations in Japanese and English can be said to be more or less congruent.

However, the particular set of communicative resources that participants have at their disposal in the respective socio-linguistic environments can lead to somewhat distinctive realisations (grammatical and otherwise) in the achievement of these generalised tasks, which in turn, can have further interactional implications. According to SSJ,

> it remains the case that examination of any particular materials will display the context-free resources of the turn-taking system to be employed, disposed in ways fitted to particulars of context. It is the context-free structure which defines how and where context-sensitivity can be displayed; the particularities of context are exhibited in systematically organized ways and places, and those are shaped by the context-free organization. (SSJ: 699, n. 8)

In this sense, the context-sensitive manifestations of the turn-taking operations are inseparable from their context-free structure. SSJ further point to the possibility that features of the local contextual fabric can "selectively" and "locally" affect the turn-taking system itself (p. 700) while leaving invariant its basic structure. Arguably, it is precisely because divergent resources in the respective socio-linguistic contexts are enlisted for accomplishing similar basic objectives that specific turn-taking practices may exhibit differences. Linguistic structure (and grammar in particular) is an integral strand in this contextual fabric which the turn-taking apparatus both accommodates and is shaped by. Accordingly, much of the book has dealt with possible differences in turn-taking practices resulting from the divergent host materials participants can avail themselves of in accomplishing the basic turn-taking operations. Outlined below are the main findings of this inquiry and areas for future research.

7.2. Distribution of syntactic, intonational, and pragmatic completion points

Chapter 3 investigated the statistical distribution of syntactic, intonational, and pragmatic completion points and their association with speaker change in Japanese through a comparison with the original study for American English by Ford and Thompson (1996) (F&T). The attempt to operationalise criteria for measurement in Japanese was beset with complications from the outset. First, operationalising the notion of syntactic completion in Japanese compatible with F&T's definition for English turned out to be unfeasible. Furthermore, this exercise highlighted the difficulty of conceptualising syntactic completion separately from a consideration of prosodic, intonational, and pragmatic factors. The method of operationalisation of syntactic completion employed for both English and Japanese would certainly benefit from refinement in the future, for instance through further clarification of the differences between analytic and conversational syntactic completion.

However, a comparison of F&T's study for conversations in American English with Japanese conversational data revealed a number of differences in the relative distribution of the various types of completion points. For English, F&T report that syntactic completion points occurred about twice as often as intonational and pragmatic completion points, but when intonational or pragmatic completion points occurred they were almost always accompanied by syntactic completion. Further, a strong correlation was found between the convergence of the three completion points (termed "complex transition relevance places" or CTRPs) and instances of speaker change. F&T therefore conclude that CTRPs are oriented to as possible TRPs by speakers in English.

In the case of the Japanese data, syntactic completion points occurred with much less frequency than in English, and matched more closely the numbers of intonational and pragmatic completion points. The results for Japanese accorded with F&T's findings in so far as Japanese participants also seem to orient to CTRPs as possible TRPs. However, there was a small but significant number of pragmatic completion points which were *not* accompanied by syntactic completion—a class of completion points which was practically non-existent in the reported results for English. Moreover, this further set of completion points was also shown to have a high correlation with speaker change in Japanese. In other words, *all* pragmatic completion points (and not just CTRPs) were identified as likely candidates for possible TRPs in Japanese.

An important difference which is suggested from the above-mentioned comparison of F&T's findings for American English and the results of the corresponding study for Japanese, then, is that possible TRPs in English almost always occur at syntactically complete points, but that potential TRPs in Japanese include points which are syntactically complete as well as some which are syntactically incomplete. A noteworthy implication of this contrast for turn-taking is that Japanese participants cannot always rely on syntactic completion as a concomitant indicator that a turn may be coming to an end. This finding was further substantiated in Chapter 6, where it was shown that syntactically incomplete turns in Japanese ending with conjunctive particles are contingently treated as complete turns.

A more detailed analysis of the turn-shapes of pragmatically complete turns in the Japanese data revealed an extraordinary degree of orderliness towards their terminal boundaries. First, the syntactically complete variety (CTRPs) consisted of turns which could roughly be classified into three types depending on their turn-ending designs: (i) those terminating with utterance-final elements (e.g. items such as copulas, final suffixes, and final particles) accounting for 62.6 per cent of all pragmatically complete turns; (ii) recompleters, consisting of 10.5 per cent of pragmatically complete turns; or (iii) the *iikiri* (truncated) form without utterance-final elements, making up 14 per cent of pragmatically complete turns. Secondly, (iv) the use of "extensions" to produce syntactically incomplete turns amounted to 11.7 per cent of all pragmatically complete turns. These figures indicate that a majority of CTRPs (and pragmatically complete turns more generally) do seem to be designed through the use of utterance-final elements, though a substantial minority are not. At present, it is not known how representative of Japanese conversation this breakdown may be. Again, this question must be carried forward to future research on a larger data set.

Though this is speculative at this stage, it was further hinted that pragmatically complete turns which are syntactically complete (or CTRPs) in Japanese are specifically fashioned to perform further social actions towards the terminal boundary of a turn including what may be called "relational work": e.g. instantiations of identity, gender, status; formulations of context along levels of formality; display of relationality between the speaker and others; display of stance, etc. (see Tanaka 1996 for a preliminary study). In other words, CTRPs can be designed to incorporate various explicit displays of relationality through the selective deployment or absence of utterance-final elements. On the other hand, pragmatically complete turns which are not accompanied by syntactic completion appear to be designed to minimise relational displays or to engage in delicate interactional tasks such as the creation of innuendoes (leaving implicit some consequence of an action). It thus appears that syntax can be managed by Japanese conversationalists for a differential display of relationality and degrees of directness. Whereas syntactic completion performs something that might be called "relational completion", syntactically incomplete turns can be associated with the minimisation of "overt" relational work. However, additional study is still required to extend the preliminary observations made here in order to gain a deeper understanding of the interactional and contextual implications of these turn-shapes.

7.3. Grammar and turn-taking: Projection of TRPs and the progressivity of turns

One of the core features of the turn-taking system providing for an orderly achievement of speaker change is the possibility of projecting the progressivity of a turn and the initial point when a turn might come to an end (i.e. the projection of possible TRPs). Chapters 4 to 6 dealt with some of the major consequences that the grammatical structure of Japanese may have on the projectable patterns of the unfolding of turns and turn-terminations in comparison with past findings relating to English. It has been noted for English that the canonical Subject-Verb-Object grammatical structure coupled with the relatively fixed word ordering overwhelmingly (though not necessarily) result in an early projection of the type of turn being produced, the action performed by a turn, as well as the likely point at which an initial TRP may arrive.

By way of contrast, aspects of Japanese grammar can sometimes render the progress of a turn more difficult to anticipate (relative to English), and therefore can delay the point at which a possible TRP can be projected. Importantly, (i) the use of postpositional particles which retroactively specify the grammatical sense of some spate of talk already produced, (ii) the possibility of employing various other suffixes to transform incrementally the grammatical form and hence the action trajectory of a turn-in-progress, and (iii) the predicate-final orientation, cumulatively imply that there may not be sufficient information towards the beginning of a turn for participants to anticipate what type of turn is emerging or what kind of action a turn may be performing. These features massively result in delayed projectability in Japanese.

This propensity for the incremental transformation of turn-shapes and delayed projectability in Japanese was further demonstrated through an examination of the properties of case and adverbial particles for projecting the unfolding of a turn in Chapter 5 and the employment of conjunctive particles for extending or terminating a turn in Chapter 6. These postpositional particles can be used to create an elaborate set of binomial relations, each incrementally projecting at least one further increment of talk through the linking of (i) a nominal with another nominal (certain case particles), (ii) a nominal with a predicate (certain case or adverbial particles), or (iii) a clause with another clause or sentence (conjunctive particles). Case, adverbial, and conjunctive particles can thus foreshadow the production of a further component by creating a binomial retrospective and prospective link between an item marked by the particle and some item not yet produced, thereby projecting a further increment. Alternatively, they can also function in the reverse direction for constructing recompleters by linking the item marked with some expression produced earlier. These particles (either in expressed or unexpressed form) inform participants of the moment-to-moment unfolding of a turn, which can at the minimum indicate if further components are still due.

More specifically, case and adverbial particles are critical tools for the projection of the incremental progressivity of a current turn. As one evidence for their significance for turn-projection, an examination of instances where these particles are unexpressed indicated that the trajectory of an emergent turn can remain equivocal. However, when these particles are physically present, they can provide a robust guide for coparticipants to anticipate one further increment of a turn-in-progress. Other examples indicated that participants frequently exploit these particles either to establish or modify the trajectory of talk. In spite of their utility for projecting a further increment of talk, it was also argued that the appearance of a case or adverbial particle does not necessarily contribute to either projecting the location within a turn where a projected component may be produced, or the ultimate trajectory of a turn.

The use of conjunctive particles to construct compound TCUs in Japanese can result in different patterns of turn-projection of multi-unit turns in the two languages. In English the compound TCU format is a pre-emptive strategy, realisable through the turn-initial placement of items such as *if* in *if X*, which foreshadows the production of a second component *then Y* (likewise for related formats such as *when X–Y* or *because X–Y*). According to Lerner (1991, 1996), this syntactic format strongly projects a second component, and the occurrence of a possible TRP on its termination. Furthermore, the fact that items such as *if* or *when* need to be placed at the beginning of the first component for the implementation of this format implies that a maximum of two main components can be projected (with a possible expansion of the first component).

In contrast, there are several factors which restrict the capacity of conjunctive particles (e.g. *dakara*, *kedo*, *kara*, *de*, *ba*) in Japanese to project a further component or to foreshadow the occurrence of a possible TRP at the end of a second component, if one is produced at all. First, conjunctive particles are occasioned post-positionally to characterise a clause retrospectively as a possible first part of a compound TCU. Secondly, conjunctive particles can be employed either to project a further component or to terminate a turn-in-progress after the first component (the latter type representing an example of a pragmatically complete but syntactically incomplete ending, as discussed in Chapter 3). Japanese participants therefore need to inspect the prosodic delivery of the particle, the contextual particulars, and other displays, to discover which of the alternative uses of conjunctive particles is intended in a particular case. Furthermore, the placement of these particles in component-final positions (together with their prospective and retroactive binomial linking property) opens up a combined possibility of an indefinitely extendible internal expansion of a turn, through the incremental and *ad hoc* addition of multiple components without passing through a TRP. One implication of this grammatical structure which contrasts with English is that recipients (and possibly speakers) cannot always project an eventual arrival of a possible TRP even after the recognisable onset of the second component.

The findings above might be fed into a future cross-linguistic study of the occurrence of "inadvertent" overlaps when multi-unit turns are constructed. When conjunctions such as *and* or *or* are employed in English to extend a current turn by connecting two sentences, the first component typically passes through a point of syntactic completion, after which another sentence can be attached. Therefore, unless some pre-emptive strategy is employed to project an extended turn, conjunctions in English may be vulnerable to "inadvertent" overlap as they regularly occur *after* a possible TRP. On the other hand, Japanese speakers can exploit the property that conjunctive particles (including the corresponding conjunctions *te* (and) and *ka* (or)) can bypass possible TRPs when they are used to connect multiple components into one TCU. Although speculative at this stage, this feature of conjunctive particles may lead to a minimisation of inadvertent overlaps in the construction of multi-component turns in Japanese (because a new increment is projectable *before* the arrival of a possible TRP). It is hoped that these possible consequences of differences in grammatical realisations of conjunctions in the respective languages can be explored in greater depth through an examination of a larger corpus of materials.

Returning to the main line of argument, because of the relative opaqueness of the trajectory of a turn and the incremental transformability of an emerging turn-shape, Japanese participants typically await clear grammatical or prosodic cues that a turn is coming to a completion; these cues are typically produced either shortly before or just as a turn reaches a possible TRP. First, the situated deployment of utterance-final elements (e.g. certain combinations of grammatical elements such as verb-suffixes, copulas, and final particles) is strongly oriented to as marking a possible TRP. Participants can co-ordinate smooth transitions from the current to next speaker with reference to the onset of such elements. Another class of turn-endings in Japanese consists of the *iikiri* (truncated) format, distinguished by an absence of utterance-final elements. These turn-endings, however, are regularly marked by pronounced prosodic contours (e.g. stressing, clipping, stretching), and appear to be oriented to as a suspension of the relevance of utterance-final elements. Thus, the commonly delayed projectability of a possible TRP and the shape of an unfolding turn in Japanese is compensated for by these turn-ending devices which contribute to the precise localisation of TRPs—once they do become imminent. The turn-endings classified in Chapter 3 can therefore be seen to exhibit an even greater degree of orderliness and significance for turn-taking than can be anticipated simply on the basis of the statistical study.

In sum, whereas important displays permitting the projectability of turn-development, the action(s) performed by a turn, and the initial TRP are found toward the beginning of a turn in English, many of these displays are concentrated towards the vicinity of the end of a turn in Japanese. As one implication of this anti-symmetric turn-structure, English conversationalists have relatively less freedom to change the course of a turn once it has begun without passing through a possible TRP; while Japanese speakers have numerous resources to revise the trajectory of talk before a turn comes to a possible completion.

7.4. Turn-taking, grammar, and styles of interaction

Finally, I return to reconsider some common conceptions held about Japanese patterns of interaction (*Nihonjinron*) in relation to the findings of this investigation. The analysis conducted in this book has highlighted some of the consequences of grammar on the projection of possible TRPs, the incremental construction of turns, and the internal expansion of turns, etc. One key to approaching cultural similarities and differences in social interaction may lie in regarding conversational syntax as a resource which participants contingently select, adapt, and exploit in situated interaction. I would like to end this book with some speculations on features of Japanese grammar and interaction which may have relevance to images of Japanese interaction as illogical, ambiguous, indirect, affiliative, etc., and also point to areas for future research.

In one sense, the syntactic resources available in Japanese seem to allow participants to engage in intendedly "logical" and "unequivocal" styles of discourse. For instance, case particles are capable not only of specifying the case of a nominal element, but also of indicating the "logical" relationship of a nominal to an ensuing nominal or predicate element. Conjunctive particles conjoin clausal components while also indicating the "logical" connection between the components. In terms of turn-projection, these particles can be enlisted to provide a "running commentary" of the progressivity of a turn through the binomial linking of various components of a turn. Moreover, the predicate-final structure and the consequent delayed projectability of turns can be considered as an in-built mechanism to motivate coparticipants to monitor carefully the progress of a turn, as the thrust is overwhelmingly left for the end of a turn—which can itself remain non-projectable until imminent. In this connection, since "critical" interactional work can be reserved for the terminal boundaries of turns, turn-beginnings may be exploited as places in which to engage in ground preparation such as stating caveats, making qualifications, setting the stage and stating the rationale for a forthcoming statement. Such preliminary tasks, moreover, can be accomplished without passing through TRPs, as it is possible to project more talk as one proceeds through the use of postpositional particles and other elements, contributing to forestalling others' attempts to appropriate the floor. Although detailed empirical work is necessary, it may be that these devices provide a greater degree of freedom or control to avoid or insert possible TRPs within talk in Japanese in comparison to English (e.g. through the avoidance of syntactic completion points). Owing to possibly expanded opportunities for engaging in explanatory work prior to taking a stand, potential misunderstandings, disagreements, and the like may be circumvented. Such features appear to render Japanese into a language which is not only "rational" but "efficient" for the purposes of social interaction.

Seen from another angle, however, the very features mentioned above may arguably be conducive to seemingly "illogical" and "ambiguous" talk. As the trajectory of talk can be structured to "develop" over the course of a turn, it may mean that relatively little pre-planning of the shape of a turn is required when starting turns at talk. Further, since there may be little expectation of an early projectability of the design or possible ending of an emerging turn, Japanese speakers can gradually build up a point, adjoining numerous elements, components, etc. As a result, there is a possibility that elements which are projected early in a turn do not get produced, but may be abandoned or cut short, as exemplified in Chapters 5 and 6. Moreover, since particles are postpositioned and link units prospectively and retrospectively, there is theoretically no limit to how many elements may be connected in this way before a turn is brought to an eventual completion. The possibility of an indefinite expansion of a turn (without passing through a TRP) may therefore engender long, winding, and ambiguous (if not seemingly illogical) arguments.

The image that the Japanese talk in an allusive, circumscribed, and indirect manner may be associated with similar turn-constructional possibilities. As mentioned above, the greater scope for accomplishing preliminary work before the onset of a predicate—and hence before the first possible TRP is reached—may render the beginnings of turns into optimal locations for the placement of "pre-pres" (see Levinson 1983) such as pre-delicates, pre-invitations, pre-disagreements, etc. The grammatical structure of Japanese is particularly amenable to the accomplishment of such operations prior to the performance of actions foreshadowed by these items, such as taking a stand on a topic being discussed. Indeed, the production of negative markers, disagreements, displays of positions such as 'I think', 'I wonder', 'I wish' etc. are regularly delayed. While engaging in preliminary matters leading up to some point, participants can potentially monitor the reactions of coparticipants —e.g. for disagreement-implicative actions or "trouble-premonitory" responses (see Jefferson 1980), etc. Consequently, an early opportunity may be presented whereby an action implicated by the "pre-pres" may be modified mid stream or ultimately avoided altogether on the basis of preliminary work. Even an action accomplished in a prior turn can subsequently be amended or reversed through further addition to a prior TCU, as illustrated in Chapter 4. Such operations are no doubt also observable in Anglo-American English, but it may be the case that the syntactical resources available in Japanese can further facilitate realignments and modifications of prior talk without the need to engage in overt repair. In particular, the possibly greater ease with which potential disagreements and other dispreferred actions may be forestalled can contribute to the notion of Japanese interaction not only as "indirect" and "allusive" but also "affiliative" and "non-confrontational". Relatedly, an important difference between Japanese and English in the organisation of turn-taking that emerges from the analysis is the greater scope for constructing complete turns which are syntactically incomplete in Japanese. By ending a turn with a case, adverbial, or conjunctive particle, participants can leave implicit the main thrust of a turn (as discussed in Chapters 3, 5, and 6). This feature may be mobilised for an indirect accomplishment of some social action.

The discussion above suggests that Japanese conversational organisation cannot be described as *inherently* illogical or logical, ambiguous or clear, indirect or direct, affiliative or disaffiliative. Rather, resources are available to enable both possibilities. The turn-taking mechanism can thus be mobilised in the interests of the performance of social actions to allow participants to tailor turn-designs to the particular tasks for which they are fitted. On the other hand, it is possible that cultural orientations may bias the employment of some resource over another, as has been suggested with respect to the occasioned avoidance of second-person pronouns (Tanaka 1996). Only a careful, close analysis of such possibilities can hope to reveal the impact of cultural features on the selection of resources.

This study has only begun to address the immense implications of the interpenetration of language, culture, and social interaction in relation to turn-taking. Although more extensive and intricate analysis is required, the work in these chapters points to a number of significant similarities and differences in turn-taking practices in Japanese and Anglo-American English which would be difficult to account for solely on the basis of cultural explanations. Moreover, since disparate resources may be directed towards the accomplishment of a basic interactional task, it is possible that apparent differences in turn-taking can mask more primordial and universal features of human interaction which may be shared across many cultures and languages. Thus, in addressing cross-cultural differences and similarities, it is important to bear in mind that what may appear to be a difference on one level might very well be a manifestation of a deeper commonality. At the same time, relatively little empirical work in CA has hitherto addressed the interrelation between culture and social action. As mentioned, workers in CA have come to realise some of the limitations of CA methodology in accounting for the relevance of social and cultural context in talk, and have begun to incorporate statistical, distributional studies of interactive phenomena. Coupled with a continued focus on the detailed analyses of individual instances, such methodological innovations promise expanded possibilities in the future for gaining access to the interpenetration of culture on the one hand, and language and social interaction on the other.

References

Amino, Y. 1993. *Nihonron no Shiza: Rettō no shakai to kokka* [Perspective on Japanology: Society and nation of the archipelago]. Tokyo: Shōgakukan.

Aoki, T. 1990. *'Nihon-Bunkaron' no Henyō* [Transformation of Theories of Japanese Culture]. Tokyo: Chūō Kōron Sha.

Atkinson, J.M., and Drew, P. (eds.) 1979. *Order in Court: The organisation of verbal interaction in judicial settings*. London: Macmillan.

Atkinson, J.M., and Heritage, J. (eds.) 1984. *Structures of Social Action: Studies in conversation analysis*. Cambridge: Cambridge University Press.

Benedict, R. 1954. *The Chrysanthemum and the Sword: Patterns of Japanese culture*. Tokyo: Tuttle [original copyright 1946].

Boden, D. 1981. "Talk International: An analysis of conversational turn taking and related phenomena in six Indo-European languages". Unpublished M.A. thesis, University of California at Santa Barbara.

—— and Zimmerman, D.H. (eds.) 1991. *Talk and Social Structure: Studies in ethnomethodology and conversation analysis*. Cambridge: Polity Press.

Button, G., and Lee, J.R.E. (eds.) 1987. *Talk and Social Organisation*. Clevedon: Multilingual Matters.

Cappella, J.N. 1979. "Talk-Silence Sequences in Informal Conversations, I". *Human Communication Research* 6: 3–17.

—— 1980. "Talk-Silence Sequences in Informal Conversations, II". *Human Communication Research* 6: 130–45.

Clancy, P.M. 1982. "Written and Spoken Style in Japanese Narratives". In D. Tannen (ed.), *Spoken and Written Language: Exploring orality and literacy*. Norwood, N.J.: Ablex, 55–76.

—— Thompson, S.A., Suzuki, R., and Tao, H. 1996. "The Conversational Use of Reactive Tokens in English, Japanese, and Mandarin". *Journal of Pragmatics* 26: 355–87.

Cook, H.M. 1990. "The Sentence-Final Particle *Ne* as a Tool for Cooperation in Japanese Conversation". *Japanese/Korean Linguistics*. Stanford: Center for the Study of Language and Information, 29–44.

—— 1992. "Meaning of Non-Referential Indexes: A case study of the Japanese sentence-final particle *ne*". *Text* 12(4): 507–39.

Couper-Kuhlen, E., and Selting, M. (eds.) *Prosody in Conversation: Interactional studies*. Cambridge: Cambridge University Press.

Crystal, D. 1985. *A Dictionary of Linguistics and Phonetics*. Oxford: Basil Blackwell.

Dale, P.N. 1986. *The Myth of Japanese Uniqueness*. London: Croom Helm and Nissan Institute for Japanese Studies.

Doi, T. 1971. *Amae no Kōzō* [Anatomy of Dependence]. Tokyo: Kōbundō.

—— 1988. *Anatomy of Self: The individual versus society*. Tokyo: Kōdansha International.

Drew, P. 1984. "Speakers' Reportings in Invitation Sequences". In Atkinson and Heritage (eds.), 129–51.

—— and Heritage, J. (eds.) 1992. *Talk at Work: Interaction in institutional settings*. Cambridge: Cambridge University Press.

Du Bois, J.W., Schuetze-Coburn, S., Paolino, D., and Cumming, S. 1993. "Outline of Discourse Transcription". In J.A. Edwards and M. D. Lampert (eds.), *Talking Data: Transcription and coding methods for language research*. Hillsdale, N.J.: Lawrence Erlbaum.

Duncan, S., Jr., and Fiske, D.W. 1977. *Face to Face Interaction: Research, methods, and theory*. Hillsdale, N.J.: Lawrence Erlbaum.

—— —— 1985. *Interaction Structure and Strategy*. Cambridge, England: Cambridge University Press.

Edwards, D. 1996. "Conversation, Cognition, and Intersubjectivity". Paper presented at the symposium *Talk and Cognition*, 15 Oct. 1996, Nottingham University.

Ford, C.E. 1993. *Grammar in Interaction: Adverbial clauses in American English conversations*. Cambridge: Cambridge University Press.

—— Fox, B.A., and Thompson, S.A. 1996. "Practices in the Construction of Turns: The 'TCU' revisited". *Pragmatics* 6(3): 427–54.

—— and Mori, J. 1994. "Causal Markers in Japanese and English Conversations: A cross-linguistic study of interactional grammar". *Pragmatics* 4(1): 31–61.

—— and Thompson, S.A. 1996. "Interactional Units in Conversation: Syntactic, intonational, and pragmatic resources for the management of turns". In Ochs, Schegloff, and Thompson (eds.), 134–84.

Fox, B.A., Hayashi, M., and Jasperson, R. 1996. "Resources and Repair: A cross-linguistic study of syntax and repair". In Ochs, Schegloff, and Thompson (eds.), 185–237.

Furo, H. 1998. "Turn-Taking in Japanese Conversation: Grammar, intonation and pragmatics". In S. Iwasaki (ed.), *Japanese/Korean Linguistics*, Vol. 7. Stanford: Center for the Study of Language and Information.

—— (to appear). "Turn-Taking in Japanese Political Debate: Syntax, intonation, and semantics". In D. Silvia (ed.), *Japanese/Korean Linguistics*, Vol. 8. Stanford: Center for the Study of Language and Information.

Garfinkel, H. 1967. *Studies in Ethnomethodology*. Englewood Cliffs, New Jersey: Prentice-Hall.

Goffman, E. 1981. "Replies and Responses". In E. Goffmann, *Forms of Talk*. Oxford: Blackwell, 5–77.

Goodwin, C. 1979a. "Review of S. Duncan, Jr. and D.W. Fiske, *Face-to-Face Interaction: Research, methods, and theory*". *Language in Society* 8(3): 439–44.

—— 1979b. "The Interactive Construction of a Sentence in Natural Conversation". In Psathas (ed.), 97–121.

—— 1981. *Conversational Organization: Interaction between speakers and hearers*. New York: Academic Press.
—— 1986. "Gesture as a Resource for the Organization of Participation". *Semiotica* 62(1/2), 29–49.
Haga, Y. 1979a. *Gengo, Ningen, Shakai* [Language, People, Society]. Tokyo: Ningen no Kagaku Sha.
—— 1979b. *Nihonjin no Hyōgen Shinri* [The Expressive Psychology of the Japanese]. Tokyo: Chūō Kōron Sha.
Hammersley, M. 1989. *The Dilemma of Qualitative Method: Herbert Blumer and the Chicago tradition*. London and New York: Routledge.
Hayashi, M. 1997. "Where Grammar and Interaction Meet: A study of co-participant completion in Japanese conversation". Paper presented at *Ethnomethodology and Conversation Analysis: East and West*, Waseda University, Tokyo, Japan, 21–23 Aug. 1997.
—— and Mori, J. 1998. "Co-Construction in Japanese Revisited: We *do* 'finish each other's sentences' ". In S. Iwasaki (ed.), *Japanese/Korean Linguistics*, Vol. 7. Stanford: Center for the Study of Language and Information.
—— —— and Takagi, T. To appear. "Contingent Achievement of Co-Tellership in a Japanese Conversation: An analysis of talk, gaze, and gesture". In C.E. Ford, B.A. Fox, and S.A. Thompson (eds.), *The Language of Turn and Sequence*. Oxford: Oxford University Press.
Heritage, J. 1984a. "A Change-of-State Token and Aspects of its Sequential Placement". In Atkinson and Heritage (eds.), 299–345.
—— 1984b. *Garfinkel and Ethnomethodology*. Cambridge: Polity Press.
—— 1988. "Explanations as Accounts". In C. Antaki (ed.), *Analysing Lay Explanation: A casebook of methods*. London: Sage, 127–44.
—— 1990/91. "Intention, Meaning and Strategy: Observations on constraints on interaction analysis". *Research on Language and Social Interaction* 24: 311–32.
—— 1995. "Conversation Analysis: Methodological aspects". In U.M. Quasthoff (ed.), *Aspects of Oral Communication*. Berlin: Walter de Gruyter, 391–418.
—— and Greatbatch, D. 1991. "On the Institutional Character of Institutional Talk: The case of news interviews". In Boden and Zimmerman (eds.), 93–137.
—— and Roth, A.L. 1995. "Grammar and Institution: Questions and questioning in the broadcast news interview". *Research on Language and Social Interaction* 28(1): 1–60.
Hinds, J. 1982. *Ellipsis in Japanese*. Carbondale and Edmonton: Linguistic Research, Inc.
Hirokawa, R.Y. 1987. "Communication within the Japanese Business Organization". In D.L. Kincaid (ed.), *Communication Theory: Eastern and Western perspectives*. London: Academic Press, 137–49.
Hopper, R. 1989. "Conversation Analysis and Social Psychology as Descriptions of Interpersonal Communication". In Roger and Bull (eds.), 48–65.
Hopper, R., and Doany, N.K. 1989. "Telephone Openings and Conversational Universals: A study in three languages". In S. Ting-Toomey and F. Korzenny (eds.), *Language, Communication, and Culture*. Newbury Park, California: Sage, 157–79.

Ito, Y. 1989. "Socio-Cultural Background of Japanese Interpersonal Communication Style". *Civilizations* 39: 101–28.

Iwasaki, S. 1993. "The Structure of the Intonation Unit in Japanese". In S. Choi (ed.), *Japanese/Korean Linguistics*, Vol. 3. Stanford: Center for the Study of Language and Information, 39–53.

Jaffe, J., and Feldstein, S. 1970. *Rhythms of Dialog*. New York: Academy Press.

Jefferson, G. 1980. "On 'Trouble-Premonitory' Responses to Inquiry". *Sociological Inquiry* 50: 153–85.

—— 1983a. "Notes on Some Orderliness of Overlap Onset". In G. Jefferson, *Two Explorations of the Organization of Overlapping Talk in Conversation:T ilburg Papers in Language and Literature* 28. Tilburg: University of Tilburg.

—— 1983b. "On a Failed Hypothesis: 'Conjunctionals' as overlap-vulnerable". In G. Jefferson, *Two Explorations of the Organization of Overlapping Talk in Conversation: Tilburg Papers in Language and Literature* 28. Tilburg: University of Tilburg.

—— 1986. "Notes on 'Latency' in Overlap Onset". *Human Studies* 9: 153–83.

—— 1987. "On Exposed and Embedded Correction in Conversation". In Button and Lee (eds.), 85–100.

—— 1989. "Preliminary Notes on a Possible Metric which Provides for a 'Standard Maximum' Silence of Approximately One Second in Conversation". In Roger and Bull (eds.), 166–96.

—— To appear. "Sketch: Some orderly aspects of overlap in natural conversation". In G. Lerner (ed.), *Conversation Analysis: Studies from the first generation*. Lanham, MD: University Press of America.

—— Sacks, H., and Schegloff, E.A. 1987. "Notes on Laughter in the Pursuit of Intimacy". In Button and Lee (eds.), 152–205.

Kataoka, K. 1995. "Affect in Japanese Women's Letter Writing: Use of sentence-final particles *ne* and *yo* and orthographic conventions". *Pragmatics* 5(4): 427–53.

Kawashima, T. 1948. *Nihon Shakai no Kazoku-teki Kōsei* [The Familial Organisation of Japanese Society]. Tokyo: Gakusei Shobō.

Kindaichi, H. 1981. *Nihongo no Tokushitsu* [Characteristics of the Japanese Language]. Tokyo: Nippon Hōsō Kyōkai.

Kōjien 1976. 2nd edn. Tokyo: Iwanami Shoten.

Kunihiro, M. 1976. "The Japanese Language and Intercultural Communication". *Japan Interpreter*, Winter: 96–108.

Kuno, S. 1973. *The Structure of the Japanese Language*. Cambridge, Mass. and London: The MIT Press.

Lebra, T.S. 1987. "The Cultural Significance of Silence in Japanese Communication". *Multilingua* 6(4): 343–57.

Lerner, G. 1987. "Collaborative Turn-Sequences: Sentence construction and social action". Unpublished Ph.D. dissertation, University of California, Irvine.

—— 1989. "Notes on Overlap Management in Conversation: The case of delayed completion". *Western Journal of Speech Communication* 53, Spring: 167–77.

—— 1991. "On the Syntax of Sentences in Progress". *Language in Society*, 20: 441–58.

—— 1996. "On the 'Semi-Permeable' Character of Grammatical Units in Conversation: Conditional entry into the turn-space of another speaker". In Ochs, Schegloff, and Thompson (eds.), 238–76.

—— and Takagi, T. To appear. "On the Place of Linguistic Resources in the Organization of Talk-in-Interaction: A co-investigation of English and Japanese grammatical practices". *Journal of Pragmatics*.

Levinson, S.C. 1983. *Pragmatics*. Cambridge: Cambridge University Press.

Loveday, L. 1986. *Explorations in Japanese Sociolinguistics*. Amsterdam: John Benjamins Publishing Company.

McClain, Y.M. 1981. *Handbook of Modern Japanese Grammar*. Tokyo: The Hokuseido Press.

McHoul, A.W. 1978. "The Organization of Turns at Formal Talk in the Classroom". *Language in Society* 7: 183–213.

Martin, S.E. 1975. *A Reference Grammar of Japanese*. New Haven and London: Yale University Press.

Maruyama, M. 1952. *Nihon Seiji Shisō Shi Kenkyū* [Research on the History of Japanese Political Thought]. Tokyo: Tōdai Shuppan Kai.

Maynard, S.K. 1986. "On Back-Channel Behavior in Japanese and English Casual Conversation". *Linguistics* 24: 1079–108.

—— 1989. *Japanese Conversation: Self-contextualization through structure and interactional management*. Norwood, New Jersey: Ablex.

—— 1990. "Conversational Management in Contrast: Listener response in Japanese and American English". *Journal of Pragmatics* 14: 397–412.

—— 1993. *Discourse Modality: Subjectivity, emotion and voice in the Japanese language*. Amsterdam: John Benjamins.

Midooka, K. 1990. Characteristics of Japanese-Style Communication. *Media, Culture and Society*, Vol. 2, 477–89.

Miller, R.A. 1982. *Japan's Modern Myth: The language and beyond*. New York: Weatherhill.

Moerman, M. 1972. "Analysis of Lue Conversation: Providing accounts, finding breaches, and taking sides". In Sudnow (ed.), 170–228.

—— 1988. *Talking Culture: Ethnography and conversation analysis*. Philadelphia: University of Pennsylvania Press.

Molotch, H.L., and Boden, D. 1985. "Talking Social Structure: Discourse, dominance and the Watergate Hearings". *American Sociological Review* 50: 273–88.

Mori, J. 1994. "Functions of the Connective *Datte* in Japanese Conversation". *Japanese/Korean Linguistics*, Vol. 4, Center for the Study of Language and Information. Stanford: Stanford University, 147–63.

—— 1996a. "Co-Constructing Complaints in Japanese Conversations: Some implications for cross-linguistic/cross-cultural studies of interaction". Paper presented at AAAL.

—— 1996b. "Negotiating Agreement and Disagreement: The use of connective expressions in Japanese conversations". Ph.D. dissertation, University of Wisconsin-Madison.

Mouer, R., and Sugimoto, Y. 1986. *Images of Japanese Society: A study in the structure of social reality*. London: KPI.

Nakane, C. 1973. *Japanese Society*. Harmondsworth: Penguin Books.

Neustupný, J. V. 1978. *Post-Structural Approaches to Language*. Tokyo: Tokyo University Press.

Nishizaka, A. 1995. "The Interactive Constitution of Interculturality: How to be a Japanese with words". *Human Studies* 18: 301–26.

Ochs, E., Schegloff, E.A., and Thompson, S.A. (eds.) 1996. *Interaction and Grammar*. Cambridge: Cambridge University Press.

Odaka, K. 1965. *Nihon no Keiei* [Japanese Management]. Tokyo: Chūō Kōron Sha.

Oide, A. 1965. *Nihongo to Ronri* [The Japanese Language and Logic]. Tokyo: Kōdansha.

Okabe, R. 1993. "Nihon no Rhetoric" [Japanese Rhetoric]. In M. Hashimoto and S. Ishii (eds.), *Nihonjin no Communication* [Japanese Communication]. Tokyo: Kirihara Shoten, 55–81.

Ono, T., and Suzuki, R. 1992. "Word Order Variability in Japanese Conversation: Motivation and grammaticization". *Text* 12(3): 429–45.

—— and Yoshida, E. 1996. "A Study of Co-Construction in Japanese: We don't finish each other's sentences". In N. Akatsuka, S. Iwasaki, and S. Strauss (eds.), *Japanese/Korean Linguistics*, Vol. 5, Stanford: Center for the Study of Language and Information, 115–29.

Oreström, B. 1983. *Turn Taking in English Conversation*. Lund, Sweden: CWK Gleerup.

Parsons, T. 1937. *The Structure of Social Action*. New York: McGraw-Hill.

Pomerantz, A.M. 1978. "Compliment Responses: Notes on the co-operation of multiple constraints". In Schenkein (ed.), 79–112.

—— 1984a. "Agreeing and Disagreeing with Assessments: Some features of preferred/dispreferred turn shapes". In Atkinson and Heritage (eds.), 57–101.

—— 1984b. "Pursuing a Response". In Atkinson and Heritage (eds.), 152–63.

Psathas, G. (ed.) 1979. *Everyday Language: Studies in ethnomethodology*. New York: Irvington.

Ren, J. 1989. "Turn-Taking in Mandarin Chinese Conversation". Unpublished M.A. thesis, University of California at Santa Barbara.

Roger, D., and Bull, P. (eds.) 1989. *Conversation: An interdisciplinary perspective*. Clevedon, Philadelphia: Multilingual Matters.

Sacks, H., Schegloff, E.A., and Jefferson, G. 1974. "A Simplest Systematics for the Organization of Turn-Taking for Conversation". *Language* 50(4): 696–735. (Reprinted in Schenkein (ed.) 1978, 7–55).

Saft, S.L. 1996. "Reassessing Cross-Cultural Comparisons of Back-Channel Behavior in Japanese and English: Arguments for an expanded notion of context". *Linguistics and Language Teaching: Proceedings of the Sixth Joint LSH-HATESL Conference*, 169–87.

Schegloff, E.A. 1968. "Sequencing in Conversational Openings". *American Anthropologist* 70: 1075–95.

—— 1972. "Notes on a Conversational Practice: Formulating place". In Sudnow (ed.), 75–119; 432–33.

—— 1979. "The Relevance of Repair to Syntax-for-Conversation". In T. Givón (ed.), *Discourse and Syntax*. New York: Academic Press, 261–88. [*Syntax and Semantics* 12].
—— 1984. "On Some Gestures' Relation to Talk". In Atkinson and Heritage (eds.), 266–96.
—— 1987a. "Between Macro and Micro: Contexts and other connections". In J. Alexander, B. Giesen, R. Munch, and N. Smelser (eds.), *The Micro-Macro Link*. Berkeley and Los Angeles: University of California Press, 207–34.
—— 1987b. "Recycled Turn Beginnings: A precise repair mechanism in conversation's turn-taking organisation". In Button and Lee (eds.), 70–85.
—— 1987c. "Analysing Single Episodes of Interaction: An exercise in conversation analysis". In D.W. Maynard (ed.), *Social Psychology Quarterly* 50(2): 101–14. [Special issue: *Language and Social Interaction*].
—— 1988. "Discourse as an Interactional Achievement, II: An exercise in conversation analysis". In D. Tannen (ed.), *Linguistics in Context: Connecting observation and understanding*. Norwood, New Jersey: Ablex, 135–58.
—— 1993. "Reflections on Quantification in the Study of Conversation". *Research on Language and Social Interaction* 26(1): 99–128.
—— 1996a. "Turn Organization: One intersection of grammar and interaction". In Ochs, Schegloff, and Thompson (eds.), 52–133.
—— 1996b. "Confirming Allusions: Toward an empirical account of action". *American Journal of Sociology* 102(1): 161–216.
—— and Sacks, H. 1973. "Opening up Closings". *Semiotica* 8: 289–327.
—— —— 1974. "Opening up Closings". In R. Turner (ed.), *Ethnomethodology*. Harmondsworth: Penguin, 233–64.
—— Jefferson, G., and Sacks, H. 1977. "The Preference for Self-Correction in the Organization of Repair in Conversation". *Language* 53(2): 361–82.
Schenkein, J. 1972. "Towards an Analysis of Natural Conversation and the Sense of *Heheh*". *Semiotica* 6: 344–77.
—— (ed.) 1978. *Studies in the Organization of Conversational Interaction*. New York, San Francisco, and London: Academic Press.
Sgall, P. 1995. "Prague School Typology". In M. Shibatani and T. Bynon (eds.), *Approaches to Language Typology*. Oxford: Clarendon Press, 47–94.
Shibagaki, T. 1984. "Nihon Bunka no Kōzō" [The Structure of Japanese Culture]. In T. Shibagaki, M. Inoue, and M. Hata (eds.), *Bunka no Hyōsō to Shinsō* [The Outer and Inner Layers of Culture]. Osaka, Japan: Sōgensha, 101–67.
Shibatani, M. 1990. *The Languages of Japan*. Cambridge: Cambridge University Press.
Simon, M.E. 1989. "An Analysis of the Postposing Construction in Japanese". Unpublished Ph.D. dissertation. University of Michigan.
Soeda, Y. 1993. *Nihon Bunka Shiron: Benedict* Kiku to Katana *wo yomu* [Essays on Japanese Culture: Reading Benedicts' *The Chrysanthemum and the Sword*]. Tokyo: Shinyōsha.
Squires, T. 1994. "A Discourse Analysis of the Japanese Particle *Sa*". Pragmatics 4(1): 1–29.

Stewart, L.P. 1993. "Organizational Communication in Japan and the United States". In W. Gudykunst (ed.), *Communication in Japan and the United States*. Albany: State University of New York Press, 215–48.

Sudnow, D. (ed.) 1972. *Studies in Social Interaction*. New York: The Free Press.

Suzuki, R. 1990. "The Role of Particles in Japanese Gossip". *Berkeley Linguistics Society* 16: 315–24.

Suzuki, T. 1975. *Tozasareta Gengo: Nihongo no sekai* [The Closed Language: The world of Japanese]. Tokyo: Shinchō-sha.

Szatrowski, P. 1993. *Structural Analysis of Japanese Discourse* [*Nihongo no Danwa no Kōzō Bunseki*]. Tokyo: Kuroshio.

Tanaka, H. 1996. "Language, Culture and Social Interaction: A comparison of turn taking in Japanese and Anglo/American English". Unpublished D.Phil. thesis, University of Oxford.

—— 1998. "Prosody and Turn-Taking in Japanese: The localisation of TRPs". Paper presented at the *6th International IPrA Conference*, Reims, France, 19–24 July 1998.

—— To appear-a. "Turn-Projection in Japanese Talk-in-Interaction". *Research on Language and Social Interaction*.

—— To appear-b. "Grammar and Social Interaction in Japanese and Anglo-American English: The display of context, social identity and social relation". *Human Studies*.

—— to appear-c. "The Particle *Ne* as a Turn-Management Device in Japanese Conversation". *Journal of Pragmatics*.

Tsujimura, A. 1987. "Some Characteristics of the Japanese Way of Communication". In D.L. Kincaid (ed.), *Communication Theory: Eastern and Western perspectives*. London: Academic Press, 115–26.

Tsunoda, T. 1978. *Nihonjin no Nō: Nō no hataraki to tōzai bunka* [The Brain Structure of the Japanese: Functions of the brain and cultures of the East and West]. Tokyo: Taishūkan.

Umegaki, M. 1988. *Nichi-ei Hikaku Gengogaku Nyūmon* [Introduction to Comparative Linguistics: Japanese and English]. Tokyo: Taishūkan Shoten.

Uyeno, T.Y. 1971. "A Study of Japanese Modality: A performative analysis of sentence-particles". Unpublished Ph.D. dissertation, University of Michigan.

Watsuji, T. 1979. *Fūdo* [Climate and Culture]. Tokyo: Iwanami Shoten, (original copyright 1935; also published as Geoffrey Bownas, transl. 1961. *Climate and Culture*. Tokyo: Hokuseidō Press.)

West, C. 1979. "Against Our Will: Male interruptions of females in cross-sex conversations". *Annals of The New York Academy of Science* 327: 81–97.

—— and Zimmerman, D.H. 1983. "Small Insults: A study of interruptions in conversations between unacquainted persons". In B. Thorne and N. Henley (eds.), *Language, Gender, and Society*. Rowley, Mass.: Newbury House, 102–17.

—— —— 1987. "Doing Gender". *Gender and Society* 1(2): 125–51.

White, S. 1989. "Backchannels Across Cultures: A study of Americans and Japanese". *Language in Society* 18: 59–76.

Wilson, T.P., Wiemann, J.M., and Zimmerman, D.H. 1984. "Models of Turn Taking in Conversational Interaction". *Journal of Language and Social Psychology* 3(3), 159–83.

—— and Zimmerman, D.H. 1986. "The Structure of Silence between Turns in Two-Party Conversation". *Discourse Processes* 9: 375–90.

Yamada, T., Yoshii, H., and Yamazaki, K. (eds. and transl.) 1987. *Ethnomethodology*. Tokyo: Serika Shobō.

Yoshii, H. (ed.) 1992. *Ethnomethodology no Genjitsu* [The Reality of Ethnomethodology]. Tokyo: Sekai Shisōsha.

Zimmerman, D.H., and West, C. 1975. "Sex Roles, Interruptions and Silences in Conversations". In B. Thorne and N. Henley (eds.), *Language and Sex: Difference and dominance*. Rowley, Mass.: Newbury House, 105–29.

Index

In the PRAGMATICS AND BEYOND NEW SERIES the following titles have been published thus far or are scheduled for publication:

1. WALTER, Bettyruth: *The Jury Summation as Speech Genre: An Ethnographic Study of What it Means to Those who Use it.* Amsterdam/Philadelphia, 1988.
2. BARTON, Ellen: *Nonsentential Constituents: A Theory of Grammatical Structure and Pragmatic Interpretation.* Amsterdam/Philadelphia, 1990.
3. OLEKSY, Wieslaw (ed.): *Contrastive Pragmatics.* Amsterdam/Philadelphia, 1989.
4. RAFFLER-ENGEL, Walburga von (ed.): *Doctor-Patient Interaction.* Amsterdam/Philadelphia, 1989.
5. THELIN, Nils B. (ed.): *Verbal Aspect in Discourse.* Amsterdam/Philadelphia, 1990.
6. VERSCHUEREN, Jef (ed.): *Selected Papers from the 1987 International Pragmatics Conference. Vol. I: Pragmatics at Issue. Vol. II: Levels of Linguistic Adaptation. Vol. III: The Pragmatics of Intercultural and International Communication* (ed. with Jan Blommaert). Amsterdam/Philadelphia, 1991.
7. LINDENFELD, Jacqueline: *Speech and Sociability at French Urban Market Places.* Amsterdam/Philadelphia, 1990.
8. YOUNG, Lynne: *Language as Behaviour, Language as Code: A Study of Academic English.* Amsterdam/Philadelphia, 1990.
9. LUKE, Kang-Kwong: *Utterance Particles in Cantonese Conversation.* Amsterdam/Philadelphia, 1990.
10. MURRAY, Denise E.: *Conversation for Action. The computer terminal as medium of communication.* Amsterdam/Philadelphia, 1991.
11. LUONG, Hy V.: *Discursive Practices and Linguistic Meanings. The Vietnamese system of person reference.* Amsterdam/Philadelphia, 1990.
12. ABRAHAM, Werner (ed.): *Discourse Particles. Descriptive and theoretical investigations on the logical, syntactic and pragmatic properties of discourse particles in German.* Amsterdam/Philadelphia, 1991.
13. NUYTS, Jan, A. Machtelt BOLKESTEIN and Co VET (eds): *Layers and Levels of Representation in Language Theory: a functional view.* Amsterdam/Philadelphia, 1990.
14. SCHWARTZ, Ursula: *Young Children's Dyadic Pretend Play.* Amsterdam/Philadelphia, 1991.
15. KOMTER, Martha: *Conflict and Cooperation in Job Interviews.* Amsterdam/Philadelphia, 1991.
16. MANN, William C. and Sandra A. THOMPSON (eds): *Discourse Description: Diverse Linguistic Analyses of a Fund-Raising Text.* Amsterdam/Philadelphia, 1992.
17. PIÉRAUT-LE BONNIEC, Gilberte and Marlene DOLITSKY (eds): *Language Bases ... Discourse Bases.* Amsterdam/Philadelphia, 1991.
18. JOHNSTONE, Barbara: *Repetition in Arabic Discourse. Paradigms, syntagms and the ecology of language.* Amsterdam/Philadelphia, 1991.
19. BAKER, Carolyn D. and Allan LUKE (eds): *Towards a Critical Sociology of Reading Pedagogy. Papers of the XII World Congress on Reading.* Amsterdam/Philadelphia, 1991.
20. NUYTS, Jan: *Aspects of a Cognitive-Pragmatic Theory of Language. On cognition, functionalism, and grammar.* Amsterdam/Philadelphia, 1992.

21. SEARLE, John R. et al.: *(On) Searle on Conversation*. Compiled and introduced by Herman Parret and Jef Verschueren. Amsterdam/Philadelphia, 1992.
22. AUER, Peter and Aldo Di LUZIO (eds): *The Contextualization of Language*. Amsterdam/Philadelphia, 1992.
23. FORTESCUE, Michael, Peter HARDER and Lars KRISTOFFERSEN (eds): *Layered Structure and Reference in a Functional Perspective. Papers from the Functional Grammar Conference, Copenhagen, 1990*. Amsterdam/Philadelphia, 1992.
24. MAYNARD, Senko K.: *Discourse Modality: Subjectivity, Emotion and Voice in the Japanese Language*. Amsterdam/Philadelphia, 1993.
25. COUPER-KUHLEN, Elizabeth: *English Speech Rhythm. Form and function in everyday verbal interaction*. Amsterdam/Philadelphia, 1993.
26. STYGALL, Gail: Trial Language. *A study in differential discourse processing*. Amsterdam/Philadelphia, 1994.
27. SUTER, Hans Jürg: *The Wedding Report: A Prototypical Approach to the Study of Traditional Text Types*. Amsterdam/Philadelphia, 1993.
28. VAN DE WALLE, Lieve: *Pragmatics and Classical Sanskrit*. Amsterdam/Philadelphia, 1993.
29. BARSKY, Robert F.: *Constructing a Productive Other: Discourse theory and the convention refugee hearing*. Amsterdam/Philadelphia, 1994.
30. WORTHAM, Stanton E.F.: *Acting Out Participant Examples in the Classroom*. Amsterdam/Philadelphia, 1994.
31. WILDGEN, Wolfgang: *Process, Image and Meaning. A realistic model of the meanings of sentences and narrative texts*. Amsterdam/Philadelphia, 1994.
32. SHIBATANI, Masayoshi and Sandra A. THOMPSON (eds): *Essays in Semantics and Pragmatics*. Amsterdam/Philadelphia, 1995.
33. GOOSSENS, Louis, Paul PAUWELS, Brygida RUDZKA-OSTYN, Anne-Marie SIMON-VANDENBERGEN and Johan VANPARYS: *By Word of Mouth. Metaphor, metonymy and linguistic action in a cognitive perspective*. Amsterdam/Philadelphia, 1995.
34. BARBE, Katharina: Irony in Context. Amsterdam/Philadelphia, 1995.
35. JUCKER, Andreas H. (ed.): *Historical Pragmatics. Pragmatic developments in the history of English*. Amsterdam/Philadelphia, 1995.
36. CHILTON, Paul, Mikhail V. ILYIN and Jacob MEY: *Political Discourse in Transition in Eastern and Western Europe (1989-1991)*. Amsterdam/Philadelphia, 1998.
37. CARSTON, Robyn and Seiji UCHIDA (eds): *Relevance Theory. Applications and implications*. Amsterdam/Philadelphia, 1998.
38. FRETHEIM, Thorstein and Jeanette K. GUNDEL (eds): *Reference and Referent Accessibility*. Amsterdam/Philadelphia, 1996.
39. HERRING, Susan (ed.): *Computer-Mediated Communication. Linguistic, social, and cross-cultural perspectives*. Amsterdam/Philadelphia, 1996.
40. DIAMOND, Julie: *Status and Power in Verbal Interaction. A study of discourse in a close-knit social network*. Amsterdam/Philadelphia, 1996.
41. VENTOLA, Eija and Anna MAURANEN, (eds): *Academic Writing. Intercultural and textual issues*. Amsterdam/Philadelphia, 1996.
42. WODAK, Ruth and Helga KOTTHOFF (eds): *Communicating Gender in Context*. Amsterdam/Philadelphia, 1997.

43. JANSSEN, Theo A.J.M. and Wim van der WURFF (eds): *Reported Speech. Forms and functions of the verb.* Amsterdam/Philadelphia, 1996.
44. BARGIELA-CHIAPPINI, Francesca and Sandra J. HARRIS: *Managing Language. The discourse of corporate meetings.* Amsterdam/Philadelphia, 1997.
45. PALTRIDGE, Brian: *Genre, Frames and Writing in Research Settings.* Amsterdam/ Philadelphia, 1997.
46. GEORGAKOPOULOU, Alexandra: *Narrative Performances. A study of Modern Greek storytelling.* Amsterdam/Philadelphia, 1997.
47. CHESTERMAN, Andrew: *Contrastive Functional Analysis.* Amsterdam/Philadelphia, 1998.
48. KAMIO, Akio: *Territory of Information.* Amsterdam/Philadelphia, 1997.
49. KURZON, Dennis: *Discourse of Silence.* Amsterdam/Philadelphia, 1998.
50. GRENOBLE, Lenore: *Deixis and Information Packaging in Russian Discourse.* Amsterdam/Philadelphia, 1998.
51. BOULIMA, Jamila: *Negotiated Interaction in Target Language Classroom Discourse.* Amsterdam/Philadelphia, 1999.
52. GILLIS, Steven and Annick DE HOUWER (eds): *The Acquisition of Dutch.* Amsterdam/Philadelphia, 1998.
53. MOSEGAARD HANSEN, Maj-Britt: *The Function of Discourse Particles. A study with special reference to spoken standard French.* Amsterdam/Philadelphia, 1998.
54. HYLAND, Ken: *Hedging in Scientific Research Articles.* Amsterdam/Philadelphia, 1998.
55. ALLWOOD, Jens and Peter Gärdenfors (eds): *Cognitive Semantics. Meaning and cognition.* Amsterdam/Philadelphia, 1999.
56. TANAKA, Hiroko: *Language, Culture and Social Interaction. Turn-taking in Japanese and Anglo-American English.* Amsterdam/Philadelphia, 1999.
57 JUCKER, Andreas H. and Yael ZIV (eds): *Discourse Markers. Descriptions and theory.* Amsterdam/Philadelphia, 1998.
58. ROUCHOTA, Villy and Andreas H. JUCKER (eds): *Current Issues in Relevance Theory.* Amsterdam/Philadelphia, 1998.
59. KAMIO, Akio and Ken-ichi TAKAMI (eds): *Function and Structure. In honor of Susumu Kuno.* 1999.
60. JACOBS, Geert: *Preformulating the News. An analysis of the metapragmatics of press releases.* 1999.
61. MILLS, Margaret H. (ed.): *Slavic Gender Linguistics.* 1999.
62. TZANNE, Angeliki: *Talking at Cross-Purposes. The dynamics of miscommunication.* n.y.p.
63. BUBLITZ, Wolfram, Uta LENK and Eija VENTOLA (eds.): *Coherence in Spoken and Written Discourse. How to create it and how to describe it.Selected papers from the International Workshop on Coherence, Augsburg, 24-27 April 1997.* 1999.
64. SVENNEVIG, Jan: *Getting Acquainted in Conversation. A study of initial interactions.* 1999.
65. COOREN, François: *The Organizing Dimension of Communication.* n.y.p.
66. JUCKER, Andreas H., Gerd FRITZ and Franz LEBSANFT (eds.): *Historical Dialogue Analysis.* 1999.